AF622008

EDUCATION IN ANCIENT INDIA

EDUCATION
IN
ANCIENT INDIA

Compiled & Edited
by
Dr. R.K. Pruthi

SONALI PUBLICATIONS
NEW DELHI-110002

Edition : 2022

ISBN 81-88836-64-8

© Editor

Published by

SONALI PUBLICATIONS
4228/1, Ansari Road,
New Delhi-110 002 (India)
Phone: 23266109, 23279245
Fax: 91-11-23253475

Printed at:
Navya Digital
Delhi-110092

Preface

The study of Educational Philosophy, its principles, its methods and its history of ancient India is immensely important for a better understanding of the present educational systems and can enable us to propound a vibrant future educational culture in India.

Aim of this work is to make available to our readers some perspectives of the ancient Indian educational culture. This we hope will enable them to understand the complexities of various aspects of education in proper perspectives. The work will be of use not only to the students and teachers but also to the general readers, educationists and policy makers.

In preparing this work we have incurred indebtness of the authorities on the subject. We record our gratitude and acknowledgments.

Librarians and their staff members have been kind and helpful. We are thankful to them.

My publisher both at printing and publishing levels have worked hard. They deserve the love and kindness of my readers

R.K. Pruthi

Contents

1

Introduction

The roots of the ancient Indian system of education[1] may be traced in the works of Vedic literature, namely, the Vedic Saṁhitās, the Brāhmaṇas, the Āraṇyakas, and the Upaniṣads. In fact these works are the products of the educational system which they reveal.

The main aim of this system is the training of the mind as an instrument of knowledge, and not simply to fill it with the furniture of objective knowledge. What weakens the mind is its contact with matter; what strengthens it is its detachment from matter and freedom from its contaminating contacts. In a word, the only way by which the mind can fulfil its innate and intrinsic potentialities is to keep itself in constant communion with the cosmic principle and open itself to its influence. It is what may be called *yoga* or the process of bringing together the individual soul and the Oversoul. The individual is the *ādhāra* (base) which is vitalized by the cosmic energy (*prakṛti, māyā,* or *śakti*) pervading the world and pouring itself into every name and form, the clod, the plant, the insect, the animal, or man. When the *ādhāra* is fully fitted to bear the inrush and impact of this divine energy, its evolution is completed, and the man becomes *siddha,* 'the fulfilled or perfected soul'.

Thus the first principle of this education was to bring into play the cosmic principle upon the individual by building up in the latter a strong store of infinite energy or divine potency through the practice of *brahmacarya* (chastity), the first necessary condition for increasing the vital force within and giving scope to its working.

Let us next proceed to analyse some salient features of the old Indian educational system. First of all, ancient schools were largely located far away from the din and bustle of cities in sylvan retreats, in an atmosphere of solitude and serenity conducive to mental concentration as the main appliance in education. From these sylvan schools and hermitages flowed the highest thought of India. Thus India's civilisation through the ages has been very largely the product of her woods and forests. It started as a rural and not as an urban civilization.[2] A significant designation of a branch of Sanskrit sacred literature is the Āraṇyaka, 'the literature of the woods', in the silence and solitude of which its meaning was revealed.

Apart from the influence of the environment, the real creative force in education came from the teacher (*guru*) as the master mind directing its entire course. His home was the school. The school was thus a natural formation and not an artificially created institution. It began where the pupil met the teacher and was admitted by him to his pupilage. The pupil was not forced upon him by the fee by which a modern school admits its pupils. The teacher's admission of the pupil was a solemn and sacred ceremony known as *upanayana* or initiation. It was not a mere meaningless ritual. The ceremony took three days, during which, as explained in the *Atharva-Veda,* the teacher held the pupil within him to impart to him a new birth, whence the pupil emerged as a *dvija* or twice-born. His first birth he owes to his parents, who gave him only his body; this is a mere physical birth. His second birth is spiritual; it unfolds his mind and soul.[3] Education was thus based upon an individual treatment of the pupil by his teacher, with whom he must live to give full scope to it. The pupil was to imbibe the inward method of the teacher, the secrets of his efficiency, the spirit of his life and work, and these things were too subtle to be taught. This individual treatment was all the more essential where the supreme purpose of education was the attainment of the highest, saving knowledge leading to *mukti* (liberation). The highest knowledge is described as *vidyā* or *parāvidyā,* as distinguished from *avidyā* or *aparāvidyā,* which is a body of contingent truths, half-truths, and fallacies.[4]

Three steps are distinguished in the attainment of supreme knowledge. These are *śravaṇa, manana,* and *nididhyāsana*. *Śravaṇa* is listening to the words or texts as they are uttered by the teacher. This was the time-honoured method of education in ancient India, the system of oral tradition, by which knowledge was transmitted from teacher to pupil by *guruparamparā* (a succession of teachers) or *sampradāya* (handing down). Such knowledge was imparted in the form known as *mantra* or *sūtra,* by which the maximum of meaning was compressed within the minimum of words, of which the crowning example was the *praṇava* or the syllable *Om* containing within itself a world of meaning. All the learning of the times was thus held between the teacher and the taught, and the teacher was the walking library and source of knowledge to be tapped directly by the student. Besides, recitation of texts as they were uttered by the teacher had its own value as a vehicle of knowledge. *Śabda* or sound of the sacred word or *mantra* has its own potency and value apart from its sense, and its intrinsic and innate implications, its rhythm, its vibrations, should be captured. *Śabda* is Brahman, 'the Word is God'.[5] The receiving of this knowledge as it was uttered by the teacher was to be followed by the process of its assimilation by *manana,* deliberation or reflection on the topic taught. But such reflection resulted only in a mere intellectual apprehension of the meaning of the text imparted by the teacher to his pupil. Therefore learning was to be completed by the third step or process—which was technically called *nididhyāsana* (meditation), leading to the realization of truth after its intellectual apprehension. As the *Muṇḍaka Upanisad* (II. 3-4) points out: A mere intellectual apprehension of truth, a reasoned conviction, is not sufficient, though it is necessary at the first stage as a sort of mark at which to shoot. *Nididhyāsana* represents the highest stage of meditation, which, with reference to Brahman or the one Reality, has been defined as 'the steady stream of consciousness of the one Reality, undisturbed by the slightest awareness of the many, of any material object such as the body, contradictory to the sense of the one, non-dual Self or Reality'.[6] The Upaniṣads prescribe certain preliminary exercises in meditation to lead up to its final stage. These are called *upāsanās,* giving training in contemplation.[7]

A set of external aids to knowledge was also formulated to supplement these inner disciplines and process and to strengthen the moral foundations for the pursuit of knowledge. The first of these has already been stated, viz. that the pupil must live with his teacher as a member of his family, so that his education may be a whole-time process and not for a stated period, as is the custom in modern schools. Living with his teacher as his *antevāsin* (companion), the pupil had to take advantage of the opportunities which opened out before him in such a school, a hermitage set in sylvan surroundings. His first duty was to walk to the woods, collect fuel, and bring it home for tending the sacred fire. The Upaniṣads frequently mention pupils approaching their teacher with fuel in hand, as a token that they are ready to serve the teacher and tend his household fire. The *Śatapatha Brāhmaṇa*[8] explains that the *brahmacārin* 'puts on fuel to enkindle the mind with fire, with holy lustre'.

The pupil's next duty was to tend the teacher's house and cattle. Tending the house was training for him in self-help, in dignity of labour, by manual service for his teacher and the student brotherhood. Tending cattle was education through a craft as a part of the highest liberal education. The pupils received a valuable training in the love of the cow as the animal most serviceable to man, and in the industry of rearing cattle and dairy-farming, with all the other advantages it gave of outdoor life and robust physical exercise.[9]

Another duty of the *brahmacārin* was to go out on a daily round of begging. It was not the selfish begging for his own benefit, but for the academic corporation to which he belonged. Its educative value is explained in the *Śatapatha Brāhmaṇa,*[10] which points out that it is meant to produce in the pupil a spirit of humility and renunciation.

Thus all these external practices operate as aids to knowledge by strengthening the potency of the mind as an instrument for acquiring knowledge, by making it less and less objective and less and less open to contamination by contact with matter. The aim of education is thus *cittavṛtti-nirodha* (control of the mental waves), by which the individual merges in the universe. It is the Union (*yoga*) of the individual soul with the oversoul.[11]

We may next notice the different types of institutions by which education was promoted in the country in the Vedic period. The first was the *āśrama* or hermitage, a home of learning with an individual teacher as its head, who admitted to his domestic school as many pupils as he found fit and could instruct. In these schools the pupils passed their period of studentship (*brahmacarya*) properly. But there might be pupils who would prefer to continue as students through life, dedicated to the pursuit of learning and religion in the spirit of the passage in the *Bṛhadāraṇyaka Upaniṣad:* 'Wishing for that world (Brahman) only, mendicants leave their homes; knowing this, the people of old did not wish for offspring... and they, having risen above the desire for sons, wealth, and new worlds, wandered about as mendicants.'[12] Such students are known as *naiṣṭhika brahmacārins*. They wandered about the country as *parivrājakas,* seeking higher knowledge by mutual discussions or contact with renowned *ṛṣis* (sages) and master minds. The Upaniṣads call these peripatetic votaries of knowledge and seekers after truth *carakas,* who were the diffusers of thought in the country. Thus Uddālaka Āruṇi, a Kuru-Pañcāla scholar, after finishing his education, went to the north and received further instruction from Ṛṣi Śaunaka. He also lived for some time in the land of the *Madras* to place himself under the instruction of Ṛṣi Patañcala Kāpya.[13]

There were also in the country institutions for advanced study known as *pariṣads*. The most famous *pariṣad* of the times was the Pañcāla *pariṣad,* which was patronized by the philosopher-king of the country, Pravāhaṇa Jaivali, who daily drove out of his palace in his royal chariot to attend its sittings.[14]

Besides these residential schools, academies for advanced study, and circles of wandering scholars given to philosophical discussions, there were the assemblies of learned men gathered together by kings at their courts. A typical example of such a conference is described in the *Bṛhadāraṇyaka Upaniṣad,* stating how Janaka, king of Videha, invited to his court the learned scholars of the Kuru-Pañcāla country, 'then known for its abundance of savants', to meet in a philosophical conference, perhaps the earliest of its kind in the world. The procedure adopted by the conference was to make its proceedings as fruitful as possible.[15] Philosophy was then represented in a variety of schools with their different doctrines, and the founders and exponents of these schools were selected to present to the conference the doctrines promulgated by each school. Eight such exponents and leading philosophers were thus chosen. They were Uddālaka Āruṇi, Aśvala, Ārtabhāga, Bhujyu, Uṣasta, Kahola, Vidagdha Śākalya, and Gārgī Vācaknavī (the woman philosopher). Of these, Uddālaka was very famous as the centre of a circle of scholars who contributed most to the philosophy of the Upaniṣads. Aśvala was the *hotṛ* priest of King Janaka.

Bhujyu was a fellow pupil of Āruṇi senior. The most learned of all was Yājñavalkya. King Janaka announced that he would award the royal prize to the philosopher who answered the most subtle and difficult questions that were put to him. Even the woman philosopher Gārgi publicly challenged his wisdom by posing two perplexing problems, but Yājñavalkya successfully answered her questions.

The standard of knowledge attained in those days is indicated in questions like the following one which was put to Yājñavalkya by the philosopher Uṣasta: 'When anyone says, "That is an ox, that is a horse", it is thereby pointed out. Point out to me the revealed, unveiled Brahman, the Ātman which dwells in every thing.'

From the story of the lady Gārgī just mentioned it appears that women were then considered as equals of men in their eligibility and capacity for achieving the highest knowledge. The Upaniṣads also tell us the study of Maitreyī, the worthy wife of Yājñavalkya, as his partner in the pursuit of the highest knowledge.[16]

II

It was during this period that the Vedic scheme of education of the three upper classes of Indo-Aryan society was expanded and systematized in the aphoristic as well as the metrical Smṛtis. In the Smṛti scheme, as has been well said by a distinguished Indian authority,[17] the teacher is 'the pivot of the whole educational system'. Though the old tradition of the father as the teacher was continued down to the times of manu and Yājñavalkya, it was the usual practice to send the boys after the ceremony of *upanayana* (investiture with the sacred thread) to live with a teacher. The texts distinguish between two types of teachers, namely, the *ācārya* (who performs the pupil's *upanayana* and teaches him the whole of the Veda) and the *upādhyāya* (who teaches the pupil only a portion of the veda or its auxiliaries). The *ācārya's* position was very high. The pupil, according to the *Āpastamba Dharma-Sūtra,*[18] was to look upon the teacher as God. In the *Viṣṇu Smṛti*[19] and *Manu Smṛti*[20] the *ācārya*, the father, and the mother are described as the three highest *gurus* of a man, deserving as such his utmost reverence. Elaborate rules are laid down in Manu[21] for a pupil's respectful behaviour towards his *guru*. The pupil, we are told,[22] must not even pronounce his *guru's* name without an honorific title; he must close his ears or leave the place when other people justly or unjustly slander his *guru;* and he who incurs the sin of slandering his *guru* will be born in a lower place of existence in his next birth. The teacher on his part is to have high qualifications of learning and character. An unlearned Brāhmana, we read,[23] is like an elephant made of wood and an antelope made of leather; the Brāhmaṇa (and this applies especially to the Brāhmaṇa teacher) must not, even though afflicted, utter harsh speech or injure anyone in thought or deed; he should constantly shrink from praise as from poison and should welcome scorn as nectar. The pupil, we are told in the same context, may abandon the teacher if he fails to teach or becomes a sinner. With the above we may compare an old text[24] which says that he whom a teacher devoid of learning initiates enters from darkness into darkness, and so does he who is himself unlearned. The texts distinguish between two types of students, namely, the *upakurvāṇa* (one who offers some remuneration to the teacher after completing his studies, and leaves to lead a home life), and the *naiṣṭhika* (one who lives perpetually with his teacher, or in the event of his death with his family). The pupil is to serve the teacher at his bath and toilette, to massage his body, and in general to do work that is pleasing and beneficial to him; he is to do a daily routine of offering fuel to the sacred fire, going round for alms, and performing his devotions at dawn and dusk, willful neglect of these duties being visited with appropriate penances. The pupil is to observe the prescribed rules about dress and mode of begging alms as well as about food and drink; he should be restrained in thought and speech, and should shun personal adornment and amusements. His behaviour should be respectful towards his superiors and guarded in the presence of women. The pupil should pay no fee to his teacher in advance, but at the end of his studies he should offer something according to his means or to the teacher's desire. The strictness of the Smṛti rule on this point is reflected in the texts of Manu and Yājñavalkya, which exclude a person teaching or learning for pay from invitation to the ceremony in memory of one's ancestors and declare him to be guilty of a minor sin.[25] The educational course comprised principally the Vedas studied in the pupil's family, other recensions of the same Veda as also other Vedas being permitted to be studied thereafter. The method of teaching was oral, so much so that reliance on books was included by Nārada[26] in a list of six obstacles to knowledge.

The scheme of training for a Vedic student given above may be supplemented by an account of the education of a Kṣatriya prince given in Kauṭilya's *Arthaśātra*. The importance of the prince's training and discipline is repeatedly emphasized at the outset by the author[27] in the interest of the king's security and success and the stability of his family. How the course of education is to be graduated for him is shown at length.[28] After his tonsure ceremony and before reaching his seventh year, he has to learn the alphabet and the accounts; after the *upanayana* ceremony he has to study the four sciences, namely, *trayī* (the Vedas with their auxiliaries), *ānvīkṣikī* (the three schools of philosophy), *vārttā* (economics), and *daṇḍa-nīti* (politics). Even after the completion of his studies, and his marriage in his sixteenth year, he has to go through a daily routine of receiving lessons in the art of war and in *Itihāsa* (historical traditions). For the rest, the prince's education is based on a sound methodology. Of the two branches of discipline (*vinaya*) namely, 'the acquired' and 'the natural', the first, we are told, should be imparted only to eager and intelligent pupils. Above all, the senses are to be brought under control by checking the mental reaction to them, or else by performance of the canonical injunctions.

The above schemes of education for the Vedic student in general, and for the Kṣatriya prince in particular, are corroborated in part by other sources. In the *Mahābhārata* we have stories of pupils who distinguished themselves by exemplary devotion to their teachers. Such are Upamanyu and Āruṇi (pupils of Dhaumya) and Utaṅka (the pupil's pupil of Dhaumya).[29] We have, again, the story of Droṇa, the Brāhmaṇa who was appointed to teach the art of war to the sons of Pāṇḍu and Dhṛtarāṣṭra by their granduncle the warrior-sage Bhīṣma. The *Milindapañha* (The questions of Menander), a celebrated Buddhist work probably of the first century after Christ, contains a remarkable account of the current curriculum of studies for a Brāhmaṇa and for a prince.[30] The Brāhmaṇa studied the four Vedas (with their auxiliaries), astronomy and astrology, materialistic philosophy, and the science of omens. By contrast, the prince learnt the arts of managing horses, elephants, and chariots, of writing and accounts, and of waging war. In other words, the Brāhmaṇa was expected to study all the known branches of literature and science, while the Kṣatriya was required to confine his attention to the practical arts of fighting and administration. Further light is thrown upon this point by the study of the early career of Nāgasena, the hero of the last-named work, who was born in a distinguished Brāhmaṇa family, and who rose to the position of the foremost Buddhist theologian of his time. The Brāhmaṇa boys, we learn,[30] commenced their education at the teacher's residence when they reached their seventh year, and they paid him their fee in advance. After the Brāhmaṇa student had completed his education, he could, if he chose, seek further knowledge from non-Brāhmaṇa teachers, and he could live thereafter as a wandering scholar, learning from (or vanquishing) distinguished scholars in the best Upaniṣad tradition.

A fresh type of education was developed during this period in the Buddhist monasteries for the training of the newly ordained monks, the rules under this head being laid down in the section of the canon concerned with monastic discipline. The difference between this system and that of the two types mentioned above is that between what may be called the domestic and the collective (or the group) systems. The monk, to begin with, was to place himself under the guidance of a teacher, after making a formal application and receiving his tacit consent. The teacher was called *ācārya* or *upādhyāya*, the former being regarded, in contrast with the Smṛtis, as a deputy or substitute for the latter. The relations between the teacher and the pupil followed the pattern of the Smṛti scheme. The pupil was daily to serve the teacher at his bath, toilette, and meals, and on his begging tour, and nurse him during his illness. The teacher on his side was to give a complete instruction to his pupils, to supply their necessaries, to nurse them during sickness, and so forth. The teacher followed the usual method of oral instruction by answering questions or delivering discourses. The pupils were to observe strict rules about food and clothing, equipment and shelter, which were based upon the combined Smṛti scheme of duties of the Vedic student and the hermit.

The ancient educational tradition of the Upaniṣads is represented during this period by a number of examples. In the *Rāmāyaṇa* we have the instance of the *āśrama* (hermitage) of Bharadvāja at Prayāga, and in the *Mahābhārata* we read of the *āśrama* of Śaunaka, distinguished as a *kulapati* or teacher of ten thousand pupils, at the Naimiṣa forest, and that of Kaṇva on the banks of the Mālinī river. The *Milindapañha* mentions a number of Buddhist hermitages of this type—such as those of Assagutta, of Dhammarakkhita at Pātaliputta, and of Āyupāla at Sāgala—which were visited by Nāgasena as a wandering scholar for the purpose of instruction or controversy.

We now turn to a new type of educational institutions which were a product of the advanced city life characteristic of this period, namely, the higher centres of learning in the metropolitan cities of our country. In the objective accounts of the Jātakas we are told how pupils from distant Mithilā and Rājagṛha in the east and from Ujjayinī in the south, not to speak of those from the Śivi and Kuru kingdoms in Uttarāpatha nearer home, flocked to Takṣaśilā, capital of the Gandhāra kingdom (in the Rawalpindi District of West Punjab), so that they might complete their education under 'world-renowned teachers'. The Jātakas also mention Banaras as a great centre of learning which was established mostly by students trained at Takṣaśilā. In the epic tradition of the *Rāmāyaṇa,* the city of Ayodhyā, capital of the Kośala kingdom, is said to have contained schools of Vedic and Purāṇic learning along with residences of the students. We may quote here two remarkable extracts pointing to a conscious appreciation of the value of foreign travel as constituting the urge of this particular development. In a Jātaka story we read how former kings used to send their sons to distant lands for completing their education, so that they might be trained to quell their pride, to endure heat and cold, and to acquire the ways of the world.[31] The *Mahābhārata*[32] quotes an adage to the effect that a Brāhmaṇa not going abroad (for study) and a king not going to war (when necessary) are swallowed up by the earth, just as creatures living in holes are devoured by serpents. We owe to the Jātakas some vivid sketches of the methods of education that were in vogue at Takṣaśilā. The admission, we learn, was open to pupils of all castes and stations in life with the sole exception of the Caṇḍālas (outcastes). The pupils lived with their teachers or attended as day scholars; the latter class included even married students. The pupils paid their fees in advance, or else served their teacher in lieu of the same. The course of studies comprised the three Vedas as also an unspecified (and evidently may be summarized as follows: The preceptor admitted his pupil by perventional) list of eighteen crafts (*silpas*). Reference is made in particular to the study of elephant lore, of charms and spells of different kinds, of divination, and (what is most important) of archery and medicine. The number of students residing with a single teacher is frequently given as five hundred. Strict discipline was enforced by the teachers among their pupils.

Along with the types of education mentioned above there arose at this period a system of vocational and technical training. The condition of medical education at the time of the rise of Buddhism is illustrated by the narrative of the career of Jīvaka (surnamed Komārabhaccha or 'master of the science of infantile treatment'), which is told in a Pali canonical work.[33] Born as the son of a courtesan at Rājagṛha and brought up by prince Abhaya of Magadha, he was sent to study medicine under a world-renowned teacher at Takṣaśilā. There he stayed for seven years, and he completed his training by passing a difficult practical test in the knowledge of medicinal plants. His subsequent career is said to have been exceptionally brilliant, as he rose to the position of court physician of Bimbisāra, king of Magadha, and established a country-wide practice in medicine and surgery. References to the current condition of medical education occur likewise in the *Milindapañha*.[34] The student, we learn, was to apprentice himself to a teacher on payment of his fee in advance, or else on the condition of offering personal service. Further, there already existed a number of distinguished teachers of the science, who wrote treatises on its different branches. We have a more detailed account in the *Suśruta Saṁhitā*, a well-known surgical work belonging to the early centuries of the Christian era. The account[35] may be summarized as follows: The preceptor admitted his pupil by performing a special *upanayana* ceremony, which was open to all the three upper classes, and according to some, to Śūdras as well. At the ceremony the pupil solemnly undertook in the presence of the sacred fire to observe a number of rules relating to physical purity and moral probity, and to obey his preceptor; the teacher on his side agreed with equal solemnity not to behave towards his pupil otherwise than teaching him properly. The pupil, it was emphatically stated, should acquire proficiency both in theory and practice, failing either of which he would be in the position of a bird clipped of one of its wings. Turning to another point, we find in two stories of the *Divyāvadāna*[36] reference to the training of the sons of rich merchants at that time. The list of studies comprised the knowledge of writing, arithmetic, coins, debts and deposits, examination of gems and residences, elephants and horses, young men and women, and so forth.

III

The old systems of higher education and advanced types of educational institutions were continued during the period of the Imperial Guptas and their successors. The later Smṛtis as also the Smṛti commentaries and digests recapitulate the old rules about education with some additional explanations. To take a few instances, perpetual studentship is included in the list of forbidden practices of the *Kaliyuga* in the *Nāradīya Purāṇa*[37] and the *Āditya Purāṇa*.[38] Acceptance fees by the preceptor from his pupil is condemned in the *Varāha Purāṇa*,[39] but it is allowed tacitly or conditionally in the commentaries of Medhātithi,[40] Aparārka,[41] and Vijñāneśvara[42] as well as in the *Smṛti-candrikā*.[43] A special title of law meaning 'non-rendition of service after entering into a contract' (*abhyupetyāśuśrūṣā*) deals in these works with the duties of the student towards his teacher. Under the general heading of attendants (*śuśrūṣakas*), are included, on the one hand, the Vedic student, the craftsman's apprentice, the hired servant, and the supervisor of labour, who belong to the class of workmen (*karmakaras*), and, on the other hand, the slaves.

The methods of princely education in vogue at this period seem to have followed the older lines. From an extract of the *Mānasollāsa*, an encyclopaedic work attributed to the Western Cālukya king Someśvara III (*c.* A.D. 1126-38), we learn that the prince on reaching his eighth or tenth year should be initiated into the vow of studentship and be instructed thereafter in the Vedas as well as in the military science.[44] After completing his training, the prince should be tested by his father for his skill in the military arts, literature, and the fine arts. The high standard of the prince's education is illustrated at its best by the examples of the scholar-kings of this period such as Samudragupta, Harṣavardhana, Mahendravarman, and Yaśovarman before A.D. 1000, and Someśvara III, Ballālasena, and, above all, Bhoja Paramāra in the centuries thereafter.

In the vivid account of the Chinese Buddhist pilgrim I-tsing, belonging to the latter half of the seventh century, we have a striking testimony to the continuance of the old type of education in a Buddhist monastery. The monastic schools, we are further told, had, besides novices, two classes of lay pupils, namely, children reading the Buddhist scriptures with the object of ordination at some future date, and those studying secular books alone without any intention of renouncing the world.

Among the monasteries of the Gupta period, that of Nālandā in Magadha attained the highest distinction because of the magnificence of its establishment and the intellectual and moral eminence of its alumni. We owe its fullest description to two Chinese Buddhist pilgrims of the seventh century, namely Hiuen Tsang and I-tsing. The buildings consisted of eight halls besides the great college, with ten thousand resident monks (according to the former account), of eight halls as well as three hundred apartments tenanted by three thousand or three thousand five hundred monks (according to the latter version). Because of their learning and high character the monks were looked upon as models all over India. Such was the fame of this great centre of learning that it attracted students from abroad, but because of the strict admission test only two or three out of ten succeeded in getting admission. In the account of I-tsing we are further told that Nālandā in eastern and Valabhī in western India were the two places in the country that were visited by advanced students for completing their education. During the rule of the Pāla kings of eastern India, a fresh group of monasteries (namely, those of Vikramaśila, Somapurī, Jagaddala, and Uddaṇḍapura) rose into eminence as great centres of learning. From these monasteries issued a rich literature of Tantrika Buddhism, much of which has been preserved in Tibetan translation. Among the alumni of these monastic universities, special mention may be made of Dīpaṅkara Śrījñāna (otherwise called Atīśa), who became in later life the founder of a reformed school of Buddhism in Tibet, and Vidyākara, who wrote a great sanskrit anthology, just published, called the *Subhāṣita-ratnakośa.*[45]

The old type of forest hermitages is represented during this period by a historical example which we owe to Bāṇa, the author of the *Harṣacarita*. In the last chapter of this work the author introduces us to a great Buddhist teacher called Divākaramitra, whose hermitage in the depths of the Vindhya forest was visited by King Harṣa in search of his long-lost sister. The author gives us a vivid picture of the cosmopolitan character of the sage's following, and the intensely scholastic atmosphere prevailing around him.

Our account of the centres of higher learning during these times will be incomplete without some reference to the numerous concrete instances of this type furnished by our historical sources. In the eleventh century the schools of Kashmir were so famous that they drew scholars from distant Gauḍa (West Bengal) for higher learning. Above all, we have a long series of inscriptions covering the whole of the period under review which record endowments of real or personal property made by individuals and communities throughout our land for the promotion of higher learning.[46]

The course of studies laid down for the Vedic student in the Smṛti works of this period follows the traditional lines. The student, says Medhātithi,[47] should study from one to three recensions of a single Veda, while the *Smṛti-candrikā* requires the student to study and follow just another recension of the Veda after going through his own. As regards primary education, the Smṛti authorities mention a sacrament called *Vidyārambha* or *akṣara-svīkṛti* (beginning of education' or 'learning the alphabet'), which was started in the boy's sixth year, or at any rate before his *upanayana*. The boy read a primer called *Mātṛkā-nyāsa* as also arithmetic. A story in the *Narmamālā*, a satirical work of the eleventh century Kashmirian writer Kṣemendra, shows that the rich householders of the time employed resident tutors for their children, sometimes with disastrous results for their own families.[48]

A complete and the most authentic account of the courses of studies during this period has come down to us from the pen of the two great Chinese Buddhist pilgrims mentioned above. According to Hiuen Tsang, the children, after mastering a short primer called 'the Twelve Chapters' or 'the *Siddha* composition', were trained in five sciences, namely, grammar, the science of arts and crafts, medicine, the science of reasoning, and the science of the internal. The curriculum of studies, according to I-tsing, comprised in graded sequence Pāṇini's grammar with the commentaries, logic, and metaphysics, in addition to which the Sūtras and the Śāstras were prescribed for monks. The parallel list of subjects studied at the Nālandā monastery comprised, according to Hiuen Tsang, not only the works of all the eighteen Buddhist schools but also the Vedas, logic, grammar, medicine, the *Atharva-vidyā,* the Sāṁkhya, and so forth.

Some light is thrown upon the training of the craftsman's apprentice by the later Smṛtis from Nārada onwards as also by the Smṛti commentaries and digests under the head mentioned above (Breach of Contract). When the apprentice, we read, had settled with his preceptor the period of his apprenticeship, the latter was to take him to his house, train him in his craft, and treat him as his son. The preceptor refusing to give him his training or making him do some other work was liable to a fine, while the apprentice deserting his flawless teacher was liable to corporal punishment or compulsory repatriation. According to the great Venetian traveller Marco Polo, who visited the extreme south of India in the closing years of the thirteenth century, the boys of the tradesmen of the Pāṇḍya kingdom, on reaching their thirteenth year, were dismissed by their parents with a small pocket-money for earning their living by trade. Thus they grew up to be very dexterous and keen traders. Testimony to the high standard of the craftsmen's training is furnished by the superb remains of art and architecture that have come down to us from this period.

Turning, lastly, to the condition of female education during these times, we have to mention that the ban on Vedic study by women and on their utterance of Vedic *mantras* at their sacraments, which had been imposed by the older Smṛtis, was continued and developed by their successors. The *Smṛti-candrikā,*[49] significantly enough, explains as belonging to a different age cycle the text of the *Hārīta Smṛti* dividinging women into two classes, namely, students of the sacred lore (*brahmavādinīs*) and those married straightway (*sadyovadhūs*). This development is no doubt connected with the tendency in the later Smṛtis to reduce progressively the marriageable age of girls. On the other hand, we know from other sources that women of the upper classes enjoyed such opportunities for education in the fine arts that some of them became accomplished poetesses and authorities on *belles-lettres*. Of such we have historical examples in Princess Rājyaśrī (sister of King Harṣavardhana of the house of Thanesar) and Avanti-sundarī, wife of the dramatist and rhetorician Rājaśekhara. The story of Princess Kādambari and Mahāśvetā in Bāṇa's prose romance[50] and that of Kāmandakī in Bhavabhūti's great drama[51] seem to suggest the existence of regular institutions where girls received their training, sometimes in the company of male students. In the stories of the *Upamiti-bhavaprapañca-Kathā,*[52] a Jaina allegorical work of the tenth century, we are told how princesses were skilled in the arts of painting, music, and versification.

—*R.K. Mookerji*

REFERENCES

1. On the subject of Indian education the following works may be consulted: *Promotion of Learning in Ancient India* by Narendra Nath Law; *Ancient Indian Education (Brāhmanical and Buddhist)* by Radha Kumud Mookerji (1947); *Education in Ancient India* (5th Ed.) by A.S. Altekar; and above all, *History of Dharmaśāstra* by P.V. Kane, Vol. II, pp. 268-415. For a survey of the whole subject during successive periods, *vide* also the chapters on education by Radha Kumud Mookerji in Vol. II and by the present writer in Vols. III-V of *The History and Culture of the Indian People.*

2. As the poet Rabindranath Tagore writes in his inimitable style: 'A most wonderful thing we notice in India is that here the forest, not the town, is the fountain-head of all its civilization. Wherever in India its earliest and most wonderful manifestations are noticed, we find that men have not come into such close contact as to be rolled or fused into a compact mass. There, trees and plants, rivers and lakes, had ample opportunity to live in close relationship with men. In these forests, though there was human society, there was enough of open space, of aloofness; there was no jostling. Still this aloofness did not produce inertia in the Indian mind, rather it rendered it all the brighter. It is the forest that has nurtured the two great ancient ages of India, the Vedic and the Buddhist. As did the Vedic *ṛṣis*. Lord Buddha also showed his teachings in the many woods of India. The current of civilization that flowed from its forests inundated the whole of India.' (Quoted in *Ancient Indian Education* (by R.K. Mookerji), p. xxxv.

3. The supreme need of a teacher is thus explained in the *Chāndogya Upaniṣad* (VI. 14. 1-2): 'Precisely, my dear sir, as a man who has been

brought blindfold from the country of Gandhāra and then set at liberty in the desert, goes astray to the east or north or south because he has been brought thither blindfold and set at liberty also blindfold; but, after that, when someone has taken off the bandage and told him, "In this direction Gandhāra lies, go in this direction", instructed and prudent, asking the road from village to village, he finds his way home to Gandhāra; even so the man who in this world has met with a teacher becomes conscious, "To this (transitory world) I shall belong only until the time of my release, thereupon I shall go home".

4. This distinction between grades of knowledge is very well described in the *Chāndogya Upanisad* (VII. I), where the Sage Nārada approaches Sanatkumāra after completing his period of studentship, during which he studied the four Vedas, the Vedāṅgas, and many practical subjects known in those days. Nārada says to Sanatkumāra: These subjects, sir, I have studied. Therefore I am learned in the scriptures (*mantravid*), but not as regards the Ātman (*Ātmavid*). Yet I have heard from personages like you that he who knows the Ātman vanquishes sorrow. I am in sorrow. Lead me then, I pray, beyond the reach of sorrow.

5. Śaṅkara in his *Viveka-cūḍāmaṇi* (Anc. Ind. Edu.; p. xxxi) further explains *śravana* as listening to the instruction of the teacher and knowing from him the primary truth that the Self is to be differentiated from non-Self appearing in various forms. Bondage is moved by knowledge. The knowledge that is thus received through the ear was aptly called *śruti*, 'what has been heard'. It was a term for revealed knowledge.

6. *Vijātīya-dehādi-pratyaya-virahito 'dvitīya-vastu-sajātīya-pravāhah.* (*Sarva-Vedānta-Siddhānta-Sāra-Saṁgraha*, V. 814).

7. In the story of Nārada (*Chā. U.*, VII. 1) sanatkumāra answered him: 'Whatever you have studied (including even the Vedas) is mere words.' Similarly, Śvetaketu, spending twelve years in a thorough study of all the Vedas, is found by his father Uddālaka Āruṇi only 'full of conceit about his erudition, without that knowledge through which everything is known'. (*Ibid.* VI. 1). Upakosala Kāmalāyana was another student who even with his twelve years' study and austerities was not considered fit by his teacher for the highest knowledge (*Ibid.*, IV. 10). Therefore the *Bṛhadāraṇyaka Upaniṣad* (IV. 4. 21) states: 'The seeker after the highest knowledge should not seek after the knowledge of the books, for that is mere weariness of the tongue.' The *Kaṭha Upaniṣad* (I. 2. 23) similarly points out: 'Not by the study of the Vedas is the Ātman attained, nor by intelligence, nor by much book-learning.'

8. XI. 5. 4. 5.

9. *Chā. U.*, (IV. 4. 1 ff; 5. 1; 6. 2; etc.) tells us the story of Satyakāma Jābāla, who was of uncertain parentage, but was admitted as a pupil by his teacher Gautama who discovered in him the real characteristics of a Brāhmaṇa, namely, spirituality and truthfulness.

10. XI. 3. 3. 5.

11. Bergson similarly insists (*Morality and Religion*, p. 6) on the withdrawal of the mind from the world of matter, which 'imposes upon it its spatial forms and thus arrests the natural creativity, inwardness, and suppleness of conscious life'. 'Consciousness,' he says, 'in shaping itself into intelligence, that is to say, in concentrating itself on matter, seems to externalize itself'. It is only when the Self 'brackets' itself out from the realm of things that the psychic processes regain their normal ways. He further points out that 'the individual's consciousness, delving downwards, reveals to him, the deeper he goes, his original personality, to which he may cling as something solid, as means of escape from a life of impulse, caprice, and regret. In our innermost selves, we may discover an equilibrium more desirable than the one on the surface. Certain aquatic plants, as they rise to the surface, are ceaselessly jostled by the current; their leaves, meeting above the water, interlace, thus imparting to them stability above. But still more stable are the roots which, firmly planted in the earth, support them from below.'

12. IV. 4. 22.

13. *Br. U.*, III. 7. 1.

13. *Anc. Ind. Ed.*, by R.K. Mookerji, p. 126.

14. *Chā, U.*, VII. 14; *Br. U.*, VI. 2. 1-7.

15. *Br. U.*, III. 8.

16. The story is that when Yājñavalkya, after rejecting King Janaka's offer of his kingdom, decided to retire at once 'from home to homelessness' and to devote himself entirely to the quest of truth, he called his wife Maitreyī to take leave of her after providing for her living. She wisely asked him the fundamental question, 'My lord, if this whole earth full of wealth belonged to me, should I be immortal with it or not?' 'No', replied Yājñavalkya, 'like the life of rich people will be your life: But there is no hope of immortality through wealth.' Knowing wealth to be only a means of enjoyment, Maitreyī at once resolved: 'What should I do with that by which I shall not become immortal?' And so she chose a life of renunciation and quest of Truth.

17. Kane, *H. Dh.*, II. p. 326.

18. I. 2. 6. 13.

19. XXXII. 1-2.
20. II. 227-37.
21. II. 69 f.
22. *Manu*, II. 199 f.
23. *Ibid.*, II. 157 f.
24. *Āp. Dh. S.*, I. 1. 1. 11.
25. *Manu*. XI. 63; *Yāj.*, II. 255.
26. Cf. *Sm. C.*, I. 167 f.
27. *Kauṭ.*, I. 5-6, 17.
28. *Ibid.*, I. 5-6.
29. *Mbh.*, I. 3.
30. IV. 3. 26; I. 9.
31. Jātaka No. 252.
32. XII. 57. 3.
33. *Mahāvagga*, VIII. 1. 4 f.
34. IV. 720; VI. 11.
35. *Suśuruta Samhitā*, I. 20-23.
36. 26. 99-100.
37. I. 24. 13-16.
38. Cf. *Sm. C.*, I. 29.
39. XIV. 5.
40. On *Manu*, III. 156.
41. Triv. Ed., I. p. 50.
42. On *Yāj.*, I. 28.
43. Vol. I. p. 140.
44. III. 1203-1304.
45. For the accounts of Hiuen Tsang and I-tsing *vide* the works *On Yuan Chwang's Travels in India* (2 vols.) by Thomas Watters, and *Record of the Buddhist Religion as Practised in India and the Malay Archipelago, by* I-tsing translated by J.A. Takakusu.
46. For a connected account of the private and public foundations of advanced centres of learning after the inscriptions of this period *vide* Chapter XII. p. 368 and Chapter XVII. pp. 510-11 of *The History and*

Culture of the Indian People by the present writer, vols. IV and V. respectively.

47. On *Manu*, III. 2.

48. *Narmamālā*, II.

49. I. 60-63.

50. *Kādambarī*, p. 240.

51. *Mālatī-Mādhava*, Act. I.

52. Ed. by Peterson and Jacobi, pp. 354, 453-59, and 875-92.

2

Vedic Education

Introduction

"The present is embedded in the past" is a well-worn truism. The glory of ancient India, while illuminating the present, is making her future fascinating. The unique feature of ancient India is that the formation of her culture was influenced not so much by political, economic or social factors as by religion. Well-nigh all the spheres of life were dominated by religion. Indian culture is suffused thoroughly by religious sentiments. The approach of our forefathers to life and their subtle analysis and codification of duties, all indicate their cherished spiritual values. Their political as well as social realities, were not circumscribed within the narrow geographical bounds. Their attitude to life was characterised by width of outlook and they identified their duty with the devotion to the ideal of 'summum bonum' of mankind.[1] India did not remain contented with the evolution of her territorial and ethnic culture; she gave birth to the conception of 'the Superonan', and the multi-faceted progress of all mankind became the sole objective of her civilization. Even today, when she is groaning under the stress of destitution, social evils and political failings, an aureole surrounds her face irradiating the internal glow of her spirit. She is still a standard-bearer of the suffering hamanity.

A novel and strange thought-current emerging from religious predominance in the political, economic and social spheres, flooded the vale of life in the Vedic India. The ancient Hindu polity, eschewing the imponderables of violence, friction and self-aggrandisement, was based on the principles of love, honourable conduct and good behaviour. The development of the individual was sought to be identified with that of the group. In the economic sphere the activities were controlled by delicate and pure religious feelings, so much so that the entire fabric of society was poised on the basic spiritual sentiments and noble principles. Life had a definite aim, an ideal; and the attainment of that ideal was thought to transcend all material achievements. The educational evolution in ancient India was also founded upon this principle. "Learning in India through the ages had been prized and pursued not for its own sake, if we may so put it, but for the sake, and as a part of religion. It was sought as the means of salvations or self-realisation, as the means to the highest end of life, viz. '*Mukti*' or emancipation."[2]

The creation of entire Indian literature, science and arts reflected but her endeavour to reach the self-same destination. The ancient Indian literature is, as it were, the vehicle of religion, as has been observed by Macdonnell: "Since the birth of the oldest Vedic poetry, we find Indian literature, for a period of more than a thousand years, bearing 'an exclusively religious stamp'; even those latest productions of the Vedic age which cannot be called directly religious are yet meant to further religious ends. This is, indeed, implied by the term *Vedic*, for *Veda*, primarily signifying *knowledge* (from root *Vid*, to know), designates 'sacred lore' as a branch of literature.[3]

Ancient Indian Education has evolved strictly on Indian epistemological and philosophic traditions. The idea of the ephemerality of life and the world, the concept of death and the futility of mundane pleasures has provided them with a special angle of vision. In fact, the entire educational tradition originated in these principles. That is why the Indian sages devoted themselves to the study of a Supra-sensible world and spiritual Diety and moulded their life accordingly. They never took the material world seriously and all their faculties instead of effecting the advancement of external being sought to create and expand the inner self. Though Death did not excite fear in them because they regarded it as an inevitable natural phenomenon, yet they conceived of an eternal life in order to get everlasting riddance from this mortal coil and death. Accordingly, the world generally appeared to them illusory, and the state of oneness of the soul with Divine Being, was regarded as the supreme reality. Thus the ultimate aim of education was *Chitti-Vritti-nirodha* (the inhibition of mental activities connected with the so-called concrete world). It might, however, be added that education did not neglect the development of the pupil's powers for his advancement.

In ancient age, the pupil, away from the haunts of din and distractions of the material world, amidst beautiful natural surroundings, sitting at the feet of his teacher would comprehend all the intricate problems of life through listening, intellection and meditation. His life was pure and chaste as snow. Life to him was nothing less than a laboratory. He would not remain contented with mere bookish learning but acquire fairly practical knowledge of the world and society through his close contact with the people. "Only the mental realisation of Truth—an analytical current of thought—would not be sufficient, though in the initial stages that too was essential as an object."[4]

Thus an attempt was made to make the ancient student, capable of experiencing the Supreme Truth himself and moulding the society accordingly.

The residence of the pupil at the house of the teacher accompanied by a sense of devoted service had been a unique tradition in ancient India. The pupil, through such a close contact with his teacher, would naturally imbibe his qualities through emulation. This was regarded as indispensable for the fullest development of his personality, because the teacher was supposed to symbolise all the good ideals, traditions and code of behaviour of the society from where the pupil hailed. Thus the close association of the teacher with the pupil made the latter fully acquainted with all the cherished social traditions.

Besides this, another characteristic of Indian educational system was that education was wedded to the practical ends of life. The pupil's residence at his teacher's house would make it possible for him to develop social intercourse as it was his sacred duty to collect fuel-wood, supply water and do other household odd jobs for the teacher. In this way, not only would he receive instructions related to family life, but also learn the concrete lesson of the dignity of labour and service. The pupil derived immense benefit of a spiritual and psychic nature by tending his teacher's cows and serving him in diverse ways. The problem of discipline among the modern students which has baffled all solutions in today's educational set-up would resolve itself automatically with added advantage to the ancient students who could receive a valuable training in the occupations of animal husbandry, agriculture and dairy-farming etc. There runs a tale in the *Chhandogaya Upanishad* about the great sage Satya Kama who, during his pupilage, used to tend his teacher's cows the number whereof grew, under his supervision, from four hundred to one thousand. Similarly the *Brihadaranyaka* tells us of Rishi Yajnavalkya who had been given one thousand cows in charity by king Janaka awarding his profound learning. It is, therefore, evident that education was not merely theoretical, but was related indissolubly to the realities of life. In the Rigveda, we come across an instance of a poet-sage whose father was a physician (*Bhishag*) and mother, a grinder of corn (*Upala-Prakashini*). Higher education was thus not inconsistent with manual labour. Our great sages had unravelled the complex problems in ordinary spheres of day-to-day life. The educational method which goes by the name 'Learning by Doing' and which is understood to have been originated in modern age by the U.S.A. was the very core and essence of education in ancient India. Life served as the laboratory for the educational experimentation, from where many noble traditions were developed.

Similarly, begging alms by the pupils for their own subsistence and service of the *Guru* (Preceptor) explained the eleemosynary characteristic of ancient educational system. The object was not to render the students dependent on others, nor did it run counter to the good of the society. On the other hand, begging by the student in ancient times, was regarded as honourable. It fostered in the pupil, noble sentiment of self-abnegation and other humanitarian virtues. This system, by sublimating all unruly passions and ego in the pupil enabled him to face the realities of life. It was, thus, a concrete lesson in the cultivation of virtue of self-help and the sense of gratitude and duty towards the society.

Thus we find that the ancient Indian educational system developed in terms of the needs of the individual and those of the society as well. Its roots were firmly implanted in the depths of society and, therefore, its efflorescence was natural. It had a definite ideal and a definite mission. The ancient educational centres, situated amidst Fauna and Flora and beauties of Nature, were the perennial and inexhaustible fountain-head of Indian civilization and culture. India owing to her indifferent attitude towards material prosperity, might have made no appreciable advancement in political and economic spheres; but in the educational field, her contribution has not been insignificant. While people of many of the western world were learning only to prattle in civilized language, India was sounding the depths of metaphysical and philosophical thought. She dispelled the gloom of ignorance and developed the capacity to illuminate the world with her knowledge. Thus she presented a measuring-rod for human civilization. The ancient Indian teachers evolved a special form of education whereby harmony was established between materialism and spiritualism; and human life thus headed towards perfection.

Before giving a detailed account of the Vedic Education, it is necessary here to make a short appraisal of the four Vedas, for the education of that period is based on them.

1. *The Rigveda:* The Rigveda is the earliest and most illuminating work of the Aryan religion in India. All the same it should be noted that no history of Indian education is traceable before the Rigveda. Though the Dravidian civilization had reached the acme of culmination even before the age of the Rigveda, yet no authentic record of educational system incorporated in it, is available. The Rigveda marks the dawn of Indian Aryan civilization. There is no doubt about the fact that it should not have been possible for India to have prematurely produced so illustrious a work as the Rigveda in the absence of the background of a high civilization. India should certainly have had to pass through several stages of gradual evolution in her attempt to reach the civilization of the period of the Rigveda. "One thing is certain", says Max Muller, namely, that there is nothing more primitive, more ancient than the hymns of the Rigveda, whether in India or the whole Aryan world. Yet it does not mark merely the dawn of its culture, but rather its meridian

where we find Indian civilization and philosophy to have attained fully maturity."

According to ancient Indian tradition, the Rigveda is that great treasure of learning which contains in germinal form the knowledge and main trends of thought of that age. In reality, Hindu civilization has been founded on the Rigveda which, in view of the triviality of materialistic prosperity, contains positive injunctions as to the introversion of all human tendencies for the attainment of eternal happiness.

The Rigveda is a history of the evolution of civilization and culture of that age. It is a compilation of one thousand and seventeen hymns known as "*Samhita*". These hymns must have been collected gradually during the course of a long period. The editors of the Rigveda Samhita should have evolved highly advanced principles with a view to collecting this vast literature dealing with different ages. The Samhita is the collection of varied types of hymns: some are related to pure literature, religion and ceremonies, still others to litanies and yajna-methods. These hymns are dedicated to the invocation of Indra, Varuna, Agni, Marut, Usha, Surya and Parijanya. There are other hymns too about various ceremonies such as those related to birth, wedding, charity, yajna and death. Lastly, we have philosophical hymns and those which contain the description of Creation by the *Virat Purusha*. The Samhita thus mirrors the culminating point of cultural development of life in its various aspects.[5]

The Rigveda is divided into ten Mandalas out of which, six Mandalas (Two to seven) having originality of pattern, have been attributed to six representative Rishis, namely: Gritsamada, Visvamitra, Vamadeva, Atri, Bhardvaja, and Vasishtha. These original Mandals multiplied in number gradually through the contributions of Rishis and their families. Every family would preserve this rich heritage. The Rigveda Samhita in its complete form, came into existence through the addition of the first, eighth, ninth and tenth Mandalas to the main and original six ones afore-mentioned. In this way the entire work includes 1,028 hymns; 10,580 verses in 70,000 lines of 1,53,826 words. Of these 70,000 lines, five thousand lines are merely repetitive. It is obvious then that the authors of the hymns of a later period were mere drawing upon the pre-existent lore of hymns which had already been afloat in the country.

Other Vedas: Following Rigveda, came into existence there three Samhitas of Sama, Yajuh and Atharva in close succession. These Vedas ushered in a new kind of literature. The order of hymns include in the Rigveda is not an accord with that of the sacrifices; so much so there are some such hymns as have no relation to the Yajna or sacrifice at all. On the contrary, in the Sama, Yajuh and Atharva, the hymns follow closely in order to sacrifice. In the very period of the Sama and Yajuh, the old Rigvedic religion had begun to evince indications of considerable development while priesthood was also gaining ground. There were three main branches of the priests: *Hotri, Udagatri* and *Adhvaryu*. In addition to these, there was a fourth group too known as *Brahman*. All these four categories of the priesthood had three assistant-priests each in addition. The entire order of priesthood was divided into sixteen members. All these priests were, in general, called *Ritvij*. In course of time, a seventeenth *Ritvij* was also added to these; *'Sadasyu'* was the designation of this person whose duty it was to superintend the whole sacrifice.

The whole order of priesthood can be classified as below:

- (1) Hotṛi
  - Maitravaruna
  - Achavaka
  - Gravastut
- (2) Udgātṛi
  - Prastotri
  - Pratihatri
  - Subra-manya
- (3) Adhvaryu
  - Pratishthatri
  - Neshtri
  - Unnetri
- (4) Brahman
  - Brahmanach
  - Agnidhak
  - Potri-chamsin

Higher education, later on related itself to priesthood and ritualistic aspect of religion. The formal and material aspects of worship and sacrifice now became so prominent that the priests had needs to specialise and train themselves regularly in these formal rituals. There was division of labour to a higher degree among the priests. In the beginning there was no such group distinction among them and every priest was deemed fit to undertake every work pertaining to Yajna.

The curriculum of education was the same for all the Brahmacharins; each of them was required to attain proficiency in the melodies of verses and ritualistic aspects of Yajna. In course of time, however, essentiality of division of labour was strongly felt owing to the growing complex nature of formal aspect of sacrifice, because any individual priest could not be expected to specialise in the triple aspects of the Yajna. The priest student in the beginning, however, received training in all the three methods; but, later on, would specialise only in any one of them. At length, the order of priesthood was divided mainly into three main divisions as mentioned above. These priests respectively represented each one of the Vedas. They had separate training centres. This was so about 1000 B.C. to 800 B. C.[6]

1. *The Hotṛi*: He belonged to the first order of priesthood that undertook to recite the sacrificial hymns. These hymns were sung in honour of certain gods as *Indra*, *Agṇi* or *Māruta*. The *Hotṛi* specialised in this duty. He was regarded as the chief priest.

2. *The Udgātṛi*: The second part of the ritual of the Yajna was related to the Soma Yajna. Soma was a sort of juice that was obtained by crushing a particular creeping shrub. It was inebrious in quality. The Āryans, therefore, imputing some mysterious power to it, began to worship it as god, for according to their views, it ensured immortality to them. Thus came into being a novel ceremony according to which the hymns began to be recited. The priests who would chant these hymns, came to be known as the *Udgatṛis*.

3. *The Adhvaryu*: The duty of these priests was closely associated with the main part of the Yajna. They would specialise in the actual performance of sacrifice full of numerous ritualistic operations.

As has already been mentioned above, the Brāhman represented, in addition to these, a fourth group of priesthood who superintended and directed the worshipping ceremony as a whole. This group acquired proficiency in all the three Vedas and was empowered to exercise decisive opinion in different parts of the performance of sacrifice; their opinion on all doubtful issues was regarded as final and authoritative.

2. *The Sāma Veda:* The *Udgatṛi* was required to acquire proficiency in all the melodies of the verses for the purpose of the ceremony of the *Soma Yajna*. The compilation of all the hymns recited on the occasion of the *Soma Yajna* came to be known by the name 'The Sāma Veda'. The *Udgatṛi* priests have contributed only seventy-eight verses out of a lot of fifteen hundred and forty-nine verses. The remaining constituting the bulk of the verses have been taken out of the eighth and the ninth Mandalas of the Rigveda. The verses of the Sāma Veda have been classified into two parts which are called the '*Ārchikas*'. Each *Ārchika* contains five hundred and eighty-five '*riks*' each of which is related to some tune or the other. The second part of the Sāma Veda known as the '*Uttarrāchika*' comprises 400 hymns mostly of three stanzas each. The text of the Sāma Veda is thus directed to the learning of melodies. It is more or less like a song book which contains the entire text of the songs.

3. *The Yajurveda:* Though the duty of chanting the hymns on the occasion of sacrifice was mainly undertaken by the *Hotṛi*, yet certain hymns related to prayer or invocation were sung by the *Adhvaryus* who were closely associated with the sacrificial operations. Consequently, a separate training school was established for the education of these priests. They adopted the Yajurveda and thus it is the prayer-book of the *Adhvaryu* order of priesthood.

The Yajurveda is the collection of prose *Mantras*, majority of them being spurious ones adopted from the Rigveda. The Yajurveda consists of two divisions called Black (*Krishna*) and White (*Sukla*). The Black Yajurveda contains, besides prose-Mantras, certain hymns in verse. The elementary prose literature of India which culminated in the Upanishadas lies in its rudimentary form in the Yajurveda. It is a unique contribution to the ancient Indian literature. The White Yajurveda consists of only those hymns, prayers and sacrificial formulae that were uttered by the priests. We get in the Yajurveda glimpses of the religious and secular aspects of life in India. It prescribed various kinds of Yajna as *Pinda Yajna*, *PitṛiYajna*, *Agnihotra*, *Chāturmāsyas*, *Rājsūya*, *Asvamedha*, *Agnichayana*, etc. There are *Mantras* in the Yajurveda for the material welfare of the country as, "*Brahmavarchase jāytām asmin rāshtre*".

4. *The Atharvaveda:* In the beginning only three Vedas were popular. In course of time a fourth Veda called the Atharvaveda was also recognised. It is more original in contents than other Vedas. Unlike its preceding Vedas, the majority of *Mantras* have not been adapted from the Rigveda. Only twelve hundred stanzas out of a lot of 6,000 have been derived from the Rigveda. The entire Veda contains 731 hymns divided into twenty books. The Atharvaveda is the earliest book extant on medical science. It refers to a number of herbs for the cure of diverse diseases. We find in the Atharvaveda a detailed account of various herbs used as efficacious remedies against many fierce diseases such as fever, anaemia, delirium, consumption, snake-bite, scrofula, etc. The ninth book refers to Astronomy. A particular part of it deals with many rituals pertaining to domestic life, *e.g.* birth, marriage or death. According to certain thinkers, the Atharvaveda deals with the magic spells, because it contains those hymns which were chanted by the priests in order to ward off and destroy certain evils such as disease, enemy, savage brutes and natural calamities. Besides, there are other hymns which were uttered to attain worldly success and prosperity; again, many others are there dealing with Kings, Assemblies, Economics, Politics and Philosophy. The Atharvaveda, thus, is thoroughly secular in character containing a vivid description of various arts and sciences.

Education in the Rigveda

Introduction: The age of the origination of the *Mantras* in the Rigveda was essentially an age of creation followed closely by that of criticism and compilation. The first age produced the Rishis who were seers of truth. It is believed that these sages, by virtue of their '*Tapas*' and asceticism or Yoga, were gifted with the vision of a clairvoyant capable of knowing about the past, the present and the future. They were, in a later age, followed by the sages known as *Srutaṛishis*. The seers would impart their *Mantras* to these *Srutaṛishis* through oral preaching (*Upde'sa*). *Tapas* was regarded as the chief means of acquiring spiritual knowledge. The saints, dwelling in the forests, attained to Eternal Bliss and knowledge by virtues of *Tapas*. The Rigveda contains the description of seven Rishis and the divine powers of their *Tapas* which is capable of raising the lowest to the highest. Rita and Satya (Truth of thought and speech) are regarded as being originated from *Tapas*; even the whole creation is thought to be the result of the *Tapas* of *Brahmā*.

When, through the *Tapas* and Yoga of the sages, the highest knowledge was acquired and stored up in the form of stanzas and hymns, there were evolved some such methods as would conserve this knowledge and bequeath it to the posterity. Every Rishi, therefore, would impart to his son or pupil that knowledge which he himself had acquired. That knowledge was regarded as the patrimony of that family. The Vedic family-schools came into existence in this fashion. The teacher made his pupils learn the text by rote. Every pupil acquired knowledge according to his individual capacity. Sāyaṇa refers to three categories of the students: the *Mahaprajñān*, the *Madhyamaprajñān*, and the *Alpaprajñānin*, i.e. very intelligent, normally intelligent and subnormal, respectively. This classification naturally points to the difference in the mental powers of various students. These pupils crammed the hymns in recitative form. The whole atmosphere would reverberate with the simultaneous recitation of the hymns. A particular hymn in the Rigveda has compared this sort of recitation to the croaking of frogs.

Educational System: The students started the recitation of the Vedic hymns in the early hours of morning before the birds announced the day-break. The chanting of *Mantras* had evolved into the form of a fine art. Special attention was paid to the correct pronunciation of words, *Pada*, or even letters. The *Chhandas* or Metre was made of *Padas* or divisions and *Padas* of letters or *Aksharas*. The Vedic knowledge was imparted by the Guru to the pupil through regulated and prescribed pronunciation which the pupil would commit to memory, having listened to it alternatively. Only that knowledge which was received from the lips of the teacher was regarded as purely Vedic; the educational system, in a way, was oral. It shows that alphabet and art of writing had not evolved till then. There has also been a tradition that *Sruti* or Veda should appeal not the eyes but the ears. The *Mahābhārata* invokes eternal damnation upon those who endeavour to write the Veda.[7] Evidence, however, is there that art of writing was in vogue even during the age of the Rigveda.

The Vedic hymns were regarded as instinct with certain mystical power. The belief was current that if the Vedic hymns were to be recited properly in accordance with the prescribed regulations, they would reveal the spiritual and divine efficacy of their own. On the other hand, the influence of such *Mantras* as were pronounced incorrectly, was destroyed; and it was believed that ruin would befall the person who recited them wrongly.[8] But it should not, however, be assumed that recitation was the main thing. Unintelligent memorisation of the Vedic hymns was regarded as utterly futile.[9] The meditation and comprehension of the *Mantras* was considered to be far more important than the mechanical recitation thereof. "He who does not realise the ultimate Truth behind the Rik and Akshara (word and letter) in which rest all gods—what will he do by merely reciting and repeating the Riks?" He, who having studied the Veda did not comprehend its meaning, could be compared to an ass that, while bearing the load of Sandal-wood, feels only its weight without being benefited by its redolence.

To sum up, the system of education which evolved in the Rigveda concerns itself with the acquisition of the Supreme Knowledge, religion and Brahma. The Rigveda does not deal with ordinary secular knowledge and the solution of commonplace worldly problems. The methodology of obtaining the knowledge of the Absolute "*Paraṁbrahmajñāna*" was not identical with that of acquiring knowledge of physical sciences, arts, and crafts. The aim of the Veda was the knowledge of the Ultimate Truth and the realisation of "*Paraṁbrahmajñāna*". The Rigveda prescribes *Tapas* as the only means of its realisation. The language of the Vedic hymns evolved out of the popular dialect. This was the elementary form of Sanskrita. Thus the great seers of the Absolute Truth, Rishis, Manishis, and Munis, having realised that knowledge through *Tapas* and Yoga revealed it in the Vedic language. These Rishis would usually, on the occasion of Sacrifices, formulate the Vedic learning and language, by their mutual discussions. The members of these Academies have been designated *Sākhās*.

In the Rigveda era, there existed small domestic schools run by the teacher himself. The pupils would lodge and board at the house of their teacher. Their mode of living was strictly guided by the prescribed disciplinary rules. The elementary education was accessible to all the Brāhmanas, whereas higher education was confined only to those who proved worthy of it. The students deemed unfit for it were sent back either to agriculture or commerce; spiritual life was forbidden to them.

Characteristics: Some special features of the educational system of the Rigveda era are summed up as below:

1. The home of the preceptor served as the institution where the pupil lived after the *Upanayana* ceremony. The teacher would, in place of the father, discharge the duties of guardian who shouldered the responsibility of his ward's maintenance.

2. The pupil was eligible to admission to the preceptor's house only on the basis of his moral fitness and unimpeachable conduct. A pupil who was considered to be belonging to a lower order of moral conduct would be forbidden to live in *Gurukulas*.

3. The discipline of *brahmacharya* was compulsory. Though a married youth was entitled to get education, yet he was denied the right of being the residential pupil.

4. It was one of the sacred duties of the pupil to serve his preceptor. Being a residential pupil, he would look to the comforts of his *Guru*. Not infrequently he would look to the domestic affairs. He pledged his devotion to his teacher in thought, speech and deed and worshipped him as his own father or God.

5. Those pupils who neglected their duties towards the preceptor or whose demeanour offended the disciplinary rules were debarred from education and expelled from the institutions.

It is a point worth marking that the Varna-system was prevalent in the Rigvedic age, but its rules were not very rigid and inflexible. It must, however, be noted that seers and hermits were generally Brāhmans; but it was not always the case. Supreme knowledge was not confined strictly to any *varna;* on the other hand, *tapas* and *asceticism* were *sine qua non* of its attainment. A number of Kshatriya kings such as Ambarisha, Trasadasyu, Sindhudvipa, Mandhātā, Sibi, etc. attained to the status of the Rishis only through their *tapas.* Women too were entitled to participate in sacrificial rites. Women-ascetics were called *Rishikas* and *Brahmavādinīs*. The names of such women-sages as Romasā, Lopāmudrā, Ghoshā, Apala, Kadru, Kamayani, Shradha, Savitri, Urvasi, Saranga, Devayani, and Gaupayana figure in all the four Vedas. Non-Aryans too, are entitled to education in the Rigveda. They are described as *Krishnā-garbha, Anasa, Pisacha,* Asura, and Dasyu. They were soon assimilated in the Aryans and began to be called Sudras by the Aryans who arranged for their educational system.

Secular Education: The Rigvedic education, being essentially religious and philosophical in character, was imparted only to those who were fit to make quest of Eternal Truth and acquire Supreme Knowledge, yet there was arrangement for secular education and vocational training for the masses. Its vogue is amply evidenced by the progress in all the departments of life—economic, political, industrial and materialistic prosperity of the age. The agriculture, trade and exchange were in a developed state. It seems, therefore, that the material prosperity of the country is ascribable to adequate provision for the masses of secular sciences and technical education. The people would receive training in diverse arts and crafts for material gain. Agriculture, pasture and animal husbandry attained to a high norm of progress. There was provision for training in handicrafts. Barter system, credit, interest, and money-lending too were in vogue. The Rigveda refers to sea-borne trade and to stone-built cities known as *Pur*. Thus we can safely conclude that the secular, social and practical form of education was in existence during the Rigveda era.

Education in other Vedas

In ancient India, studentship evolved itself into the form of a science and an art. It was founded upon well regulated and well-established ideals and did not admit any change according to age or kingdom. The term 'student' was substituted by a more appropriate one '*brahmachari*'. The institution of *Brahmacharya* forms the foundation stone of the grand fabric of Hindu thought which has solidly been built through ages.

The Atharvaveda contains a detailed account of the educational system prescribed for the Brahmachari. The pupil's career begins with the performance of *Upnayana* (the ceremony of initiation). The pupil, at this time, dwells with his preceptor for three days whereafter, being imparted a new birth by his Guru, emerges in the form of a *dvija*, i.e. the twice-born. His second birth is spiritual which he owes to his preceptor. Only after the initiation ceremony, he is entitled to be called a *Brahmachari* implying that he is changed within as without. He, then, is distinguishable from other social beings in conduct and vestment. He wears a girdle (*mekhala*) of *kusa* grass, deer-skin, and carries with him sacred fuel (*Samidhā*) to offer to Agni both in morning and evening. Besides, there are certain distinct inner attributes as *Srama*, *tapas* and *dīksha* that help bloom particular permanent virtues in his life. Thus the ancient Indian pupil is the true embodiment of renunciation, asceticism, humility and purity. He is required to follow both physical as well as spiritual discipline; and as such, he has to dedicate himself to a strictly regulated and consecrated life which demanded its sustenance through begging by the pupils equipped with external paraphernalia such as kusa-girdle, deer skin and long hair. He cultivates inner discipline through self possession, practice of austerities, serving the preceptor, and renunciation, and thus becomes a 'residential'[10] pupil.

The discipline of *brahmacharya* was followed by girls too in ancient times. The maidens, through the cultivation of brahmacharya during their pupilage, would win youths in matrimony and then entering upon practical life undertook responsible duties towards the nation as the Scriptures say, *"Brahmacharyeṇ kanya yuvanaṁ vindate patiṁ."*

It is to be noted that in the Vedic schools there was provision for observing certain holidays. Teaching was suspended on the occasion of festivals, and in cloudy and stormy weather.[11]

Conclusion

Thus we see the ideal of the Vedic education was lofty. Ample opportunities were provided for the development of personality. The preceptors took personal care of the pupils which resulted inevitably in a multifaceted development of the pupil's personality. The Yajurveda refers to a trinity of debts: debt to Rishis, debt to gods, and debt to ancestors which he is required to discharge through *brahmacharya*, *yajna* and begetting of progeny respectively. The pupils would endeavour to develop their personality physically, mentally and morally by residing at their preceptor's home and their devotional service. The educational system of vedic period achieved a pronounced success in connection with character-formation, development of personality, contribution to knowledge in all branches of learning as well as social well-being and material prosperity. Though the literary and scientific progress of this period could not reach a stage of perfect solidarity and maturity, yet it marks an insatiable ambition to extend the spheres of knowledge. They felt their objective would not be accomplished only through chanting the hymns; on the other hand, it was thought essential to acquire proficiency in comprehending, appreciating and analysing their deeper significance. One who was incapable of comprehending the meaning of Vedas, was regarded as Sudra.[12] The vedic education was essentially spiritual and religious in character, yet, as has been mentioned above, it did not ignore the material aspect. The evidence whereof is available in the Yajurveda and the Atharvaveda. Thus it points unmistakably to the future evolution of Aryan culture.

REFERENCES

1. सर्वभूत हिते रताः
2. Dr. Radha Kumud Mookerjee: *Ancient Indian Education*. Macmillan & Co., London (1947) Prologue XXI.
3. Macdonnell: *Sanskrit Literature*: p. 39.
4. *Mundakopanishad* (2, 2, 24)
5. Dr. Radha Kumud Mukerjee: *Ancient Indian Education*. Macmillan & Co., London (1947) p. 22.
6. F.E. Keay: *Indian Education, Ancient and Later Times*. p. 5: Humphrey Milford Oxford University Press (1942).
7. वेदानां लेखकाश्चैव ते वै निरय गामिनः (Māhābharat Ādi parva 106/92).
8. मन्त्रो हीनः स्वरतो वर्णतो वा मिथ्या प्रयुक्तो न तमर्थमाह।
   स वाग्वज्रो यमजानं हिनस्ति यथेन्द्रशत्रु स्वरोऽपरात्।।

9. नानुवाकहता बुद्धिर्व्यवहार क्षमातभवेत्।
अनुवाकहता या तु न सा सर्वत्रगामिनी।। शुक्र, ३,२६२।

10. आचार्याकुलवासौ।

11. कर्णश्रवेऽनले रात्रौ दिवा पांशु समूहने,
एतौ स्वनध्यायावध्या' यज्ञाः प्रचक्षते।
विद्युत स्तनित वर्षायु महोल्का नाश्च संप्लवे,
आकालिक मनध्याय मेतेशु मनुरब्रवत।
X X X X
एताना कालिकान् विद्यादनध्याया नृतावपि

12. योऽधीत्य विधिवद्वेद वेद्गार्थ न विचारयेत
स संमूढ़ षूदकल्प पात्रतां न प्रपद्यते। (पद्म पुराण, आदिखण्ड ८३, ८६)

3

Education and Culture

Whenever a people's culture has been fully sustained by its religious tradition, education has not been a separate branch of activity. It has been a part of the total life with its social duties and its beliefs about God, Man, and the Universe. For this reason, we cannot find in ancient cultures of the East special books on the subject of education; rather we have to search for it in the sacred books which explain the religious and moral law to the people.

Such sacred texts of the Indians were the Vedas—poetic testament of a people's collective reaction to the wonder and awe of existence; the Upanishads which shift the emphasis from the wonder of the outside universe to the significance of the Self within; the Bhagavad Gita with its emphasis on the joyful fulfilment of one's specific Dharma, or destiny; and Buddha's 'Dhammapada' which expounds the technique of the Middle Way. 'Truth is one; [though] the wise call it by various names.'[1]

In the East, 'the destiny of man is to know himself, to make himself profoundly human and thereby further the universal life of which he is an integral element.'[2] We agree with Basil Matthews when he says, 'we give religious systems separate names but they are not separate; they are not closed globules. They merge in the universal human faith in the divine being.'[3]

In order to understand the philosophical thought of India, it is necessary for us to understand the spirit of Hinduism. Religion and philosophy are inseparable. This emphasis on the spiritual life has important bearings on the educative process.

It is in the light of this fundamental spirit which is more fully expressed in the highest, though it is present in the very lowest, that we can understand the whole movement of educational progress in India and the countries in the East.

With the perception of the unity of life, not only the philosophy of education but also the achievement of oriental culture falls into correct perspective. It is this essential spirit that Hinduism seeks to express, the spirit that its institutions imperfectly set forth, the spirit that we need to develop more adequately in the world of today.

Religion in the East is experience and power, and not merely an intellectual idea. The aim of religion is the practical realization of the highest truth. It is intuition of Reality and direct apprehension of Reality (*Brahmasākshātkāra*). The experience is what is felt by the individual in his deepest being, and this is valid for all time. Thus the spiritual discoveries contained in the Vedas, Upanishads, Bhagavad Gita, and other Scriptures stir us to an apprehension of the divine. 'The symbols are the concepts framed by the heart, thought, and mind. We cannot dispense with them as they are the ways by which we envisage the eternal under the forms of time, the unchanging counsels of God under the forms of the changing world.'[4]

In the East, the supreme aim of education has been not only the conservation and transmission of traditional culture but also the need for the renewal of experiences in the personal lives of successive generations. When a spiritual aim is put forward, it does not imply that spiritual life is a retreat from men and things as some Western thinkers seem to interpret.[5] The aim is to build up the personality of man radiant with power and energy. The freedom of the human mind and spirit is the special responsibility of the educator. The strength of a society depends largely on the fund of goodwill and freedom enjoyed by its members. It is only when we establish the realm of an *inner* order that we can build a purposeful *outer* order. There is a community and continuity of life between man and man which it is the business of education to foster, 'so that man and his becoming is in harmony with man and his being.[6]

'More and more are we beginning to realize the innumerable contacts throughout the course of history between East and West and their mutual indebtedness in language, literature, art, and philosophy.

As time goes on, it will be increasingly realized that a knowledge of the history and culture of India is essential to the proper understanding of the origin and growth of western civilization.'[7] Even before the dawn of history, there was a close community of culture between Indian and Babylonian, Egyptian and Mediterranean cultures. There is similarity between the society depicted in the Homeric and Vedic poems. The theory of metempsychosis plays almost as great a part in Greek as in Indian religious thought. The doctrine of Karma is the 'Cycle of Necessity' in Plato as we see in the famous 'Apologue of Er the Pamphylian' with which Plato appropriately ends the Republic. The absorption of the individual into the World Soul is expressed by Plotinus, the founder of the Neo-Platonic School. 'Neoplatonism has many points of contact with Buddhism.'[8]

'India claims and has the right to glory in an ancient and long enduring culture, an age of centuries in which Art and Science, Literature, and Philosophy flourished and the influence of Indian thought spread far beyond the bounds of the Indian world.'[9] C.E. Trevelyan regarded the coming of western learning to the East, not as an invasion but as a home-coming. 'The time has arrived when the ancient debt of civilization which Europe owes to Asia is about to be repaid.'[10] The dominant fact in the consciousness of Europe is the will to act, in that of India the will to know; and the peculiar emphasis of each has profoundly influenced the growth of their civilization. Such has been the verdict of the historians on India's legacy. It is characterized by a particular attitude towards life.

Man has been continually thinking of what the fundamental immortal principle at the root of this visible and perishable world is, and how he can reach it. 'The fate of Socrates had a determining influence on Plato's vision. If such a fate could be meted out to a great and just man, is it any use in interesting oneself in the world's business? From a world in which there could be no justice, purpose, good and truth, Plato turned to a world of ideas, the super-sensible world, and sought therein the supreme blessing.'[11] In his allegory of the Cave, Plato conceived the Ascent into Knowledge as a gradual progression from the world of common experience to a realm of ideas where the philosopher achieves a vision of the meaning of existence and a glimpse of the source of all life and of the standard of right conduct.

Even though we drew certain similarities in Hellenistic and Indian thought, India's version of the vision of the good is not the same as that of Plato. In Greece man saw the world as cosmos. In India man was primarily concerned with the innermost reality of the Self. 'Atman became the expression for what we call the Self and consequently goes back to the common human experience of our situation in the world which we characterize by saying that the living individual unit, aware of his identity, finds himself as a "Self" among other living individual units.'[12]

Kant's fundamental aim was to lead philosophy into the safe road of science, and he inquired into the possibility of philosophy as a science with the intention of formulating its conditions. 'The "nature" with which we deal in science and everyday life is due to the work of the understanding which arranges the multiplicity of sense in an orderly world according to a logic which Kant distinguished as synthetic from the traditional analytic logic.'[13] In Hegel, logic ceases to be a mere theory of thought but becomes an account of reality. Different are the ways of cognitive experience. Sense experience helps us to know the outer characters of the external world. Logical knowledge is obtained by the processes of analysis and synthesis. Both sense knowledge and logical knowledge are the means by which we acquire for practical purposes a control over our environment.

In India, there was no tension between the microcosm and the macrocosm. There is a knowledge which is different from the conceptual, a knowledge by which we see things as they are, and Hindu thinkers use the term '*Sākshātkāra*' for intuitive insight. This is knowledge of Being, and it is awareness of the truth of things by identity. We become one with the truth; the object known is seen not as an object outside the self, but as a part of the self. What intuition reveals is not so much a doctrine as a consciousness. Knowledge is an intense and close communion between the knower and the known.

The great illustration of intuitive knowledge given by the eastern seers is the knowledge of self. Self-knowledge is inseparable from self-existence. 'We have in this immediate apprehension a knowledge of acquaintance with being, and not knowledge about its essence or nature. The Self immediately known in experience is known as a "that" and not a "what".'[14] The early Indian seers sought more and more a centre of reference in their own consciousness to the cosmic challenge of the visible universe.

A study of some fundamental aspects of the testimony of the Orient is amply rewarding as it takes us back to first principles. We begin to see our purpose as teachers today when we listen to the affirmation of those 'Guru-Kula' teachers—that the creative deeds, the inspiration of the poets, the vision of the artists, and the genius of the men of science are in reality the utterance of the Eternal through man. In all of man's activity and experience, man draws from this universal source; the source of power expresses itself through him. That the human community is forever in tune with the creative spirit of the universe, in a sense of fellowship, that Truth shall make us free is the compelling message of the East.

All created beings must also possess a desiring reason which is pure. But as there is no other external measure except a man's conduct for finding the state of his reason, the words '*Jnāna*' (Knowledge) or '*Samabuddhi*' are usually made to include the pure discerning reason, the pure desiring reason and pure conduct.

This significant factor must be borne in mind in considering the ideals of education in classical India. Bookish knowledge and learned discourses do not constitute wisdom unless that man has become internally and externally pure, that is equable in mind. All the change takes place only in the quality of 'form'. Although these names and forms change every moment, yet there is underlying them some substance which is different from that name and form and which never changes. But though this elementary substance which is the foundation of the entire universe may be imperceptible, i.e. uncognizable by the organs, yet our Reason has drawn the definite inference that it is 'Sat' that is really and eternally to be found in and under this name and form, and never ceases to exist.

It is important for us to grasp the unity of knowledge in order to appreciate the growth of the educational philosophy based on it. It has been stated in the Upanishads that 'This Atman is not reached by giving discourses nor by intelligence nor by great learning.'[15] In the Upanishads, *education served-to aid the individual in his supreme duty to achieve the expansion into the absolute* and not merely the acquisition of mere objective knowledge. This fact has not been understood by some western philosophers who speak of 'the Easterner who formulates logically subtle and systematic systems even when referring to immediately apprehended factors.'[16] The Upanishad Seers sought the source of all life and knowledge. The world was young and factual knowledge was limited and so they withdrew their minds inward, away from the world of matter to seek the knowledge of the whole. They felt that individuation, acquiring knowledge, piece-meal by the study of objects shut out omniscience. Perception of life in the perspective of the whole is what they called '*Mukti*' or emancipation.

REFERENCES

1. *Rig Veda*, 1, 164, 46.
2. S. Radhakrishnan, *Eastern Religions and Western Thought*, O.U.P., 1940, p. 35.
3. Basil Matthews, *Roads to the City of God*, 1928, p. 43.
4. S. Radhakrishnan, *Religion and Society*, Allen & Unwin, 1947, p.52.
5. See Georg Misch, *The Dawn of Philosophy*, ed. in English R.F.C. Hull, Kegan Paul, 1950, pp. 150-2; and *Albert Schweitzer - An Anthology*, ed. Charles Joy, p. 62.
6. Rene Guenon, *Man and His Becoming According to the Vedanta*, Luzac, p. 35.
7. H.G. Rawlinson, *India in European Literature and Thought*, O.U.P., p. 37.
8. For the parallels between Platonism and Indian Philosophy, see B.J. Urwick, *The Message of Plato*, London, 1920.
9. L.S.S. O'Malley, *Modern India and the West*, O.U.P., 1941, p. 138.
10. C.E. Trevelyan, *The Education of the People of India*, p. 168.
11. S. Radhakrishnan, *Religion and Society*, Allen & Unwin, 1947, p. 74.
12. Georg Misch, *The Dawn of Philosophy*, ed. in English R.F.C Hull, Kegan Paul, 1950, p. 133.
13. S. Radhakrishnan, *An Idealist View of Life*, Allen & Unwin, 1947, p. 132.
14. Ibid. p. 140.
15. *Katha Upinishad*, i. 2. 23, Max Muller's Translation.
16. F.S.C. Northrop, *The Meeting of East and West* : An Inquiry concerning world understanding, Macmillan, New York, 1947, p. 364

4

The Bhagavad Gita and Education

"I stand secure, my doubts dispelled...

I will do thy bidding."

—Gita

The Upanishads though they measured the highest reaches of the philosophic imagination of the Oriental, were in their approach too intellectual; man can never be wholly fulfilled through self-discipline and knowledge; a more human approach lies through love, which easily withdraws most of the obstacles that the Self interposes between the contemplator and the contemplated, though love too needs self-discipline for its disinterested expression. The synthesis of the different disciplines of 'Yoga' which finds perfect expression in the Bhagavad Gita, has special significance for education. The Gita expounds the harmony between the diverse approaches to Reality, through knowledge (Jnana), through love (Bhakti), through righteous and detached living (*Nishkāma Karma*) and develops the thesis that diverse are the means that help the human being's spiritual fulfilment. 'The Gita is one of the clearest and most comprehensive summaries of the Perennial Philosophy ever to have been made. Hence its enduring value, not only for Indians, but for all mankind.'[1]

In the Gita, the different elements, competing with each other within the Hindu system, are brought together and integrated into a comprehensive synthesis. The Upanishad teaching of the transcendent Brahman, the Bhagavata theism and tender piety, the Samkhya dualism, and the Yoga meditation are all drawn into an organic unity. The perception of the truth results in the renewal of life. The realm of the spirit is not cut off from the realm of life. To divide man into outer desire and inner quality is to violate the integrity of human life. The two orders of Reality, the transcendent and the empirical, are closely related. Man, by developing his inner spiritual nature, gains a new kind of relatedness to the world and grows into that freedom where the integrity of the Self is not compromised. He becomes aware of himself as an active, creative individual, living not by the discipline of external authority but by the inward rule of free devotion to truth.

The Gita Way

The Gita dwells on the problem facing man, 'which is the integration of his personality, the development of a divine existence in which the spiritual principle has the mastery over all the powers of soul and body. This integral life is created by the spirit...There is a vital unity of soul and body in man. The real dualism is between spirit and nature, between freedom and necessity. In the integrated personality, we have the victory of the spirit over nature, of freedom over necessity...Man is the possessor of freedom—*Svatantrah Karta*...The whole teaching of the Gita requires man to choose the good and realise it by conscious effort.'[2] While the movements of matter are controlled more completely, man has understanding which enables him to cooperate consciously with the work of the world. Spontaneous acting is not compulsive activity to which the individual is driven by his own isolation. It is the free acting of the total Self. The individual should strive to reach a fundamental integration, for spontaneous creative activity to be possible. 'To action alone hast thou a right and never at all to its fruits; let not the fruits of action be thy motive; neither let there be in thee any attachment to inaction.' (*Gita II.47*)[3]

It is also urged that desireless action based on spiritual knowledge so as to effect a fusion between intelligence, love, and physical capacity does not conflict with the solidarity of the world (*Lokasamgraha*) nor with that of scientific humanism. An individual who follows this way of life comes to see his own knowledge as a part of and yet transcended by the wider knowledge of his own fellows who espoused the same way of life; and this sum total of human knowledge, itself a part of and yet transcended by that yet greater body of knowledge, which is slowly being brought into existence both by the devoted lives of Guru-teachers, living in the community of Ashrams (educational centres) or by the seekers after truth in the realm of science—this in short is the full significance of the term *'Lokasamgraha'*, in the context of the modern world.

If one considers the multitudinous activities of the world today, the majority of the people are in quest of various forms of happiness based on desire of power, on obtaining this fruit or that and engrossed in selfish interests which keep fluctuating. Therefore the Gita propounds the performance of action desirelessly; those who perform action in a spirit of dedication to *'Paramesvara'* (Lord) (*Gita II. 47*), with the equable frame of mind, acquire this equable reason; this equability of reason is known as Yoga, that is, the unitive device of performing action. That person whose reason has become equable in this way is called one steadfast in *'Samatvam'* (inner poise) (*Gita II. 48*). It follows that the aim of education is to create in the pupils 'Insight' (Yogamavapsyasi) (*Gita II. 53*) to perform action for the benefit of others (*Lokasamgraha*). It is in this light that we understand the Lord's bidding 'Dedicate all action to me.' (*Gita III. 30*).

Thus the energetic doctrine of the Gita provides for the exercise of intelligence, faith, and action. Faith and knowledge have always been linked together in the East. The mind and reason are both manifestations of the three constituents of Matter; each of them falls into three classes, *'Sattvika, Rajasa,* and *Tamasa'*; and though the combination of mind and reason be permanent, the natures, beliefs, and actions of different persons will differ in the proportion in which these are more or less pure. If reason itself is impure or *'Tamasa'*, then the decision made by it as to a particular thing being good or bad will be wrong; in which case Faith though it may be *'Sattvika'* or pure will be misguided; on the other hand if Faith is itself impure, then the fact that Reason is 'Sattvika' is useless; because in these circumstances, Faith will not listen to the dictates of Reason. But ordinarily Mind and Reason are not individually impure. This subject matter has been dealt with comprehensively in the XVII and XVIII Chapters of the Bhagavad Gita, as interpreted ably by B.G. Tilak in his *Gita Rahasya*

It becomes necessary to explain at this juncture what is meant by Pure Reason—that which decides what is right and what is wrong. As both mind (Manas) and Reason (Buddhi) are evolutes (Vikara) or Matter (Prakrti), they can inherently be of three kinds. The Gita has said that that reasoning faculty which realizes the form of the permanent Atman which is beyond the congnisance of Reason which (form) is common to all created things, is to be called the pure or the Sattvika Reason in the philosophy of action. The Sattvika Reason is also known as the Equable Reason, meaning thereby that which recognises and realises the unity of the Atman, which pervades all created things. Thus this equability of Reason is the most important factor in determining questions of morality and in order to find out whether or not Reason is pure and equable, one must in the first instance consider the external actions of man. The true Knower of Brahman has to be recognized by considering his nature. Therefore, as man cannot exhibit his nature except in relationship with other people, we consider the purity of his practical Reason as relating to his actions. In this sense the Gita says, 'Reason is superior to action.' (*Gita II.49*)[4]

In order to elucidate the significance of religion as not mere believing or reasoning, but being and becoming, we have to understand the full content of the three Gunas or fundamental qualities, which make up the nature of an individual. 'According to Hindu philosophy, divine energy manifests itself in different degrees according to the preponderance of the three gunas which are (1) Sattva or light, which fully reveals the divine element within and stands for purity; (2) Rajas or passion, which partially veils the light within and promotes activity; (3) Tamas or darkness which obscures the light within. The temperament of an individual is determined according to the predominance in him of one or other of these three constituent principles.'[5]

It follows that for his own salvation as well as for social efficiency, man should be allowed to develop along the lines best suited to his natural endowments and that he on his part should perform the duties assigned to him in accordance with the predominant quality in his nature. The Gitá says *'Sattva'* binds man to his body by conscious happiness and knowledge, *'Rajas'* by restlessness and misery, *'Tamas'* by heedlessness and lethargy (*XVI. 5.7*). Knowledge, light, and happiness indicate the predominance of

'Sattva'; greed, restlessness, ambition indicate the predominance of *'Rajas'*; dullness and inactivity of *'Tamas'*.

The terms are further applied to represent modes, aspects, tendencies and character of men and things, of activity and temperament—*'Sattvika'* indicating the highest state of selflessness, *'Rajas'* that of calculating selfishness, and *'Tamasa'* of blind indifference. If we imagine as many combinations as possible of infinitely varying degrees of these constituents, we have an explanation of the astonishing diversity that we find on earth. He who has seen the play and interplay of these *'gunas'* and who can detach himself from them, he who can isolate himself from them and realize the unity as the basis of this diversity is the 'self-realized man'. He has known the truth of things; he is free and his action does not bind him.

The readers in the West will understand the distinction between the changing *'gunas'* and the unchanging Self, the shadows and the substance by reference to these lines of Shakespeare from *Julius Caesar*:

> Between the acting of a dreadful thing
> And the first motion, all the interim is
> Like a phantasma, or a hideous dream;
> The Genius and the Mortal Instruments
> Are then in Council; and the state of man,
> Like to a little kingdom, suffers then
> The nature of an insurrection.

Shakespeare with his grip on the fundamentals of things has sensed the distinction between the genius (i.e. in the language of the Gita, the unchanging, *Atman* or Self) and the mortal instruments (i.e. in the language of the Gita, the *Gunas*) and no word could be happier than the word 'instruments' which indeed all gunas are, in the hands of the genius or the Self.[6] The self-controlled, the self-possessed, does have an experience of the insurrection, but he quells it by making the instruments—gunas—act according to his will.

Now this state of self-control and ultimate peace can proceed from Self-realization or knowledge which is the fruit of endeavour. This is the supreme task of education to see that man works himself upwards, towards *'Sattva'*, dedicating all his activity and endeavour to the giver of all good and ultimately reaching beyond the three gunas. This state is the state of true wisdom and freedom. The perfect man *(Siddha)* whose Reason has become unattached and pure as a result of the realization of the *Atma,* according to the Gita, is an example of the sublime purity of human intelligence and of the immensity of human strength required to balance the inexhaustible powers of the Mind, while at the same time carrying on the duties and manifold activities of the world.

The fundamental basis of righteous action is the change which takes place in the nature of a man or his character as a result of the particular Peace which is acquired by the human self by the ceaseless worship and direct experience of that immortal Reality which is at the root of the world. In this way the tension between individual good and social good is resolved. The educative process demands a withdrawal from practical activity only in order to permit concentration or reflection, intellectual or emotional, so that this withdrawal into individual solitariness expresses the need for an active return to the life of society.[7] The tragedy of Eastern education came when it mistook apathy and lassitude for exalted equilibrium.

What is Dharma?

'The principles which we have to observe in our daily life and social relations are constituted by what is called *"Dharma"*. It is truth's embodiment in life and power to refashion our nature.'[8] *We may define Dharma as the whole duty of man in relation to life. Dharma is the effective pointer to the realization of the dignity of the human spirit, which is the dwelling place of the Supreme.* That the Supreme Spirit abides in the heart of every living creature is the basic principle of Dharma. Under the concept of Dharma, the Hindu means that which binds human beings to each other in bonds of love, mutual rights, and duties and binds them to God. Dharma enables man to keep his mind fixed on the Supreme Principle of Unity amidst the pressure of his daily work so that he might do his work with proper balance and righteousnes. To unify man's diverse activities and interests is the purpose of Dharma. It becomes the aim of education as well. The principle of Dharma makes us aware of life's relationships. It is also a triple way, subdivided into the path of knowledge, of devotion, and of work. It is also the way which leads to happiness, to peace, and to freedom. Spiritual well-being and social good are not opposed to one another.[9]

It is the message of the Gita that it is the highest duty of every human being in this world to acquire supreme knowledge both of the Self and Brahman. But as the binding together of one's own Self also includes exerting oneself to the fullest extent of one's abilities, the Gita goes further and says that the realization of the identity of Brahman and Atman ultimately resolves itself into bringing about the universal welfare of society (Lokasamgraha). 'The true object of all human action is "Lokasamgraha" or the holding together of the human race in its evolution.'[10] Dharma tells us that while our life is in the first instance for our own satisfaction, it is more essentially for the community and most of all for that universal self which is in each of us and all beings. Ethical life is the means to spiritual freedom, as well as its expression on earth. Dharma and its observance are neither the beginning nor the end of human life, for beyond the law is spiritual freedom, not merely a noble manhood but universality, the aim which ennobles the whole life of the individual and the whole order of society.[11]

The Gita has reiterated in Chapter XVIII that a man after acquisition of knowledge should continue to perform his duty for the universal welfare. Nevertheless this action beneficial to society must not be performed with a selfish motive. The Gita is emphatic on this point. 'Man must perform action keeping in sight public welfare' (*Gita III. 20*). It is true that action beneficial to society is an important duty of man. But it must not be forgotten that the advice given by Krisna to Arjuna in III—19 that all acts should be performed without attachment, applies equally to *'Lokasamgraha'*. Action done devotedly and whole-heartedly, without attachment to the results, makes for perfection.

The western readers will follow the line of thought outlined by us on Dharma better if we elucidate it with a further explanation given of 'Dharma' by a western scholar F.W. Thomas, in *The Legacy of India*.[12] 'Dharma is the mode or fashion in which anything does behave. When stress is laid upon the "does", the nuance of meaning may be in the direction of truth; when it is on the "behave", we may get the opposite idea of mere phenomenon or aspect. But it is when the idea of obligation, social, moral, or religious, is included that the term assumes its great practical importance, as denoting the manner in which a person ought to behave. In the earlier occurrences of the term, the notion is the general idea of righteous conduct......It is in this wide sense that the doctrine of self-less performance of duty was preached in the Bhagavad Gita.'

Thus we come to see that the play of the 'gunas' is reflected in the principle of social perfection. The highest knowledge is to abide in God. When this is realized, it is the same thing whether we say that self-less action leads to self-purification or social purification or that self-less action leads to self-realization or freedom. 'He who by his action, mind and speech is continually engrossed in the welfare of others and who is always a friend of others, knows the essence of Duty—(*Dharma*)' (*Santiparva 261. 9*). The core of the individual's life takes him beyond the social forms, though he has need of them. The social life as envisaged in Gita is a movement in the march of time and not a terminus. So to uphold the Hindu 'dharma'—way of life—as enunciated in Gita is not to stand still. It believes that all true growth preserves unity through change. Man does the duty expected of him—'Kartavyam Karma', with freedom and spontaneity. Our 'Svadharma' (outward life) and Svabhava (inner being) must answer to each other.[13] Only then will action be free, easy and spontaneous. Thus Gita insists on the unity of the life of the spirit which cannot be resolved, into philosophic wisdom, devoted love or strenuous action. Work, knowledge and personal relationships are complementary.

No study of the Hindu way of life will be complete without a reference to caste and untouchability. There was much to commend the traditional ethics underlying the caste system which originated in the occupational needs and diverse range of individual talents and temperaments. The caste system when instituted was a social unity in which the different peoples could live together in mutual harmony while enjoying the freedom to maintain their differences. The caste system aimed at universal brotherhood and love. Rise in the social scale was determined not by increase in wealth but by ascent of spirit.

The 'Brahmins' formed the trustees of learning and tradition and were the conservers of the religious spirit. The highest place was given to the philosopher who found his life work in search for truth, artistic creation, and moral endeavour. The *'Ksatriyas'* belonged to the warrior class who preserved peace and administered the country justly. The *'Vaisyas'* were the skilled traders and agriculturists who performed various essential services efficiently and the *'Sudras'* were the semi-skilled and unskilled labourers who had no definite assignment of any particular work. The institution of caste represented the cultural, political, economic, and industrial levels of the Hindu communal life and was based on trust and tolerance.

A custom that had its genesis in the preservation of the social organisation of India, based on the principle of reconciliation and not discord, strangely enough has today deteriorated into social rigidity and immobility, and the soul of India has to be delivered from its besetting evils. The caste system has failed to recognize the flow of life, the mobility of mind, and the mutability of characteristics. This one good custom has worked so much havoc and corruption in the heart of Hindu Orient that the Occident finds it difficult to reconcile it to our belief in the universal spirit of love and wisdom.

In the integral social order of the East today, caste has not only become valueless but the oppression, intolerance, and injustice perpetrated in its name for countless decades require not redemptive measures of social legislation but the consecrated service of all classes of men and women, in the cause of the suppressed and downtrodden. The solution lies in the steadfast occupancy of the higher human, or spiritual point of view. This was the signal service rendered by Mahatma Gandhi and the social reformers of modern India before and after him. Gandhiji's valuable work on untouchability has succeeded to some degree in purging the traditional Hindu Dharma of all its dross so that, once again, it may shine in its pristine purity. His atonement stands out as the highlight of philosophic insight and has made the *'Sarvodaya'* movement a reality today. The *Bhoodan* (land-gift) reform under the spiritual leadership of Acharya Vinoba Bhave is revolutionizing the social order. The *'Sarvodaya'* ideal of universal service is built upon the dignity and freedom of the individual. The reshaping of the social order, the silent transformation of the attitude of the silent masses, the rapidity of the spread of *'Bhoodan'* into *'Gramdan'* are all in the air, bearing a silent testimony to the process of spiritualizing the 'exploiter and the exploited.' The greatest gift of life is the dream of a higher life not in the next world but here and now. So believes Acharya Vinoba, the living commentary of Hinduism rediscovered.

The Bhagavad Gita is a valuable aid for the understanding of the supreme ends of education. The intellectual expression and the psychological idiom are the products of time while the permanent truths are capable of being lived and seen by a higher than intellectual vision at all times. All great doctrines as they are repeated in the course of centuries, are coloured by the reflections of the age in which they appear and bear the imprint of the individual who restates them. We may well accept the verdict of Dr. Barnett: 'If the greatness of a book can be measured by its power over the souls of men, then assuredly the Gita is a great book.'[14]

REFERENCES

1. Swami Prabhavananda and Christopher Isherwood, *The Bhagavad Gita*, Introduction by Aldous Huxley, 1945.
2. *Vide* S. Radhakrishnan, *The Bhagavad Gita*, Introductory Essay, Allen & Unwin, 1948, pp. 45-6.
3. S. Radhakrishnan, *The Bhagavad Gita*, p. 119.
4. *Vide* Reference, B.G. Tilak, *Gita Rahasya*, Vol. II, pp. 667-74.
5. *The Legacy of India*, ed. G.T. Garratt, Clarendon Press, 1937, p. 133.
6. For detailed exposition on the subject of the gunas *see* B.G. Tilak, *Gita Rahasya*, Vol. II, Tilak Bros., Poona, 1935, pp. 652-63.
7. *Vide* Mahadev Desai, *The Gospel of the Bhagavad Gita according to Mahatma Gandhi*, Introduction; and M.K. Gandhi, *Gita, the Mother*, Kitab Press, 1938.
8. S. Radhakrishnan, *Religion and Society*, p. 104.
9. For fuller explanation of the concept of Dharma in relation to life *see* Dr. G.U. Pope's Translation of *Thirukural*; also M.N. Dutt, *Dharma Sastra*, Vol. I, 1906.
10. S. Radhakrishnan, *Eastern Religions and Western Thought*, O.U.P., 1940, p. 357.
11. Ibid. pp. 353-4.
12. *Vide* F.W. Thomas in *The Legacy of India*, ed. G.T. Garratt, p. 186.
13. *Vide* Sankaracharya --*Gita Bhaysa*, ed. Belvakar, Poona, 1906.
14. *Bhagavad Gita or The Lord's Song*, translated by L.D. Barnett, The Temple Classics, p. 79.

5

Post-Vedic Education (1000 B.C.—200 B.C.)

Sources

In Vedic period, the educational sphere was inordinately dominated by priesthood and knowledge pertaining to sacrificial rituals had considerably advanced. There were scholars and thinkers who had developed an attitude characterized by mysticism towards life and meditated on speculative subjects such as God, Soul and Universe, Life and Death, etc. In later vedic age this trend of speculative thought grew intense and vehement. The philosopher-sages, dwelling in the shady solitude of forests, would meditate upon self-realization. Their mystical experiences manifested themselves throught the *Brahmaṇas* and *Araṇyaks*, the latter being like the *Brahmaṇas* of the *Vaṇprastha* sages. The *Upanishads* were next to emerge into being. They are the archives preserving ancient culture and civilization. The *Vedanta*, an important trend in philosophical thought which can rightly be regarded as the culminating point of the Vedic knowledge, was revealed through the pages of the Upanishads. Philosophical and metaphysical propositions have in detail been analysed and discussed in them. The *Brahmaṇas*, *Araṇyakas* and *Upanishads* are the main sources that acquaint us with the post-Vedic education and civilization. The spread and propagation of the post-Vedic education was effected through diverse institutions known as *Sakhas*, *Charaṇas*, *Parishads*, *Kulas* and *Gotras*—an improvement on the oral tradition of the Vedic literature. These institutions were religious and academic in character functioning as schools in the Vedic period.

Propagation of Learning

The knowledge conserved in the Vedic *Saṁhitas*, the *Brahmaṇas*, *Araṇyaka* and the *Upanishads* was bequeathed by successive generations of teachers and pupils till it spread in every part of the country. The entire country was a network of the vedic schools which specialised in separate Vedas. These diverse centres of learning mirror forth the ancient Indian life in its true and genuine form. The real aim of education, the consummate development of all aspects of life, seems to have been realized by them. Modern education leads us astray in the direction of materialism which seeks to sever the essential bond of unity among mankind and divide it into heterogenous groups. The Vedic education, on the contrary, establishes the unity and concord of humanity through its teaching.

This education was not exclusively confined to religion only; but it illuminated all obscure and dark corners of life. These institutions aptly regarded as religious, academic and cultural centres, were the main spring whence emerged a civilization which surviving all the fierce cataclysmic changes through the ages, is still serving as beacon-light to the floundering humanity. This, indeed, is the unique feature of the Vedic education. These centres of Aryan civilization were giving the lesson of spiritualism and human perfection to the world.

Educational System and Svadhyaya

As pointed out above, education was not regarded as an end in itself; it was fundamentally related to life. Its aim was the attainment of *Brahmavarchasa*, *i.e.* knowledge of the Absolute. The performance of Sacrifice and other ritualistic operations were directed to the same end, but special emphasis was laid on the study of the Scriptures, technically known as *Svadhyaya*. *Svadhyaya* was a sort of Sacrifice to *Brahma* whereby the attainment of an imperishable world was possible. The *Araṇyakas* attach magnitudinous significance to *Svadhyaya*. The efficacy of *Svadhyaya* was such, the belief was prevalent, as to make one capable of establishing harmony with *Brahma* through the attainment of spiritual knowledge. It should, however, be noted in this context that any time or any place was not suitable for *Svadhyaya*. The *Brahmacharis*, in order to derive the utmost benefit of *Svadhyaya*, would leave the haunts of noisy distractions and retire to the peaceful lap of Nature and study the Vedas, Aranyaka, Brahmanas, Itihasa, Puranas and Upanishadas. It would be perfectly legitimate to note in this context that earlier prohibitions of Vedic study, *i.e.* in cloudy and stormy weather, under the shade of trees and amidst the cattle etc. were prevalent and followed in the later period too.

Importance of the Teacher

Though the vogue of *Svadhyaya* or self-study was commonly prevalent, yet the need and importance of the teacher for the student could by no means be ignored or dispensed with. The *Katho-Upanishad* lays special stress on the indispensability of the teacher. The teacher was expected to be in possession of the essential qualities, viz. profundity of erudition, clairvoyant vision and dwelling entirely in *Brahma*. The teacher gave an inner vision and intellectual regeneration. He was regarded as the builder, guide and leader of the society. Only his son or the pupil was entitled to receive education from him. After the *Upanayana* or 'initiation ceremony' the preceptor considered the pupil his son and both of them would be bound together in spiritual relation. The *Guru* would accept only those as his pupils who were eligible on the grounds of individual ability and sense of personal service to the teacher.

The Upanishadas abound in examples of the pupils presenting themselves to their teachers with fuel in hand. Besides these, there were irregular or peripatetic teachers who imparted education to the pupils without the performance of initiation ceremony. Yajñavalkya instructed his wife Maitreye and Gargi in theology in this manner. Not only that, examples exist of fathers initiating and educating their sons. Svetaketu received higher knowledge from his own father; likewise, Bhragu too was taught by Varuna, his father. We thus find that educational system, while recognising the magnitude of *Svadhyaya* or self-study admitted of the necessity of the teacher.

Admission

In fact, studentship of a boy naturally began only after 'Upanayana' or ceremony of initiation. He was usually called *Brahmacharin* upto the age of twenty-five (the period of celibacy). The initiation ceremony marked the second birth of the pupil;

thenceforward he entered upon spiritual career having been initiated by his preceptor. It was customary for the preceptor to admit and initiate his pupils only after having inquired into their birth, individual merits and sense of personal service and sacrifice for the teacher. The period of studentship would usually extend to twelve years. There are examples of such eminent students as Svetaketū and Upkausal Kamalanayana who lived at their teacher's housẹ for a period of twelve years. Moreover, education would begin at the age of twelve years. Many students extended the period of their academic career even beyond twelve years so much so that there is an extreme instance of hundred and one years as the period of studentship.[1] But such a long period was only commensurate with the acquisition of higher education dedicated to supreme knowledge.

Duties of Students

The first condition, in fact, was the essentiality of the pupil's residence at the house of the preceptor; hence the applicability of the epithet "*Acharya-kulavasin*" to the students. Further, he had to go about begging alms for the support of his *Guru* and himself. This tradition was carried out invariably by all, be he poor or rich, prince or peasant. This would beget in the students the virtue of humility and thereby he learnt the concrete lesson of charitable good done to him by the society and in return his sense of obligation to it. History cannot boast of such unique example of humility to be found elsewhere.

Tending of the sacred fire of his preceptor's house and keeping it aflame was another of important duties of the pupils. They collected sacred fuel '*Samidha*' from the forest to feed the fire. The sacred flame was symbolic of intellectual and spiritual illumination of the pupil.

The next duty to be performed by them was that of tending the herds of cows belonging to the *Guru* and grazing them in the forests. In this way, a major fraction of pupils' time was devoted to the service of the *Guru*. These duties were mainly undertaken by poor students alone. The well-to-do disciples would usually present gifts to the teacher.

Along with these external duties, study was the primary duty of the pupil. The study of the Vedas would initiate their education; in other words, it involved a knowledge of pronunciation, phonology, prosody and elementary grammar. Of these, grammar and correct pronunciation were attached special importance to, for future correctness of the Vedas ultimately rested upon their formal purity and faultlessness.

The external impositions thus created inner discipline in the pupil. He had to overcome certain passions and evil habits of mind, such as sensuality, extravagant desire, lust for mundane glory, as well as excessive sleep, anger, taste for fragrance and love of physical adornment etc. The pupil, prior to receiving education, was called upon to prove that he was peaceful, continent, patient and tenacious of purpose.[2] In short, "simple living and high thinking" was the motto of his life.

It is to be remembered here that pupils considered it to be their sacred duty to acquire higher knowledge. The austere practices of academic career made them capable of realization of Supreme knowledge of *Brahma*. This inevitably necessitated the dedication of a whole life and not merely a fraction of it. Svetaketū, despite the studies of twelve long years failed to attain the Supreme knowledge and as such had to devote more time to it thereafter. In many cases, it is noteworthy, that persons devoted the entire term of their life to the cause of knowledge following strictly the prescribed regulations of *brahmacharya*. They were usually called *Naisṭhika* or perpetual *brahmacharin*.

At the completion of their educational period, the teachers would deliver convocational address to the students which sought to remind them of the duties in practical life they stood at the threshold of. This was known as '*Samavartana*' ceremony. These duties embodied primarily speaking of truth, performance of duties, study of the Veda, maintenance of good health, performance of sacrifice, service to parents and the teacher, charity and other similar good deeds.[3] These final addresses of the teachers of ancient India can be compared to the Convocation Addresses of modern universities with the only difference that while ancient addresses invited the attention to its inner spirit, *i.e.* spiritual and ethical aspects, the modern ones remain confined to mere formal and external aspects.

Duties of the Teacher

The entire ancient Indian civilization is a reflection of the spiritual and ethical attributes of the teachers of that age. The teacher was expected to possess all moral and spiritual qualifications. His profession made it indispensable to master the Vedic knowledge thoroughly and dwell entirely in the *Brahma* (*brahmanishtha*). He illumined the inner being of his pupils with his own spiritual enlightenment.

In ancient times only that person was deemed worthy of teachership who must himself have been an ideal student during his academic career. The man who possessed the qualities of guiding the society on right lines and profound scholarship, appropriated to him rightly the title of teacher. When a fit pupil approached him, it was the duty of the teacher to impart to him the highest knowledge. Whatever knowledge was possessed by the teacher, was transmitted to the pupil without any concealment or reserve. Nevertheless, examples are extant about secret learning revealed only to special students in view of the unfitness of ordinary students. It is, indeed, appreciably remarkable to note that when a teacher considered himself to be deficient in knowledge of a particular subject, he regarded it as his sacred duty to reveal it to his students.

It was traditional to transfer knowledge to pupils through a succession of teachers which came to be known as *Guru-parampara*. The teachers felt the natural desire that their truths and principles, learning and experience should survive them and promote good of the society. The life of the teacher served as a model for the pupil to follow and imitate. "Lead from Darkness into Light" was their sacred duty. The teacher functioned as a spiritual and intellectual father of the pupils. If, however, the pupil fell a prey to moral turpitude or spiritual deviation, the teacher was likely to be held responsible for it. The teacher evinced his paternal care and interest in matters of looking after the students generally, financial help to the indigent pupils, care of the ailing students and other like emergency.

Modes of Teaching

During Vedic period, education was imparted directly to the pupil. The teacher played the main role in this system. But in the later Vedic education, the pupil was the main factor. The method of teaching was characterized by catechism which involved the elucidation of a particular subject through a graduated series of questions and answers between the pupil and the teacher. The teacher put forth certain propositions to the pupil or the latter himself asked questions and being answered duly by his teacher removed all doubts thereabout. Thus the solutions of the proposed problems and answers to questions constituted the chief method of education. The educational system in the Upanishadas is discursive and argumentative. All the intricate and difficult mysteries were unravelled through intelligent and leading questions. Instructions were imparted orally in general, though art of writing too was progressing. Some of the important methods of teaching that were employed are catechism, stories, allegories, parables, etc. The discursive method of study led to the development of Logic (*Tarka-Sastra*) in the period of Upanishadas. Later on, its development contributed to the evolution of *Nyaya Sastra*.

During the course of discussion, the pupil was not merely a passive listener to his teacher; on the contrary, he had to remain mentally active and conscious. He had to cogitate answers to the question through the process of introspection and meditation. Accordingly, his mental faculty and imagination received exercise and training indirectly. It was usual for the teacher to provide some leading and important hints and ask the pupil to work them out himself; and the pupil reached the destination of his proposition through *Svadhyaya* (self study), *Manana* (intellection) and *Chintana* (meditation). The Taittiriya Upanishad refers to a very interesting mode of teaching whereby Varuna, the father of Bhrigu, during the course of instructing the latter, gives only general hints and directions about the Absolute four times, and leaves him to find its content. It is only in the fifth turn that Bhrigu himself gets at the knowledge of the Absolute. Similarly Svetaketu too had acquired a practical knowledge from his father concerning Mind and its various faculties and interdependence of psychological conditions. It is evident, therefore, that in the drama of learning the pupil played the role of the protagonist; the teacher, however, acted as a mere guide to him.

In the Brihadaranyaka Upanishad there is the record of three main processes of learning, viz. (i) *Sravana*, (ii) *Manana*, and (iii)

Nididhyasana. *Sravana* or listening itself called for six specified auxiliaries: (a) *Upakrama*, a formal ceremony performed preceding the study of the Veda, (b) *Abhyasa*, recitation of the text, (c) *Apurvata*, ready grasp of the meaning, (d) *Phala*, a comprehension of outcome, (e) *Arthavada*, the reading of elucidatory texts, (f) *Upapatti*, attainment of final conclusion. The process of *Manana* was an unfailing aid to learning. Besides these methods, knowledge of the Absolute could be realized through *Tapas* and *Yoga*.

Forms of Educational Institutions

Broadly speaking, there existed three types of institutions namely, '*Gurukulas*', *Parishads*' (Academies) and '*Sammelana*' (conferences) in that age.

(i) The Gurukulas

The main reason of keeping a student at the *gurukula* was that he availed himself of the opportunity to mould his life and character on the pattern of idealistic life of his teacher by living in close contact with him. The preceptor serves as a model for the child. Through the closest and constant contact with the teacher the possibility of assimilation by the pupil of all those virtues which have served as the guiding-force of his teacher's life itself grows in intensity. An additional benefit that accrued from this contact with the teacher was that the pupil would get the practical knowledge of domestic affairs because, the teachers, generally, were settled family-holders. This explains the vogue of receiving education at the *gurukulas*. The child, with first streaks of consciousness, would leave his natural parents for the house of his spiritual father. There, having undergone the initiation ceremony, he was admitted to the stage of life known as *brahmacharaya*. He would receive education for a period of twelve years doing multifarious duties at the house of his preceptor such as tending cows, collecting fuel and keeping the sacred fire aflame, etc. Thereafter, growing into a profound scholar, he would take leave of his Guru. This system was just like the vedic period.

(ii) Parishad (Academies)

These academies were the main forums where students belonging to higher order of learning gathered and quenched their insatiable thirst for knowledge through discussions and talks. Those students who would not terminate their scholastic career earlier and remained in quest of truth and supreme knowledge, enriched their mind in these academies. Mutual discussion and argumentation alone was not the method to learn; the pupils would invite erudite scholars and literary celebrities to these gatherings and go about journeying through the country The *Brahmanas,* the *Aranyakas* and the *Upanishadas* abound in such instances. It is a point worth marking that the *Upanishadas* themselves, in a sense, were the outcome of such disputations. They are, so to say, a representation of the various philosophical investigations of the scholars of higher order whose main pursuit was characterized by incessant quest after Truth and *Atman.*

(iii) Sammelan (Conference)

Besides the local circles or academies of disputants, there were invited occasionally by some great king, several scholars, Rishis, philosophers, theologians and psychologists to a national gathering for the sake of discussions and debate. The ablest and best scholars, speakers, philosophers and thinkers were awarded special prizes for their merits.[4] It should be remembered that along with the Brahmanas, their learned ladies accompanied them to participate in these debates and wielded the weapon of their intellectual acuteness in the contest.

In addition to the above-mentioned forms of educational institutions, courts of kings too served as important centres of learning where several scholars and philosophers, hailing from different countries, would flock together, talk, discuss and throw light on metaphysical and theological problems. There were certain sylvan institutions which were situated in the peaceful solitude of forests amidst beauties of nature. The pupils, coming together would study the veda. The Araṇyakas, as the very name suggests, originated naturally from these places. They are so called inasmuch as they had to be read in these forests. In reality, the fountain-head of Aryan civilization lies in these forests. It was here that ancient Indian civilization originated. It would not, however, be impertinent to say that all the centres of learning were not to be traceable to forest. No doubt, sages regarded it as more creditable and ennobling to practise asceticism in the solitude of forests where the environment was most suitable for their mystic devotion; yet in the later vedic period we find such teachers as, while managing their household affairs taught their pupils at their own houses in the villages or towns. These very places would ultimately grow and develop into the *gurukulas* as mentioned above. Later on, we find that educational institutions were established only in important cities.

The Age of Sutra Literature

Curriculum

The period of the Vedic literature was followed by that of *Sūtra* literature. The literature of Brahmana period had by now been fully systematised. The period of Sūtra literature falls between 600 B.C. and 200 B.C. The Vedas and Upanishadas had reached the fullest extent of expansion and development till the advent of Sūtra period. The growth of Vedic literature had become so vast and diffused, that the need was strongly felt that there should be evolved some such practicable method as may epitomise conveniently the huge mass of the Vedic literature. The need of the fulfilment of this aim, therefore, brought a new type of literature, the *Sūtras*, into being. These *Sūtras* revealed great principles and truths in a very compressed and succinct form. It was natural hence to grasp the meaning of the *Sūtras* without the help of analysis and elucidation. Often their significance was abstruse and profound. The style of the *Sūtras* was so condensed and terse that, to put it wittily, an author experienced as much joy in economising even half a short vowel as in the birth of a son.

In this age, the rules and regulations of education were manifested mainly in the form of *Dharama-Sūtras*. These *Dharama-Sūtras* embody the principles of social conduct and a code of duties for the teachers and students. The authors of *Sūtras* evince no originality of invention; they simply made a scientific study of the pre-existing Vedic literature and endeavoured to bring the contents of that literature within the easy reach of masses through the results of their studies. Therefore, the Sūtra literature seriously lacks in imaginativeness and poetic charm and appeal. Due care was taken not to sacrifice brevity and economy of expression for the sake of literary flourishes. In this way the *Sūtras-karas* comprised much within the shortest compass in the *Sūtras*. Another important reason to be noted in connection with the growth of the Sutra literature is the ascendency of Buddhism which proved a formidable menace to the Vedic literature and *Brahmanism*. Hence they were forced to forge a mighty weapon for self defence against any possible onslaught of Buddhism in the form of easier and popular medium of imparting instructions in moral and religious principles so that they might easily be propagated among the masses and thus be immortalised. These efforts naturally culminated in the creation of the *Sūtra* literature.

To acquaint our readers with the number and variety of the subjects of study in existence at that time, the *Srauta-Sūtras* were first to come into being. They may be regarded as continuation of the *Brahmanas* specially in their ritualistic and formal aspect. The next in order were the *Grihya Sūtras* dealing with multifarious ceremonies pertaining to domestic life such as birth, marriage and death etc. They pass by another name too *i.e. Smriti* (that which is a matter of memory as contrasted with *Sruti*). The third offshoot of the *Sūtra* literature is known as *Dharma-Sūtra* which treats of various customs and ways of our daily social life. The last form of the *Sūtras* is *Sulva-Sūtras* which tell us of measurement required for the construction of the *Vedi* (altar). They are to be regarded as the earliest form of mathematical literature of India incorporating an advanced knowledge of geometry and algebrical propositions.

The entire Sūtra literature consists of mainly six divisions better known as *Vedaṅgas*. A pre-knowledge of various subjects such as *Siksha Chhaṅdas, Vyakarana Nirukta, Kalpa* and *Jyotisha* was indispensable for the sake of comprehending the Vedas. These aforementioned six subjects were called the *Vedaṅgas*. One special feature of education of this period is specialization of students in different branches of learning. In reality, this period is the most important one from the viewpoint of its constructive and creative aspects in ancient Indian education inasmuch as such important branches of learning as Geometry, Algebra, Astronomy, Astrology, Physiology, Grammar and Philology reached culminating point in this age. The growth of Astronomy is ascribable to religious factors. The knowledge of the position and movement of stars and planets was essential to appoint suitable days and hours for the performance of sacrifice. The science of Anatomy or surgery was founded on the dissection of the animal to be immolated. The universally acclaimed Grammar of Pānini is the creation of this very period. In a sense, we can regard Pānini as the pioneer of the Sūtra period. Katayayana and Patañjali, the two eminent literary celebrities should also be mentioned in this period.

The commentary of Pantanjali is an immortal creation of ancient India. Along with this the '*Arthaśastra*' (economic treatise) the authorship of which is ascribable to Kautilya popularly known as Chanakya, the supreme councillor of king Chandragupta Maurya, deals with the social, political and educational systems of the age. It was a unique contribution of this period. Kautilya divided his work into four divisions—(i) *Ānvikshakī*, (ii) *Trayī*, (iii) *Varta*, (iv) *Daṅda-Niti* or penal-code. There is, in it, the record of three main trends of philosophic thought, *i.e.* the *Samkhya*, *Yoga* and *Lokayata*. The *Trayī* refers to the three Vedas—the Rik, the Yajuh, and the Sama. Chanakya has visualised a well-regulated system for the students. Education was compulsory for the first three castes. The students were provided with an elaborate schedule of their duties, viz. study of the Vedas, worship of fire, begging alms, and service of the preceptor etc. In a similar way, we find a detailed account of duties of the king, different castes and those of the people in the '*Arthaśastra*' of Kautilya.

The *Nyaya and Mimansa* Sastras too were the production of this age. Besides these works, the *Smritis* were written for the proper guidance of life. The edicts of the *Manu-smriti* are regarded as gospel truth by the Indian masses. Religion was busy in this age creating and solidifying literature, though there was comparatively greater freedom in the sphere of thought. Mental life was running on parallel lines with spiritual life. Several fine arts, viz. dancing, histrionics, music, as well as economics and other secular sciences were attaining a high-water mark of perfection; these arts were cultivated mainly by women and Sūdras. These treasuries of knowledge were known as '*Up-vedas*' which had linked up other branches of knowledge with the Vedas.

System of Education during Sutra Period

The education system during the *Sūtra* period was identical with that of Upanishad period. It is worth marking that *Sūtras* did not originate or evolve any new school of philosophical thought; they are so many little solid beads of universally accepted principles held together in the rosary of antique religion. All the current unwritten regulations, social and religious traditions and long-standing conventions had been compiled in the *Sūtras* in a well-arranged and systematic order. This newly created literature became the proper course of study for the students. Some of the rituals were performed and conventions carried out by the students prior to the beginning of education; one of these ceremonies was the recitation of *Savitṛi* Mantra. The initiation ceremony or the *Upnayana* and *Chūda-karma* were performed after the beginning of education. Later on, the initiation ceremony was unexceptionably imposed on the entire Aryan race. This helped considerably the spread of education. The necessity of regular institutions was felt for higher education. The discipline of *brahmacharya* was still inexorably rigid and inflexible. With the passage of time, on account of decrease in the level of marriageable age of girls, women education received a severe shock. Generally, the women received education at home. Their teaching work was undertaken by their father or brother. Trade and commerce were imprisoned in the water-tight compartments of caste or community; but a certain measure of individual freedom was, however, permissible in matters of adopting any profession according to one's liking and aptitude. Various sciences and arts such as handicrafts, medicine, sculpture and architecture had attained the acme of their development. Thus we see that the sole objective of the entire system of education during this period was character-formation, development of personality and protection of ancient culture.

One special feature of the literature of the *Sūtra* period is the unprecedented progress of philosophy. Theories of philosophy have enjoyed an uninterrupted career since the Vedic age. The period of Upanishadas can well be regarded as the meridian of philosophy. But the period of the *Sūtras* witnessed the consummation of its progress. In this period, the current of philosophical thought flowed out chiefly in six different channels. In this way developed six systems of philosophy, viz. (i) the *Saṁkhya* of Kapila, (ii) the *Yoga* of Patanjali, (iii) the *Nyaya* of Gautama, (iv) the *Vaiśeshika* of Kaṇada, (v) *Karma* or Pūrva-Mimaṅsa of Jaimini, (v) *Uttara Mimaṅsa* or Vedanta of Badarayana.

It is to be remembered that these afore-mentioned seers or Rishis were not the originators of these systems of philosophy; on the other hand, these systems were already in existence. Their contribution in this matter was, however, confined to imparting a final shape to them through the process of analysis and elucidation of these systems. Only those students were entitled to the study of philosophy who had acquired eligibility or *'Adhikara'* to it. The generality of the students could rest contented only with the study of secular sciences. Max Mūller in his 'Lecture' on Vedanta Philosophy' has rightly observed, "one who had not thoroughly overcome his passions, was not deemed fit for the study of philosophy."

In this way the study of philosophy was complete in itself. It presented a correct solution to the problems of discipline, humanity and supreme knowledge. Indian philosophy is a unique contribution of our country to humanity at large. It was a system of thought that kept the flame of Indian culture ablaze through a succession of stormy ages by virtue of its simplicity and practicability.

Education in the Epics

Method and Curriculum

The *Ramayan and the Mahabharata* are the main Epics of ancient India. These epics give us glimpses into the creed of militarism of that age; nevertheless, there are in them scattered facts which throw light upon the education of the period. For instance, there are references to principles underlying different *Varṅas and Asramas*, definition of ideal studentship and hermitage as well as centres of learning and military education of the Kshatriya youths and princes.

As regards the education of Brahmins, there were prescribed definite rules as already laid down in the *Dharma-Sutras* as indicated above. They were required to fulfil certain conditions and acquire special qualifications, *e.g.* purity of soul, unimpeachability of character, study of Vedas, self-restraint and humility were the general attributes of Brahmins. The duties of the Brahmin pupils were: devotional service of the preceptor, discipline of brahmacharya, and mendicancy. Along with these duties of a spiritual import there were other modes of conduct pertaining to daily routine. The student would study by sitting at the feet of his master; he would, besides, not take meals or go to bed before his *guru*. The disciple thus having spent twenty-five years in his study and service of the preceptor would, according to ordinance, bid farewell and return home to shoulder the responsibilities of a settled householder. He offered the fees to his guru according to his capacity. We come across in this age certain illustrious examples of ideal studentship; outstanding names being those of Āruni, Utaṅka and Upamanyu. Along with the reference to disciples, there is the mention of certain eminent teachers, *i.e.* Kanva, Vyas, Vasishtha, Visvamitra, Droṇa, etc. Dronacharya was a celebrated military teacher. Here it should be recalled that Varna system had assumed an inflexible rigidity. The Sūdras by this time had been deprived of their rights of the study of Vedas and high military training. Ekalavya, a Sudra boy, had been denied by Dronacharya, the military teacher, the claim to receiving military training along with the Kshatriya princes. There are certain occupations and duties common to all the classes designated *'Dvija'* or the twice born, *e.g.* studying, sacrificing and charity. In addition to these there are certain duties peculiar to all the four classes: the Brahmins, undertook the special duties of teaching, performance of *Yaīña* for others and receiving gifts; the Kshatriyas those of defence and protection of the people. In the same way, the '*Vaisays* had their own special occupation appropriate to their own classes, *e.g.* trade, commerce, animal husbandry and agriculture; the Sudras undertook to serve the first three classes.[5] All these four castes had their special curricula appropriate to their occupations. The Kshatriya had compulsorily to learn the art of archery '*Dhanurveda*'.[6] The generic term *Dhanurveda* embraced all military art and science of the period. To quote only a few instances, Rama, Parasurama, Bhishma, Arjuna and Karṇa were the outstanding specialists in the *Dhanurveda*. Some of the important and great centres of learning were those at Prayaga, Kasi and Ayodhya. We may mention here one of the biggest and most famous hermitages of that period, the Āsrama of Rishi Bharadvaja at Prayaga which was the biggest centre of education of northern India.

Female Education

The post-Vedic system of female-education did not differ in essentials from that of the Vedic period; it was more or less identical. One of the special features of Indian culture which is conspicuous by its absence elsewhere in the world is that woman in India has always constituted an educated, cultured and respected limb of the society inseparable from it. In the Rigvedic age, women enjoyed freedom to the highest degree. They would participate in the performance of Sacrifice with men somuch so that no *Yajna* was considered to be complete without the active participation of women called '*Ardhangini*' for the matter of that. Several of the *Richas* of the Rigveda were ascribed to women-poetesses. The Rigvedic literature refers to many a learned and scholarly woman-Rishi, *e.g.* Visvavara, Ghosha, Romasa, Lopamudra, Urvasi and Apala. In the age of Upanishadas, women were under no restraint to receive education. The two wives of Yajnavalkyas—Gargi and Maitreyi—were both erudite and scholarly ladies. The evidence is available that once there was a learned discussion between Maitreyi and her husband on metaphysical and spiritual problems of Divinity, Creation and Soul (*Atman*). In the Upanishadas there is description about such women as undertook the duty of teaching and were designated. '*Sikshikas*'. In some of the Smriti-texts women were called '*Brahma-Vadini*', Some of the thinkers divide women into two categories : (i) *Brahma-Vadini* and (ii) *Sadyobadhu*. The former is eligible to *Upanayana* or initiation ceremony, *Agnyadhana* (Sacrifice to Fire), study of Vedas, and practice of mendicancy within the household; whereas the latter had to perform *Upanayana* in some form before her marriage. The subjects proper for her study were the Veda Mantras, music, dancing, and the cultivation of other fine arts. The *Grihya-Sūtras* too lay down that the wife should be educated necessarily to the extent of being capable of participating with her husband in the performance of sacrifice and other religious ceremonies. It is, indeed, a truism to say that both men and women were entirely free in matters of the performance of sacrifice. Dr. Radha Kumud Mookerji, citing the statement of Hemadri, observes that "Kumaris or unmarried girls should be taught *Vidya* and *Dharmaniti*. An educated virgin brings good to the families of both her father and husband. So she should be married to a learned husband (manishi), as she is a *Vidushi*.

In the period of the Sutras too, women were not prohibited from receiving education. They studied and were well versed in the Vedic literature. Women teachers were called *Upadhayaya* and *Ācharya*. The father's ambition was to see his daughter grow into a *Vidushi* or a learned woman. "Women seem also to have been admitted to military training, as indicated by the formation, '*Saktiki*', mentioned by Patanjali (iv, 1, 15) (6), which means a female spear-bearer." (Dr. Radha Kumud Mookerji's *Ancient Indian Education*). Again, we come across in the Epic age too many illustrious examples of women of profound learning and unquestionably high moral character. By this time, superiority of the husband had been established and his deification by the wife had come into vogue fully. Sita is the most glorious example in the case occurring in the Ramayana. These women were fully conversant with the Vedic knowledge. It is said of Kunti that she had acquired thorough and comprehensive knowledge of the Atharvaveda.

It must, however, be observed that no distinction whatsoever was made between the educational system applicable to men and that of women. Since the Upanayana ceremony was an essential condition to the recitation of the Vedic hymns, women too were not absolved of the imposition of the ceremony of initiation. They studied following all the necessary regulations of *brahmacharya*. The *Manu-Smritī* lays down the indispensability of the *Upanayana* for womenfolk. Study of the Vedas was the prescribed course of education for women; but the extent of their study was restricted only to those hymns which were necessary for the Yajna or other ritualistic operations. Besides the study of the Vedas, women could read the Mimańsa and specialise in its knowledge. The age of the Upanishadas produced many learned women philosophers; the most eminent ones of them were Maitreyi and Gargi who participated in discussions with sages and philosophers in the court of King Janaka. The Uttar-Ramacharit relates of Atraiyi who had studied the Vedanta with Lava and Kusa in the hermitages of Balmiki and Agastya.

Thus we see women were highly respected and honoured in the post-Vedic period. They had fullest extent of freedom to develop their personality. The Upanayana was as essential for girls as for boys, hence women-education was compulsory. Girls belonging mainly to noble families, were essentially required to receive education in the Vedic literature. As time wore on, the superiority of men affected the social status of women adversely. The conviction was taking firm roots that women folk were not fit for the Vedic education. Child-marriage was strictly forbidden during the Vedic age. Certain women were there who would study pledging the serious vow of life-long celibacy. But in the last phase of the later Vedic age, child-marriage seems to have come into vogue. The rules of the Upanayana applicable to women were also relaxed gradually. The ratio of women-education was, therefore, on a constant and steady decline. Consequently, the role of women as the mistress of the household was being stressed by the social thinkers. Provision of all domestic comforts for the husband by virtue of her proficiency in all the household affairs came to be regarded as the sole purpose and significance of a woman's life. The natural consequences of such views were that importance and social status of women proceeded on a downward slope of its career. It was thought proper that the Vedic education, even the recitation of the Vedic hymns, should be prescribed for the women, for the belief had been current that they could not recite the Vedic Mantras according to phonetic regulations. It was essential, therefore, that women-folk should regard the Vedic education as the Forbidden Fruit for themselves, if the sanctity of the Vedic-texts were to be preserved intact. Along with this idea, the superstitious notion that improper and defective recitation of the Scriptures would spell ruin to some individual or his family, or some catastrophe would overtake them, had been unshakably rooted in the hearts of the people. Sanskrita which had served as the medium of expression in the Vedas and other religious Scriptures, was the *lingua franca* of the people. Henceforward, both the languages, at a certain point parted company. The popular language was steadily degrading itself into colloquial and slang dialect known as 'Prakrat'. Under such circumstances, the difficulty of correct accent should inevitably have emerged. This explains partly the prohibition of women-folk from the Vedic education. It is unmistakably manifest that this phenomenon is undoubtedly ascribable to the apathetic attitude of the society towards women, because if the women were to be encouraged to receive education and adequate facilities were provided as was done in the vedic or the post-vedic era, they could be capable of acquiring proficiency and adeptness in the art of correct and chaste recitation of the Vedic Mantras, for the intellectual faculty of women could develop *pari passu* with that of man provided that suitable opportunities were ensured. Women were famous for their mental acuteness and perspicacity from the very beginning. But the evolution and currency of the belief that women are inferior to men intellectually dealt a serious blow to the education of women and they were deprived of the fundamental right of developing their personality for ages to come.

Industrial Education

Division According to Caste-system

From the earlier period, the Aryans had felt that progress of the society was inconceivable without a judicious division of duties. Accordingly, they classified the entire body of society mainly into four categories '*Varnas*': (i) Brahmins (ii) Kshatriyas (iii) Vaisyas (iv) Sudras. This classification based itself purely on the division of work; and every caste was allocated a particular duty. Primarily the caste-system was not so rigid; and a change from one class to another was not difficult or impracticable, but in course of time their duties assumed strict inflexibility and caste-system was reduced to mere conventionalism.

1. *The Brahmins:* The main duties of the Brahmins were: studying and teaching of the Vedas, performance of the Yajna for himself as well as for others, receiving and giving gifts. In the beginning, knowledge alone was the criterion of determining and judging of the class of Brahmins; the element of birth and parentage did not enter into it. Gradually, however, with the passage of time the custom of children's education by some learned preceptor came into vogue. Thus the continuity of the profession of priesthood from father to son, gave birth to a distinct and separate class of priests. There are certain exceptions to it and there have been examples of certain Kshatriyas who were honoured and respected as brahmins for their wide learning. King Janaka and Ajatsatru are the glorious specimens in the case. The Brahmins ultimately had to undertake the responsibility of the education of the Kshatriya and Vaisyas in view of their specialization in the profession of teaching. This responsibility heightened the level of their honour and dignity in the society. They came to be regarded as the guide and teacher of the entire community. The intellectual superiority of the Brahmins ensured first rank to them; they began to be compared to the brain of social organism. Their presence was considered to be indispensable on the occasions of religious ceremonies and rituals such as birth, Upanayana

marriage, death, etc. Thus, it is evident that the social background of priesthood is essentially economic and occupational. The priests thought it necessary to train their progeny in the art of efficiently conducting the priestly profession. For centuries to come this profession remained the special preserve of the Brahmins; and even today, the relics are to be found in the society.

2. *The Kshatriyas:* It has already been observed that with the passage of time the Vedic study came to be regarded as of secondary importance by the Kshatriyas and Vaisyas. They thought it sufficient for them to have acquired merely superficial knowledge of the Vedas, Vedangas, and the Upanishadas. The Vedangas had originated near about 500 B.C. and institutions for conducting education in grammar and law were gradually established. The *Dharama Sutras* and *Dharama Sastras* were produced during the age of the Sūtras. These works were the main law and political treatises which dealt with the rights and duties of the Kshatriya kings. In a later period, the *Niti-Sastra* (Ethics) and the *Artha-Sastra* (Economics) were produced based on the ideas underlying the aforementioned Sastras. Though we find no reference to the subjects of study proper for the Kshatriya princes in the *Dharama-Sutras* written by Apstṁbha, Buddhayana or Vasistha. But Gautama, on the other hand, has clearly laid down that a prince ought to be thoroughly conversant with the three Vedas and *Tarka Sastra* (Logic). As a matter of fact, the sphere of duties appropriate to the Kshatriya was limited only to defence, protection of people and administration. For the efficient performance of such responsible task, the training of intellectual faculties was indisputably essential; but still of greater magnitude and significance was the military training for the princes. This explains the co-ordination of the Vedic-education with military education involving a sound training in the art of wielding various weapons and knowledge of war strategies. Therefore, a major fraction of their life was appropriated by military education. The Ramayana contains a reference to the military training of king Dasaratha's sons during their boyhood.[7] Rama regarded it as his sacred duty to help and rescue the distressed by weeding out all evil forces. From time to time he displayed his superior military skill by killing such immorally evil persons as Bali, Kumbhakarna and Ravana with a view to establishing the reign of religion and

sinlessness. In the Mahabharata, we find the ancient Indian military art to have reached its cluminating point. In history, it was probably the first Great War that had been conducted on so wide a scale. The account of the military training of Kauravas and Pandavas by Dronacharya is found in the Mahabharata. It is to be remembered that certain Brahmins were proficient and learned not only in liberal arts and sciences but also in certain highly specialized ones such as military skill. This fact can well be borne out by the examples of such outstanding soldierly personalities as Parasurama and Guru Dronacharya. To say that military education was forbidden to the Sudras may be an extreme view; nevertheless, it is an undisputed fact that the Sudra boys were not permitted to receive military training along with the boys belonging to higher classes of society, the Brahmins and the Kshatriyas.

The Sutra age evolved an elaborate schedule of the rights and duties of the Kshatriyas and consequently it helped to develop their education. The *Arthasastra* of Kautilya is traceable to this period. It contains a detailed description of the education for the Kshatriyas. We may quote here the example of Chanakya who was the main cause of the overthrow of the empire held by Nanda dynasty. It is he who had trained Chandragupta, a Kshatriya prince, in political and military sciences and art of administration and ultimately encouraged and instigated him to build a new mighty empire over the ruins of Nanda dynasty.

Kautilya's *Arthasastra* refers to four kinds of sciences prescribed for the education of princes : (i) *Anvikshaki*, involving three systems of thought and philosophy, viz. Saṁkhya, Yoga, and Lokayata, (ii) *Trayi, i.e.* the three Vedas, Sama, Rik, and Yajuh; (iii) *Varta, i.e.* subjects related to agriculture, animal husbandry and commerce; (iv) *Dandaniti, i.e.* Science and art of penal administration. There was well-arranged time-table for the training of different arts and sciences. Forenoon was fixed for the training pertaining to the military art related to four departments of the army, *i.e.* the elephant, the horse, the chariot and the infantry implying the art of wielding various sorts of arms of war. The afternoon was devoted to the study and listening to discourses on *Itihāsa* which comprised, according to Kautilya, the following subjects as Puraṇa, Akhyayika, Itivritta, Udaharna, Dharmasastra and Arthasastra. The princes were educated in the science of politics through parables and fables as is evidenced by the Akhyayikas contained in Panchatantra and Hitopadesa as well as those of Jatakas belonging to a later period.

Thus we find that the Kshatriya princes were imparted a practicable knowledge which had an important bearing upon the duties of their future life. Not only that, a Kshatriya king had necessarily to acquaint himself with the thorough knowledge meant for other three classes, their occupation and educational system. In addition to the princes, the common Kshatriya masses had to undergo the *Upanayana* compulsorily. The study of the Vedas and Upanishadas was not so binding in the case of the Kshatriya youth as it was in that of a Brahmin lad. But military education formed essentially an integral part of their education. Generally, military occupation was the chief occupation of the Kshatriyas. These people would help the Kshatriya kings and chieftains in the work of administration and defence of the nation by their recruitment in the army and participation in the court activities. The duty of teaching had been reserved by the Brahmins to themselves and precluded other classes from it. They wielded intellectual despotism over the society, so that even after the coronation of princes, their domination over them persisted; and the Brahmins often interfered with their administrative, religious, social, internal and personal affairs. It is also to be observed that in the initial stage of the Vedic education when caste system had not assumed strict rigidity, non-Brahmins too undertook to teach the vedic subjects. In the third mandal of the Rigveda there are Mantras attributed to the authorship of the progeny of Kshatriya-Rishi Visvamitra. In the same way the contribution of the Kshatriya teachers to the expansion and analytical commentary upon the philosophical thought of the Upanishadas cannot be overestimated. In this connection, it is worthy of note that in some cases the Brahmin disciples would go to the Kshatriya teachers and philosophers for the sake of acquiring knowledge. Of these teachers, Asvapati, Janaka, and Pravahan Jevali are worth mentioning. In similar way, the custom of teaching certain non-Vedic subjects by the Brahmins was popular. Of the non-Vedic studies, the most significant ones are military education, industrial and commercial education and medicine, etc.

3. *The Vaisya:* It is an incontrovertible fact that education solves the problem of the future profession of a particular individual or class. As regards the Vaisyas, agriculture and trade was their chief occupation; and as such they were given technical education of agriculture, animal husbandry and trade. Education of the Vaisyas too was under the direct control and supervision of the Brahmins. Not unlike the Brahmins and the Kshatriyas, the Vaisyas too were not immune from the ceremony of initiation prior to the beginning of education. They were bound to gain elementary Vedic education, but, as has already been indicated, their main occupation was agriculture, cattle-rearing and trade and hence utility of practical and technical knowledge was of greater importance to them. Study of the Vedas was regarded as of secondary magnitude by them. For them there was provision of technical education because it suited their needs. It is said that a person belonging to Vaisya class should never think that he should never keep cattle. He was required to possess knowledge pertaining to a variety of occupational things such as price of precious jewels and the knowledge of the method of their test, that of cotton yarn, spices and scents. Besides these, they had a competent knowledge of good and bad fields, manure, paraphernalia for weighing and measuring and also that of fluctuating level of profit and loss in trade under varying marketing conditions. In this connection they had to study economics and commercial geography. Besides, they had to remain in constant touch with the growing demand and mode of supplying the manufactured goods in different countries of the world in order to maintain commercial relations with them. Knowledge of various languages, rates of wages, rules applicable to purchase and sale of commodities, was regarded as indispensable for the Vaisyas. To acquire this cumulative information, the study of arithmetic, general geography as well as economic and commercial geography, science of agriculture and business-method was extremely essential. Generally, this knowledge was acquired by the children from their father in a practical form. But for the study of the Vedas they had to join pre-established regular institutions. Knowledge of agriculture and commerce was usually picked up through practice and direct experience.

4 *The Sudras:* There was no provision of higher education for them. Service was their occupation. Nonetheless their education

resembled more or less that of the Vaisyas. Like Vaisyas, the Sudras too learnt agriculture, cattle rearing, dairyfarming, multifarious arts and crafts and handicrafts etc. Thus the contribution of the Sudras to the economic development of the country cannot be too highly estimated. They learnt *devajana* Vidya which, according to Samkara, included dancing, vocal music, orchestral music, perfumery and dyeing of clothes. In addition to these, they were engaged in the work of spinning, weaving, and printing of cloths. No established technical institutions were in existence for the sake of imparting technical education, but their knowledge was transferred from generation to generation as heritage. Manufacturing of weapons and their ammunitions, chariots, architecture, sculpture and painting—these and other similar occupations were suitably appropriated by the Sudras. Description of teachers thereof is available in some of the works. Narada, for example, himself was one of such teachers. Some of the Brahmin teachers have been stated to have undertaken the duty of imparting training in these secular sciences. Fishermen, snake-charmers and fowlers too were included in the category of the Sudras. They inherited these arts from their forefathers through the system of transference by heritage.

Thus we find that different castes had separate schedule of duties and occupations. All the classes of society were doing the work of building up the nation by performing their duties conscientiously. The Aryans had established and recognised the superiority of caste system. In addition to these, there were prevalent certain arts and sciences which could be regarded as nonpareil in the history of that period. Some of these sciences are described as below.

Ayurveda or Science of Medicine

Science of medicine holds a prominent place amongst all the sciences of India. Its gradual progress had begun as early as the Rigvedic period and by the time of the invasion of Alexander, it had reached its climax. We find several references to medical science in the parables of the Jatakas. In the University of Taxila, surgical operations of serious nature were performed. Education therein was imparted by individual teachers. Knowledge of Sanskrita was essential for the students, because all the works of Ayurveda were written in that language. The student of this science was required to undergo a special Upanayana ceremony even though he might have undergone the ordinary initiation ceremony. Only that student who possessed perfect health and high moral character was entitled to the Ayurvedic Upanayana. It lays special emphasis on properly formed limbs of the body such as eyes, nose, ears, tongue and teeth. The student was required to possess moral courage, patience, humility, intelligence, generosity, perseverance, tenacity of purpose, fortitude and other ethical qualities. In modern age too, a pre-medical test is held which aims at examining the elementary qualifications of a medical student for this profession. When we cast our glance back at the ancient methods, we are simply amazed at the perfection of knowledge of the people in this profession. They seem to have fully realized that good health, physical charm and unimpeachable character are the essential attributes of an ideal physician; besides, they should cultivate the cardinal virtues of truthfulness, freedom from avarice, disinterested service, and to crown all, humility directed to relieve the suffering humanity. Qualities such as intelligence, zeal, imagination, patience and perseverance which are the veritable *sine qua non* of scientific investigation, were regarded as the essential virtues of a medical student. This partly explains the phenomenon of appreciable progress of this science in ancient India. In modern times, intellectual superiority at the cost of moral virtues is specially stressed, and regarded as the sole criterion of the eligibility of a student to this profession. The spiritual aspect ignored, it loses its utility for life. Emphasis on intellectual aspect alone in this science has led us to very serious and far-reaching consequences; most of the physicians of modern age have sacrificed their mission of the service of humanity to their insatiable lust for its economic exploitation.

The Ayurvedic Upanayana was open to the members of all the four classes. The initiated students were required to pledge a vow to follow certain injunctions. Education followed the ceremony of initiation. Following their study of Āyurvedic *Padas* and *Slokas* under the guidance of the preceptor, the students in due course of time finished their study of all Āyurvedic works. They were required not merely to cram the books but to comprehend their meaning too. The practice of mere unintelligent memorisation was vehemently condemned.

The study of the Āyurvedic comprised diverse aspects of medical science such as pathology, medicine, surgery, toxicology, snake-bite, blood-test and study of bones and the like. The student belonging to a particular department would go to the teachers of other departments for the sake of advice and practical knowledge in those branches. A medical practitioner was essentially required to be '*Bahu-Sruta*', *i.e.* he could not achieve marked success in his profession unless he had mastered several branches of the science. The entire science was divided mainly into two divisions: *Sastra* (Theory) and *Prayoga* (Practice). A medical student was bound to acquire a double proficiency in both the aspects. A quack who practised his profession without the proper knowledge of either aspect, was penalised strictly by the State.

Here, it would be pertinent to quote profitably the views of Prof. Altekar about the methods of training in surgery 'Salya'. He observes, "The beginners who taught how to hold and use the surgical instruments by practising upon pumpkins, cucumbers, watermelons, etc. under the teacher's directions. Puncturing was demonstrated on the veins of dead animals, the manner of holding the probe on dry Alabu fruits, carrification on stretched pieces of leather covered with hair, sewing on thin pieces of cloth or skin, application of bandages on stuffed human figures and the use of caustics on soft pieces of flesh. The novice was then gradually initiated in real cases and allowed to extract darts, cleanse wounds, and use the knife in piercing and cutting diseased parts of the body."[8] Mere theoretical knowledge in surgery picked up from books was not adequate; it was supplemented by practical dissection of corpses. The evidence in this connection are available in the Susrutas. In course of time, with the advent and propagation of Buddhism and Jainism in India, the science of Anatomy was given a shocking blow and went gradually out of vogue, because the exponents of the creed of nonviolence nurtured a cordial aversion to it. Generally, the students would receive training in surgery and medicine through the individual teachers; but there are instances of institutions for the training of Āyurveda or medical science with important hospitals attached to them. In the great city of Pataliputra, there was a hospital where the medical students received practical training in medical science. Reference to Taxila has already been made.

Usually, the curriculum in the Ayurveda absorbed a considerably long period of time. Most of the students acquired knowledge of the entire Āyurveda; but exceptions there are of those students who, having specialised in a particular disease, would practise medicine in the same branch. The termination of the course was followed by examination. Incompetent and unauthorized practitioners were forbidden by the state from practising their profession. Only that person who had been issued letter patent (king's license) by the king was authorised to follow the profession of medical practice.

This era witnessed an unprecedented progress in medical science. The students had the ideal of selfless service of humanity before them. The teacher would send the alumni in the world having inspired them with high ideals pertaining to that profession on the occasion of convocation or Samavartana. The physicians and other medical professionalists had a high standard of knowledge which spread their fame even to foreign countries. It is a point worth noting that in 8th century A.D. the Caliph of Arab had invited physicians from India to undertake teaching work in the State hospital. "Khalifa Harun sent several scholars to India to study Hindu medicine and pharmacology and induced about 20 doctors to come to Baghdad to become chief medical officers of State hospitals and to translate Sanskrit medical works into Arabic.[9] Manikya was the most famous of all these doctors.

There was many a master of the *Ayurveda, i.e.* Charaka, Susruta and Dhanvantari of whom it is said that there was no disease whatsoever which could not have been cured by them. In short, we can safely assert that ancient Indian medical science was essentially an adequately developed and useful science of which India may rightly boast.

Veterinary Science

Side by side with medical science for human beings, veterinary science too developed considerably. *Salihotra* can be regarded as the origin of it. The two Pandava brothers, Nakula and Sahdeva, were considered to be experts of horse-diseases and their cure. From ancient times, India has been mainly an agricultural country where agriculture is done on a small scale with the help of draught animals, hence a knowledge of their diseases and cure thereof was deemed indispensable. Moreover, kings had an organisation of horse and elephant armies. It was necessary, under such circumstances, to train veterinary experts to deal with diseases of these animals. Naturally, this science progressed with long strides. But nowhere do we find any reference to regular veterinary institutions to impart education in it. It is possible that the students learnt it from expert persons through heritage system of practical knowledge.

Military Education

Military science was generally called *Dhanurveda*. According to *Dhanurveda-Samhita* ascribed to the authorship of Vasishtha, the ceremony of initiation was usually performed by a military student who was offered a weapon accompanied by the utterance of a Vedic Mantra by the preceptor. The Kshatriyas were specially made skilful in military art; though the examples are extant which relate that even Brahmins and Sudras too learnt it. The duty of instructing in the art was undertaken mainly by Brahmins, but occasionally the non-Brahmin instructors also performed this duty. In the beginning of the Vedic age the art and science of war progressed appreciably because the Aryans had to fight with the Dravidians. The weapons that were used in warfare were mainly bow and arrow, sword, club, shield and lance, etc. Chariot-war was in vogue in that period. The Mahabharata marks the culmination of military art and science. We find in the Mahabharata examples of weapons which may well be compared with the extremely destructive weapons of modern times. Again the fact can be corroborated by the Ramayaṇa giving an account of many a strange weapon employed in the battle between Rama and Ravana. In the Upanishadas we find scattered references to War-ships too.

In ancient times, military education was not only organised by the state; but on the other hand, private individual instructors too would undertake this duty. In every village, there were military training camps where villagers were given military education for self-defence. This custom was wide-spread throughout the country. In addition to these, there existed certain regular centres carrying on the work of military training. On the North Western frontiers of India, Taxila, an important city, attracted students for military training from all parts of the country. Following in the wake of Alexander's invasion, military education assumed a new form in the country. Some persons started regular institutions in their individual capacity. These teachers provided trained soldiers to be kings at critical juncture and would, in return, be awarded land, money and horses. The kings would send their sons for military education to distant-placed centres where expert teachers invited from different regions of the country imparted training to the students. Thus it is evident that in ancient India, military standard was very high. The ancient military education was a veritable boon to all in the guise of a settled occupation and powerful and efficacious means of protection of the country.

Fine Arts (Lalit Kalas) and Crafts

Mainly speaking, dancing, music, painting, sculpture, architecture, carpentry, and smithery were some such arts and crafts as helped a major fraction of the population of the country earn their livelihood. These antique arts and crafts of India are famous all over the world even today. In the early Vedic age handicrafts and agriculture were held in high esteem. Agriculture was the chief occupation of the Aryans. Both in the Rigveda and the Atharvaveda there are prayer hymns for success in multifarious agricultural processes, proper rainfall and suitability of seasons. With the passage of time, as caste-system became impenetrably rigid, these arts were affected by an ebb-tide as their popularity and public esteem, and training in them was restricted to Sudras alone. The Vaisyas and Sudra learnt these crafts and subsisted on their cultivation, a fact explanatory of low public esteem of these two classes. People belonging to higher order of society began to look down upon their work so much so that even manual work was regarded as an accompanying mark of social degradation. Consequently, in India fine arts and useful handicrafts began to decline in view of the total absence of public patronage.

The work of coaching in these arts and crafts was not conducted by any regular and well-established institutions. The student would generally serve a term of apprenticeship under a person who had followed that occupation for a long period of time and thus he acquired proficiency trough practical knowledge in that craft. Generally these arts and crafts assumed a communal aspect and the father would impart coaching to his son in a particular art. In every village there inhabited masons, tanners, carpenters, blacksmiths and goldsmiths who fulfilled the needs of the society. Even today this social system is continuing because modern India is as dependent on agriculture as ancient India. The occupations of the carpenter, tanners, blacksmith, potters as well as washermen are helping factors to that of agriculture; hence they have been still surviving through centuries though the degree of proficiency in these arts has dwindled in comparison to that of ancient times.

It must, however, be noted here that in the Rigvedic period occupations were not dependent on caste-system. At that time the nature of education was religious; but this sort of education was meant only for those persons who, rising above the mundane interests, were capable of attaining spiritual heights. The ordinary stratum of society was deemed inequal to spiritual enterprise and hence the purpose and character of their education was different. Ordinary people were still engaged to advance the material well-being of the society. There was adequate provision of secular sciences for the sake of economic development of the community. The Rigvedic age is exemplary for its economic, political and religious progress and famous for various arts and crafts (essential attributes of civilized life), agriculture, commerce and trade.

It naturally leads us to the inevitable inference that the period must have evolved an elaborate system of industrial, scientific and commercial education. As a matter of course, the development of these arts and handicrafts must have given birth to caste-system based primarily on the notion of division of labour. Even the great spiritualists and saints did not appreciate the idea of keeping their entire family limited to priestly occupations. There is an example in the Upanishadas of a poet-sage whose mother was a well versed housewife doing the work of grinding corn (*Upala-Prakshṇi*) and the father an itinerant physician (*Bhishag*). Only those persons who were capable and worthy of spiritual duties, would study the religious scriptures and guide the society. On the other hand, people who were deemed unfit for such missions, were asked to depend on the plough or the loom. Further, we come across such words as *Vanij* or *Vanijya* in the Rigveda which clearly indicates that commercial education was, as mentioned above, an integral part of the system for the economic welfare of the country in that period.

In the post-Vedic period there was full freedom as regards the choice of arts and handicrafts provided the guardians of the boys gave their consent to it. The basic foundation of Indian education is high philosophy; and its aim has never been degraded to economic or material prosperity; but on the contrary, it has always been regarded as an essential means to the achievement of a higher ideal "emancipation of soul". Therefore, even in the last phase of the Vedic age, the inner tendency of the people continued to be spiritual and religious. It consequently influenced the arts of sculpture and architecture. The artists being inspired by spiritual thoughts produced superb specimens of art. Thus they created an art which has continued through ages to be the object of emulation for the entire civilized world. These artists had regarded art as manifestation of supreme Deity.

As has been stated above, the work of coaching in these arts and crafts was done by the artisans at their houses functioning as schools. In addition to these the collective interests of a particular craft were administered by an organisation called *'Sreṇi'* (guild). There were established different guilds for particular craft.[10] The Smritis give us an elaborate classification of these guilds. These guilds are mainly those of cultivators, Herdsmen, Traders, Moneylenders, Artisans to which Bṛihspati has added two guilds that of Artists or *Chitra-karas*, and that of the Dancers. Thus all these taken collectively functioned as schools of Fine Arts and Crafts directed to cottage industries. It was in these guilds where the students of crafts were imparted their primary education.

Besides this, the ancient Indian literature contains mention of sixty-four *Kalas* (Arts). These references are found in Bhagvata-Purana, the Ramayana, Mahabhashya and Kamasutra. Magha Vamana and Bhavabhuti have given an account of them. In the Buddhist and Jain works, such as Lalitvistara, Jatakamala, Kalpasutra, Aupapatika-Sutra or Prasnavyakaraṇa-Sutra, you will find frequent references to these arts. Some of the main arts out of these are : Dancing, music, skill at toilette, painting, histrionic art, sculpture, etc.; and important handicrafts are: spinning and weaving, art of manufacturing boats, chariots, science and art of tanning leather, making ornaments of gold, carpentry, sewing, art of laundry and the art of ploughing and many others of different kinds.

Early Pāli literature mentions eighty arts (*Sippas*). According to *Milinda-Pañha* there are nineteen *sippas*; they are : Holy Tradition, Law, Samkhya Nyaya, Vaiseshika, Arithmetic, Music, Medicine, four Vedas, Purāṇas, Itihāsa, Astronomy, Spells Hetuvidya, Military Art and Poetry etc. Kautilya's *Arthasastra* belonging to Maurya period refers to the Arts of that age. According to Chānakya, there used to be Heads (*Adhyakshas*) for the supervision of different industries. All the Arts and Crafts were ùnder the direct control of central administration. Of these heads, there was the superintendent of Treasury (Koshādhyksha) who dealt with the Art known as *Ratna-Parīkshā*. He wielded his power on the business in pearls of all sorts derived from oyster shells, conch shells, and different sorts of gems and diamonds. In addition to these, there is reference to trade connected with sandalwood, other woods, hides, wool as well as that pertaining to cotton and silken clothes such as *Dukñla* (fine), *Kshauma* (coarse), Kauseya (silk) or Chinpatta or Chinese. Metallurgical industry was superintended by the Head of the Department of Mines known as Ākārādhyaksha. He was expected to be well proficient in '*Sulbadhātusāstra*' having a competent knowledge of copper and distillation and condensation of mercury. He was assisted in his duty by a body of experts in Metallurgy equipped with essential apparatus. The industry of Metallurgy and Mining marked a high level of progress in that age. In addition to these Heads, there was *Lohādhyakshya*, Superintendent of Metals, whose duty it was to deal with such metals as copper, lead, iron, tin, mercury, brass, zinc, bronze, etc. He was subordinate to *Ākaradhyakshya*. The industry of extracting and collecting pearls, oyster shells and other precious stones out of the womb of ocean as well as manufacture of salt was also carried on in that period. There was a separate department in the state dealing with and controlling the industry of salt-manufacturing. In the *Arthasastra*, there is reference to the superintendent of gold and silver. Again the Director of Agriculture would look to various branches of that industry, and the *Naukadhyaksha* or Director of Navigation controlled all traffic and transport by water. He collected tolls imposed on all ferries, supplied government boats on rent basis as well as collected proceeds from all fisheries. Gambling too was regarded as one of the Arts which called for direct state control; it was under the direct control of the Superintendent of Gambling known as *Dyutadhyaksha*, dealing with all the aspects of this Art. Thus, on the whole, in Kautilya's *Arthasastra* we get a vivid description of the economic development of the society and Arts and Handicrafts of that period. Besides, it apprises us of the fact that State control was exercised on all the important useful industries.

Conclusion

To sum up, in ancient India industrial and vocational training was essentially a practical and useful education. There was complete absence of formal paraphernalia of education required in modern times; education was imparted by the father to his son according to practical and direct method. The father would usually transfer without reserve or concealment the entire fund of his knowledge to his son in an affectionate and enthusiastic way. The people would undertake industrial occupation and carry it, being inspired by religious sentiments as in other walks of life. These industrial activities not only involved and served their economic interests, but on the other hand, spiritual factor too was an important ingredient therewith. As a matter of fact, art mirrors forth the personality of the artist. This is why ancient Indian art still today illumines the pages of history. Indian artists have bequeathed to the world many fine artistic creations which will be regarded as the valuable treasure of the past, present as well as future.

REFERENCES

1. The Chhandogya Upanishad related how Indra had dwelt with Prajapati for a period of 101 years for the sake of gaining Absolute knowledge.
2. सुखार्थिनः कुतो विद्या नास्ति विद्यार्थिनः सुखम्।
   नान्योद्योगवत्ता न चाप्रवसता नात्मानमुत्कर्षता।
   नालत्यापहतेन नामयवता नाचायविद्वेषिणा।
   लज्जाशोल विनम्र सुन्दरमुखी सोमन्तिनी नेच्छुता।
   लोके रूपातिकरः सतामभिमतो विद्यागुणः प्राप्यते। (सुभाषित)
3. सत्यंवद। धर्मंचर। स्वाध्यान्मा प्रमदः।
   आचार्य प्रिय धनमाहत्य प्रजातन्तु मा व्यवछेत्सीः।

सत्यान्न प्रमदितव्यम्। धर्मान्न प्रमदितव्यम्

कुशलान्न प्रमदितव्यम्। भूत्यै न प्रमदितव्यम्

स्वाध्याय प्रवचनाभ्यां न प्रमदितव्यम्

---- ---- ---- ----

एतदनुशासनम्। एवमुपासितव्यम्। एवमुचैतदुपास्यम्।

4. The *Satapatha-Brahman* relates the story of king Janaka inviting all the Brahmaṇas of Kuru-Panchala on the occasion of horse-sacrifice wherein the king offered a prize of 1000 cows with horns covered with gold to the most learned scholars; Yajnavalkya had appropriated this prize.

5. वेदोभ्यासो ब्र ह्णस्य क्षत्रियस्य च रक्षणम्

वार्ता कर्मेव वैशस्य विशिषृटानि स्वकर्मषु

6. कृषि गोरक्षमास्थाय जावे द्वैष्यस्य जीविकाम्। (मनुस्मृति १०।७८०)

ततो द्रोणः पाण्डु पुत्रानस्त्राणि विविधान चे

द्रौणः संकीर्ण युध्ये च शिक्षयाम स कौरवान्। (महाभारत आ.प. ११८)

7. पिता दशरथो दष्ठो ब्रह्म लोकाधिपो यथा

ते चापि मनुज व्याघ्रा वैदिकाध्ययने रतः

पितृ शुश्रूशणारता धनुर्वेदे च निष्ठिताः (बालकाण्ड अ.१८)

8. Dr. A.S. Altekar: *Education in Ancient India;* Nand Kishore Bros. Benaras (1948) p. 186.

9. Dr. A.S. Altekar: *Education in Ancient India;* (1948) p. 189.

10. "एकेनशिल्पेन पणयेन वा ये जीवन्ति तेषां समूहाः श्रेणी" पाणिनी

6

Education and the Upanishads

"Asato ma sad gamaya,
Tamaso ma Jyotir gamaya,
Mrtyor ma amrtam gamaya."

"Lead me from the unreal to the real,
Lead me from darkness to light,
Lead me from death to immortality."

—BRIHĀDARANYAKA UPANISHAD
1. iii. 27-8

Indian educational thought and practice must be understood as being ultimately the outcome of the Indian theory of knowledge. The Upanishads speak of the highest knowledge called *'Paravidya'* as distinguished from all other knowledge termed 'Apara' (*Munduka 1. i. 5*). *'Paravidya'* is that knowledge through which the ultimate reality is known and it forms the real subject matter of the Upanishads. With the fundamental vision of the unity of all life, the knowing subject is not conceived purely as a thinking being. Sense perception is included in the concept of knowing. Our knowledge of the world is not some gross object which is actually perceived by the organs, but that knowledge is the result of the synthesis of the various impressions received by the mind, which is made by the 'observing *Atman'*; and for the same reason, wisdom has been defined as *'Avibhaktam Vibhaktesu'*, 'That is true wisdom by means of which we realise the non-diversity or unity in that which is diverse.'[1] (*Gita 18.20*)

True knowledge may be said to have been acquired when noble emotions like humility (*Amānitva*), peacefulness (*Sānti*), self-control (*Ātmanigrahah*), equability of mind (*Samabuddhi*) are awakened whereby the total purification of the mind is continually expressed in conduct (*Gita 13.7-11*). That man whose discerning reason has become devoted to the Self, that is, has become steady in the contemplation on the Self and Non-self, and who has realized the identity of the Atman.

The principal aim therefore of the Upanishadic education is to educate the mind itself as the creative principle in man, the creative principle of his culture and civilization. The mind is its supreme concern and objective, the chief subject of its treatment. It seeks to train the mind as the medium and instrument of knowledge rather than fill the mind with a store of learned lumber. It addresses itself more to the 'principle of knowing', the roots from which knowledge springs and grows, than to the objective content of knowledge. Whenever and wherever the complete realization of the Atman comes, 'Release' is obtained at that very moment, because liberation is the fundamental pure state of the Atman.

It is the mission of the Upanishads to plead for the recognition of the dignity and freedom of the human spirit. It proclaims the truth in such a way that it involves no offence to the spirit of science. While the truth of the spirit excels reason, it does not exclude it. The culture based on Upanishads stands for the unity of spirit. It must be emphasized that traditional association of eastern philosophies with religious outlook became the common belief of everyone. In the many episodes dealing with the education of the pupils in the Upanishads, education and especially its application of the more objective, dispassionate method of science, even to the study of religions and humanities, was the chief means by which the climax of self-knowledge (*Atmajnana*) and of self-happiness (*Atmananda*) and the highest fulfilment of human life is attained.

The supreme knowledge cannot be gained by mere speculation but only by revelation as the result of the proper degree of self-growth. The acquisition of such knowledge which means emancipation is not a matter of study for a few years in a school, but of life. Truly, education was not only conceived but carried out with the faith of an education for life. 'Hinduism represents an effort at comprehension and co-operation. It recognizes the diversity in man's approach towards, and realization of the one Supreme Reality. For it, the essence of religion consists in man's hold on what is eternal and immanent in all being.'[2] Since the acquisition of factual knowledge is only secondary, and as the individual—subject—is the centre of education, individual treatment of pupils becomes essential in Indian education. Maturation of the self which depends on the uniqueness of personal equipment and freedom of choice, revolves on the personal relationship between the teacher and the pupil. As we become more acutely conscious of the real heart and spiritual centre of education, we build in our education upon and around the ideal of a free personality and the teacher assumes a central importance.

Education thus is a process of control of mind to direct it to its deeper layers. We shall now consider the methods by which the scientific attitude of the mind can be cultivated with respect to human values. The technique of spiritual discipline is called 'Yoga' meaning 'union' and stands for the method of concentration by which the psychoses of the mind can be sublimated and the reality can be intuitively realized. The only knowledge which is immediate is Self-knowledge and we call this intuitive experience *'Anubhuti'*. The practice of Yoga has been developed in India through the method of experimentation, observation and verification. Yoga never asks an aspirant to surrender his reason. He should put to the test of reason the instructions of his teacher and the scriptures. *Since Yoga disciplines the mind in concentration, it is a useful technique in education.*

The disciplines of Yoga are suited to different temperaments. For the intellectual type, Yoga prescribes the method of philosophical discrimination along with the cultivation of the equable mind. The learner listens to the instructions of his teacher, reasons about them, and finally contemplates them. For the second psychic type, Yoga lays down the path of self-analysis and concentration. This system is closely allied to the intellectual Yoga and the educational scheme gets merged into it. Through self-control and one-pointed meditation, he destroys ignorance and attains to truth.

Such was the technique advocated in the Upanishads for the attainment of higher knowledge. This particular scheme of education has for its object, the purification of the mind through intense concentration for the realization of the Self. It seeks to treat the mind so as to render it the vehicle and instrument of supreme knowledge, of relieving it of the tension and depression both physical and mental, arising from the continual process of sensory and motor adjustments to stimuli, to which it is normally exposed. The mind is thus led to a state of equipoise and serenity which belongs to its true nature and is restored to its innate strength and clarity of vision. 'The fundamental assumption of this scheme is that mental life is not entirely bound up with or completely dependent upon the realm of objects. It seeks to open up other avenues of knowledge than the mere brain, or the outer senses, through sustained concentration and meditation, in the life of the spirit.'[3] The Upanishadic period developed *'Atmic'* (spiritual) educational values in the institutions of learning called 'Ashramas'.

'What gives to the Upanishads their human appeal is an earnest sincerity of tone, as of friends conferring upon matters of deep concern.'[4] The quest for Reality compels man to explore the infinite depth of the Soul in which the central principle of creation is reflected. Thus we see that the Seers of the East in the first millennium B.C. saw the necessity for an inner conquest of the Self, by the Self, before human desires may safely be given freedom to weave their fabrics in the world of experience. 'If the technique of science, which is in truth neither eastern nor western and the truth of Vedanta (as revealed in the Upanishads) which is similarly so, could be harnessed to the solution of problems, both individual and collective, and if they find increasing expression in social action, all will be well with man and we shall have the Kingdom of Heaven established on earth.' Sir John Stewart Wallace writing in the Hibbert Journal says: 'Many pray that new vision may be given by that mighty atonement of science, philosophy and religion for which the greatest thinkers of our time are calling. Among these great thinkers, Indian minds are pre-eminent. In achieving this atonement, Vedanta has a great contribution to make. It is already perhaps the most noteworthy synthesis of thought to be found in the world.'[5]

REFERENCES

1. *Bhagavad Gita*, 18, 20, ed. Mahadev Desai, 1946.
2. S. Radhakrishnan, *Religion and Society*, Allen & Unwin, 1947, p. 52.
3. R.K. Mookerji, *Ancient Indian Education*, Macmillan, London, 1947, p. 288.
4. *The Legacy of India*, ed. G.T. Garratt, Clarendon Press, 1937, p. 62.
5. Dr. T.M.P. Mahadevan. 'Western Civilisation and Vedantic Culture', *The Call Divine*, May 1954.

7

Brahmanical Education

Progress of any nation is mirrored in her literature. The ancient Indian education is indicative of ancient culture and civilization which having originated in forests is still illuminating the world like the lighthouse inside the ocean. The motto of education here, has always been 'Leading from Darkness unto Light' which serves as the beacon-light in the journey of life. The Brahmanical education sought to promote material prosperity and help attain human beings' Salvation. The Vedic teachers had long ago realized the significance of the *obiter dictum* "*Vidyātu Vaidushyāmuparjāyantī jāgarti lokadvaya sādhanāya*" (with the attainment of learning both the worlds of a man are illumined); or "*Vidyā vihīnah pasuh*" (human being without knowledge is like an animal).[1] Hence they made education widespread and comprehensive in extent and left no aspect of human existence unrelated to it. As a matter of fact, the highest aim of education was an all round development of life, *i.e.* physical, mental and spiritual development of personality. Though, true it is, that the Vedic education was pre-eminently religious in character, yet, secular aspect of it was not totally ignored. The Atharvaveda abounds in examples of secular education. In short, formation of moral character, purity of heart, development of personality, knowledge of sociability and citizenship, preservation of national culture and last but not the least of all, material prosperity are the main objects of the Vedic education. It is true, of course, that in order to apprehend all the salient features of the Vedic education in right perspective, it is essential to take a bird's eye-view of its fundamental principles, methodology, the teacher-pupil relations, curricula as well as its achievements and failings.

Principles of Education

It is difficult for us to obtain the basic principles of ancient education in systematic and regular form in any volume. We can put them forth in systematic order only after gleaning them from a vast mass of scattered literature. To put them succintly, they are as below:

1. The primary object of education was to train and prepare the boy for the struggle of life. Collective education was not much in vogue; personal attention was devoted to individual students. Accordingly, all the latent faculties of the student were fully developed; hence the practical utility of education for life. Education was not purely academic; on the other hand, it aimed at providing practical knowledge for the future responsibilities of life.

2. Those candidates that were deemed fit and eligible for education, were imparted instructions according to their taste and aptitude. The ceremony of initiation (Upanayana ceremony) was compulsory both for men and women. This explains the universality of education. Moreover, education was regarded as the only means to absolve oneself of the debt of the Rishis. Hence it was the sacred duty of all to receive education.

3. The virtue of innate humility was prescribed as the essential attribute of a pupil to make him eligible for receiving education. During studentship period the pupil had to follow the discipline of *brahmacharya* strictly. His life was a period of inexorable austerities which precluded any possibility of pleasure for him. He was bound to lead an extremely austere life. He would not indulge in frivolities as the students of modern times do. The practice of self-possession and austere restraint helped the development of their personality immeasurably.

4. The ancient educationists fully realized the importance of the beginning of education at the opportune time; the *Upanayana* ceremony, therefore, was performed either in fifth or eighth year at the latest. The studentship period was not co-eval and co-terminous with educational period. Whatever was learnt by the student during his pupilage had

essentially to be rescued from oblivion; else failure therein was regarded as a sin. The rainy season was specially fixed for the purpose of revising the old study and keeping it fresh.

5. The Vedic education tends to impart education primarily on psychological principles. Corporal punishment was prohibited strictly; its infliction was regarded as a crime. Great preceptors such as Āpastamba, Manu, Gautama, and Vishnu have vehemently opposed corporal punishment. True, the utility of punishment has been acknowledged by such Rishis as Yajnavalkya, Manu and Gautama, but it is to be adopted as a last resort.[2] According to the views of Gautama, any teacher that administers corporal punishment to his pupils, should be legally prosecuted by the State.

6. The pupil remained in directly close contact with his preceptor. The preceptor, therefore, would get ample opportunity to study the mental calibre and inherent faculties of his pupil. He sowed the seed of good moral habits in the mind of the pupil. Even modern educationists have recognised the significance of habits. The habits formed during the period of childhood remain with a person all through his life and mould and influence his activities. Therefore, the formation of such beneficial habits as early-rising and sleeping, simple living and high thinking were indispensable for the maintenance of perfect discipline. The daily round of the pupil's duties was fixed and regularised which assumed, in course of time, the form of habit. This considerably helped them in the development of their personality. Bath, performance of yajna, worship, begging alms, service of the preceptor, recitation of the Vedic hymns—these and a number of like duties formed an inseparably integral part of their daily routine which were performed unconsciously and automatically.

7. In the sphere of education, there has remained a longstanding disputable issue as to which of heredity and environment plays more important role in the development of a student's personality. Even modern educationists, as a matter of fact, are not unanimous on this point. In spite of the discrepancy in the views of the educationists of the

Vedic period in this connection, they laid greater emphasis on environment and upbringing. It has unequivocally been adduced by the Atharvaveda that, given proper facilities for upbringing and education, there is nothing whatsoever the child cannot accomplish. In this context the instance of Indra is significant. (*Indroh brahmacharyen daivebhya svarā bhavata*). But later on with the evolution of the theory of *Karma* and the theory of transmigration of Soul (Metempsychosis), the educationists had to change their views. They now realized the significance of long-standing heredity. Now, in turn, heredity and habit asserted their claim in the formation of the individuality of a child, as is evidenced by "*Malayepi sthito venurvenureva na chandanah*". This theory was firmly established with the growing rigidity of caste-system; the provision for the education of the boys belonging to all the four classes was made on the basis of caste-system. This system affected curriculum too. This in the Vedic education, the theory of Karma and rigidity of caste-system assumed the shape of impenetrable conventionalism.

System of Education

During the Vedic age, entire teaching was done orally since the art of writing had not evolved upto that time. The pupils were caused to learn the Vedic Mantras by rote. It is interesting to note that even after the evolution of art of writing, the superstition persisted that to record the Vedas was nothing short of sinfulness. In the absence of printing press and paper, books were written with the hand on the leaves of the *Tala* or *Bhoja*; hence they were difficult to be available for the masses. In course of time, the copper plates began to be used for the purpose. Under the circumstances it was not possible that students might be educated with the help of books. This explains the fact that the ancient preceptors caused their pupils to memorise the Vedic hymns orally and it was thus that the vast treasury of knowledge was transferred from generation to generation successively.

In view of the non-existence of regular and established institutions, education was imparted by individual preceptors. The teacher would sit with one or two pupils at his feet; the study work followed invariably the act of obeisance by the pupils to the preceptor. The preceptor recited the Vedic Mantras first and the pupils followed. In this way the whole of the stanza was learnt. The pupils uttered the Mantras loudly and due attention was paid to the correc'ness of pronunciation. According to this procedure, verse, stanza and then chapters were gradually finished. The teacher, on the request of the pupils, would analyse, elucidate, comment upon the Vedic Mantras along with causing them to be memorised orally. The comprehension of the meaning of Mantras by the pupils was very essential. Besides the Vedas, they studied the Sūtras which called for elaborate elucidation by the teacher owing to the abstruseness of their meaning. In this way, the pupils learnt Pānini's *vyakarana* (grammar), *Nyaya* of Manu along with the Sutras of Smritis and Jyotisha (Astronomy). They were allotted some study-work to be done at home which consisted mainly of the revision of the Mantras and their intellection.

The ancient educationists endeavoured to facilitate the work of memorising the Mantras. This was why they versified all the subjects of study. Even such insipid subjects having a practical utility as *Vyakaraṇa*, *Āyurveda*, *Jyotisha*, Nyāya Sāstra, etc. too were composed in verse form. It rendered the task of memorising considerably easier.

In addition to this method of imparting education to pupils, that of disputation too proved no less efficacious and beneficial. Several *Parishadas* were organised where learned teachers and scholars delivered erudite talks on philosophical and metaphysical problems. Later on, in the period of the *Hitopadesha* and *Panchatantra*, a new teaching method was evolved according to which supreme spiritual truths were made easy and intelligible to the students through tales and anecdotes and proverbial moralisations. The method of personal contact too proved extremely beneficial and efficacious. Unlike the modern educational system according to which a teacher lectures mechanically to a number of students seated before him and at the expiry of the period departs, remaining, thereby, in majority of cases, quite unacquainted with them. The ancient preceptor was very close to his pupils and devoted individual attention to them. There was spiritual relationship existing between the preceptor and his pupils while the latter sitting at the feet of their teacher learnt their lessons.

Test was the daily feature of their studies. This kept the pupils always active and conscious. The intelligent students were entirely free to make headway by virtue of sharpness of their intellect and assiduity. They experienced, therefore, no setback to the development of their personality. In the end, we come across some such examples of certain capable sons who in the absence of their father undertook the duty of teaching according to the method through which he himself had been educated.

Pupil-Preceptor Relations

The unique feature of the Vedic education lies in its pupil-preceptor relations. In modern times, when a student desires admission to any institution, he after having filled in the admission form presents himself before an unknown teacher and money in the form of fees constitutes the primary link between him and his educator. Naturally enough, such relation is not built on the foundation stone of humility, love and faith which are largely conspicuous by their absence in modern age. In ancient times, the pupil could present himself to his *Guru* with *Samidha* (sacred fuel) in his hand which was essentially indicative of his sense of devotional service to his preceptor. Just as the sacred fuel is converted into light, being consumed by fire, in like manner, the pupil was prepared to be admitted to the Light of Knowledge by his preceptor. The teacher too, on his part, would impart without reserve to his pupil whatever knowledge he possessed regarding him as his own son. In some cases, the father himself would teach his son. There is the famous instance of Svetaketu being taught by his father mysteries of 'Supreme Knowledge'. Devotional service the preceptor was the cardinal duty of the pupils. Examples are extant of certain pupils who, being unable to present gifts to the preceptor, would serve their *Guru* all the time and devote whatsoever little spare time they could avail of to their studies. Even pupils of noble descent and high birth served, as a matter of course, their teacher in various ways, *i.e.* tending the cows, collecting fuel, kindling the fire, begging alms and doing a number of other odd household jobs. Service of the *Guru* was considered to be one of the most efficacious means of spiritual progress.

The system of the *Gurukulas* is the nonpareil contribution of the Vedic education. Since the performance of the *Upanayana* (ceremony of initiation) till the ceremony of *Samavartana* (convocation) the pupil studied at the house of his master and carried on his education accordingly. The pupil would leave his bed in the morning before his teacher and go to sleep after his retiring to bed at the time of night. In this way there was always direct personal contact between the pupil and *Guru* enabling them to develop mutual understanding. Usually the pupil stayed at the *Gurukula* for a period of twelve years whereafter he would return home having finished his academic career. At the time of departure the teacher preached to his pupils certain duties in the form of Convocation Address, *i.e.* "Speak Truth ; perform thy duties; do not neglect the study of Vedas", etc. But it is worth marking that even after the expiry of the educational period the relations between the pupil and the preceptor would remain intact.

Curriculum

In the beginning of the Vedic age, the art of writing had not evolved. Usually education was imparted orally. At that time education was essentially religious in character. From the very beginning, the Vedic Mantras, the method of Sacrifice and religious hymns were caused to be memorised by the pupils. The knowledge of the nuance between long and short syllables, *Saṁdhi*, vowel and consonant and correct pronunciation was given from the inceptive stage of educational period. This knowledge stood the pupil in good stead when he undertook the study of the Vedas. Though the Vedic literature dominated the entire period up to 1500 B.C., yet Itihasa, Purāṇas and Epics too were flourishing along. We find diverse references to them in the Atharvaveda. The students were encouraged to learn the rules of prosody and rhetorics which aided the memorisation of the Vedic Mantras. Later on, the Brahmanical literature came into being. The Samhitas evolved as the compiled form of the vedic literature. The order of priesthood appeared in the form of profession. This age was remarkable as regards the creation of literature pertaining to ritualistic ceremonies of sacrifice. Geometry too existed to help the symmetrical construction of the sacred Altar. The *Pingala Sastra* (Prosody) was progressing with long strides. Vyakarana and philosophy too were found in rudimentary form in this age.

The post-Vedic period witnessed a marked expansion and development in curriculum. The study of religious scriptures was compulsory and indispensable. Besides, there were certain other branches of learning which were very popular: *Vyākarana* (grammar) Arithmetic, Geometry, Astronomy, Poetry, *Itihāsa, Akhyāyika,* Philosophy, *Arthasāstra* (Economics), Political Science, Agricultural Science, Sculpture, Architecture, Painting, Military art and science, Animal husbandry, *Ayurveda, Sālva-Sāstra* (Surgery), *Nyaya Sāstra,* etc. were some of the subjects which progressed considerably in this age. The Brāhmanas, Āranyakas and Upanishadas which are veritably the treasure of philosophical knowledge and have been the unfailing source of philosophic inspiration to India through successive ages, were the contribution of this very period. Caste-system had begun to assume regidity in this age; hence the curriculum was fixed according to the genius of different classes. The curriculum included certain secular sciences and crafts according to the caste-system along with the religious and Vedic study. The Brahmanical education, we find thus, was not one-sided; but on the other hand, it helped the all-round development of the society.

Nārada, an eminent Ṛishi, has given a list of the subjects of study under the Brahmanical education to Sanatakumara as has been recorded in the Chhandogya Upanishad (VII/1/1/2). He goes to Sanatakumara for the sake of receiving education. On being queried by Sanatakumara about his previous knowledge of any subjects, Nārada replies, "I have studied subjects like Rigveda, the Yajurveda, the Samaveda, and the Atharvaveda as fourth, Itihāsa, Purana as the fifth Veda, Grammar (called *Vedanam Vedam, i.e.* the Veda of Vedas), Necromancy (*Pitrya*), *Deva vidya* (Theology), *Brahmavidya* (Doctrine of prayer), *Siksha* (Phonetics), *Kalpa* (Ceremonial), *Chhandas* (Metrics, prosody), *Bhuta vidya* (Biology), *Nakshatra-vidya* (Astronomy), *Sarpa-vidya* (Study of snake venoms), and *Devajana vidya* (Fine Arts)......" This list makes it clear how the Brahmanical education was expanding gradually. Thus this education goes a long way in making life prosperous and happy in all aspects.

A Criticism

Merits: We have observed all the aspects of the Brahmanical education during the course of its elaborate analysis. We have seen how the culture of ancient India evolved through her educational system. The undimmed refulgence of Indian culture and civilization is rightly attributable to her educational system. Amidst cataclysmic changes which brought about rise and fall of many a mighty empire, Indian civilization and culture has survived all the vicissitudes of fortune; and even today when the horizon of the world has been shrouded in the dark pall of stormy clouds of destruction, India is preaching gospel of love, non-violence and peace to the panic-stricken humanity.

The chief aim of the Vedic education was to guide life in the direction of spiritual prefection—'Salvation'—through inner and outer purity of being. The Vedic education achieved a marked degree of success in this noble objective. It showed glorious results in the sphere of character-formation. The pupils dwelling in the *Gurukulas* situated in enchanting sylvan surroundings, would study religion, philosophy, secular sciences and crafts at the feet of their preceptor. The cultivation of inner discipline was specially emphasised. But it did not mean the creation of artificial sense of fear to force a mechanical behaviourism among the pupils; far from that, it had a very intimate relation to the inner being of the pupil. Discipline or sense of humility was characterized by an inner urge which reflected itself through manifold activities of life. Besides, means were available for the sake of spiritual discipline and the development of character. Unlike modern students, they were strictly forbidden to indulge in the excesses of pleasure. Very hard regulations were prescribed for the daily routine of life. They were required to rise early in the morning, bathe, sleep on the ground, remain bare-footed, put on scanty clothes and take little food. They were thoroughly prohibited from using such things as sweets, scents, flowers, shoes and indulging in sentiments of love, anger, avarice as well as dancing which are the veritable agents of luxurious and sensuous life. They had to observe perfect *Neshṭhika brahmacharya*. Self-possession and control of desires were the essential attributes of the pupils of that period. All these regulations brought about expected benefits and advantages. Character-formation and mental, physical as well as moral development of personality were immensely helped. The creation of a vast literature by the society of that time can well be ascribed to purity and austerity of life and observance of strict discipline. Life seemed to have been pervaded by divinity, purity and nobility. Thus the Vedic education can be regarded as having fulfilled the objective of making human life essentially symbolic of True, the Beautiful and the Good (*Satyam, Sivam* and *Sundaram*).

In addition to this we find that another object of the Vedic education was the creation and preservation of ancient literature. "When we consider the enormous bulk of the sacred literature, it would seem an almost impossible task for it to have been preserved all through so many centuries in this way. Still we know it was done and is being done down to the present time."[3]

It is a creditable thing for ancient Indian literature and culture to have survived through ages when we consider that in the Vedic or post-Vedic age the art of writing had not come into existence and art of printing along with the rest of the paraphernalia for the purpose was conspicuous by its absence. The ancient sages and Rishis preserved such a vast literature through memorisation and orally transferred it to successive generations. As in ancient times, so to a certain measure in modern age too, the main reason for the cultural unity and harmony can be traceable to the especiality of Indian educational system.

This education bore fine fruits in the sphere of material prosperity of the society. As has already been indicated, the curriculum was not exclusively religious. Our forebearers of the Vedic period did not ignore worldly and material welfare in spite of the predominance of religion in education. The Vedic education was not totally blind to its responsibilities towards citizens and social welfare and it achieved a pronounced success in it.

Defects: In spite of the important role played by the Vedic education in the all-round development of human life, it certainly was not devoid of some defects and flaws which could be revealed by a moment's critical analysis and reflection. It would be perfectly legitimate to describe them here briefly. Not unlike ancient European educationists, Indian educationists also laid great stress on religion. Religion forms the basis of every act of theirs, so much so that even ordinary common day affairs reflected religiosity. Every activity was suffused with a kind of priestly tinge. Majority of the teachers were

Brahmin priests. The entire educational structure was pervaded by sacrificial rituals and religious ceremonies. The development and evolution of *Itihasa, Arthasastra* (economics), Politics, Arithmetic and physical sciences could not overpower the fields of religion, philosophy and religious ceremonies. The reaction of it did not occur till then; still in course of time religion came to exercise a profound influence upon life, and people in their religious bigotry lost all regard and care for material prosperity. For the persons thoroughly imbued with religiosity, religion was the sole incentive to action and struggle of life, but the general masses could not soar too high. Common people regarded Deity as the only Truth and looked askance at the world which was nothing short of illusion to them. This attitude dealt a very fatal blow to mundane progress.

According to the views of certain critics, the Vedic education helped the people turn other-worldly and spiritual visionaries; but this view is untenable. The Vedic literature has always stressed emphatically the struggle of life and duties connected therewith. Moreover, that age was characterized by constructive activities. The age produced a very vast and great literature. The sages formulated certain regulations for the guidance of practical life, strict compliance wherewith could make life prosperous. It is true that entire atmosphere was surcharged by religiosity and spiritualism and life was imbued to the marrow with formalities of religious ceremonies. At the same time it should be remembered that material success was only a means to an end, *i.e.* Emancipation of Soul and not an end in itself. This spiritual tendency pervaded the very soul of India and its reflection is visible in the thought of modern Indian masses.

Besides this, in the vedic education an appreciable importance was attached to the Sāstras. The Purānas and the Smṛitis were quoted as authoritative books. There was the firm conviction prevailing amongst the masses that whatever had been recorded in the Sastras could never be false or vice versa. This tendency weakened the reason and imagination of the people. The authority of Sastras was regarded as self-sufficient and final word, and hence the test of propriety or impropriety of a thing born of circumstances was utterly scarce. But this phenomenon occurred only in later times; otherwise logic and reasoning had reached its climax during the Vedic and Upanishadic period. As a matter of fact, the Upanishadas mainly exhibit intellectual development and display of subtle disputations. The literature of the Sutras too is not far behind in this respect and evidences the height of intellectual development of the age.

Further, it is to be noted that Arts and Handicrafts collectively known as '*Devajana-Vidyā*' were held in low esteem partly owing to the predomination of the Brahmans and partly to the inflexible rigidity of caste-system. The superiority of those doing mental work over the manual workers was regarded as an established fact. It naturally resulted in serious lack of patronage of Arts by the higher order of the society. Handicrafts were regarded as the main occupation of the Sudras while dancing, music, and painting those of women and the Sudras both. This rigidity and conventionality assumed a more serious aspect later on.

Another criticism that is levelled against the Vedic education is that it lacks seriously in co-ordination and harmony amongst diverse branches of learning. Specialization in separate subjects had been attempted from the very beginning. The result was that though the depths of particular subjects had been sounded and probed thoroughly, yet vastness and universality of the subjects was ignored and not attended to.

Besides these, the negligence of women-education during the post-vedic period, lack of mass education as well as absence of common language are some of the shortcomings of Brahmanical education. But, as has been indicated in the preceding pages, these charges are far from being wholly applicable; they contain only a modicum of truth in them. Women-folk were held in high esteem by the society; some of them were very learned and scholarly. Sanskrit was the *lingua franca* and all the Vedic literature, the Puranās, the Upanishadas and the Sūtra-literature were written in it. Education was compulsory for all as is proved by the indispensability and universality of the Upanayana ceremony (the ceremony of initiations) for all. It is true, nevertheless, that certain defects and flaws crept silently into it when the language of the common people became different from Sanskrit and people grew lax as regards the essentiality of the Upanayana ceremony or when the level of the marriageable age for girls was decreased. All these things did happen during the Vedic age. The phenomena occurred with the growing influence and popularity of Buddhism which will be described in the following chapters.

Conclusion

Thus we can put it shortly that most of the aspects of human existence found fullest scope for development and evolution during the period of the Vedic education. The Vedic educational system has its own peculiar importance as regards the harmonious development of physical, mental and spiritual aspects of human life. It helped a lot in the development of character and individuality of human beings. At the same time its contribution to material prosperity cannot be too highly valued. Some of its special features such as pupil-teacher relations, moral discipline, individual attention to the pupils, intellectual freedom, universality of the ceremony of initiation, women-education and the tradition of the Gurukulas etc. are in fullest accord with the principles of education and have invariably proved beneficial and advantageous.

REFERENCES

1. शुनः पुच्छमिव व्यर्थजीवितं विद्यया विना।
   न गुह्य गोपने शक्त न च दंश निवारणे
   [Sabhasit Ratna Bhandar 31-18].
2. अन्यत्र पुत्राच्छिष्याद्वा शिष्टयर्थ ताडयेत तो Manusmriti 4-164.
   न निन्दा ताडने कुर्यात् पुत्रं शिष्यं चताडयेत्। Yajnavalkya 1-115.
3. F.E. Keay: *Indian Education in Ancient and Later Times:* p. 34; Humphrey Milford, 1942.

8

Educational Wisdom in Buddhism

"The perception of the beautiful is at the heart of the Buddhist philosophy and religion."

"From earnest contemplation is wisdom born,
From lack of earnest contemplation wisdom wanes,
Knowing this twofold path, by becoming and by de-becoming
He may so give Self a home that wisdom waxes."[1]

—DHAMMAPADA 282

The history of Buddhism in the history of the development of religious thought in India begins from the sixth and seventh centuries before Christ. This age was outstanding for the application of human reason to the solution of the great problems of life and death, of the nature and object of the universe and its search for an ultimate cause to explain the riddle of existence. Buddhism was originally conceived and imparted as an ethical principle for the purification of the mind. Buddhism and Christianity arose as a reform movement and aimed at overcoming the formalism of Hinduism and Judaism. Both revolted against the pretence of authority, whether in Brahmin or Scribe, who held a monopoly of acting as a toll-gate on the way to God.

The doctrines of the Buddha must be interpreted against this background. Gautama Buddha lived and moved and had his being in Hindu society and found it wanting in many things. 'As a consequence, the Buddha takes it upon himself to return men to the initial and basic Hindu insight of the Upanishads. Thus the basic identity between the conceptions of the divine in Hinduism and Buddhism, together with the fact that Buddhism was a reform movement growing out of Hindu traditions are both explained.'[2] Buddhism appears during centuries as a 'Buddhification' of institutions, ideas, or feelings which were simply Indian. 'Buddhism is only the "Buddhized" aspect of contemporaneous Hinduism.'[3] Buddha emphasized the importance of 'Bodhi' or enlightenment. One cannot think one's way into reality but only live into it.

Professor Max Muller, Paul Deussen, and Mrs. Rhys Davids maintained that Buddhism was a natural development of the Indian mind in its various manifestations, religious, philosophical, social, and political. Philosophy or religion, specially in India, has always been lived and not merely contemplated, and so it has always developed its outer side in strict accordance with the inner. The two developments must always run parallel to each other in vital harmony. 'Far from discarding and denouncing the Brahmanic ideal of life, Buddhism achieved in one sense the full realization of this Brahmanic ideal. Buddhist society is far more the fulfilment than the denial of the ancient schemes and dreams of the Brahmanic law-givers.'[4]

That Buddhism in its original and ancient form is rooted deeply in the pre-existing Hindu systems of thought and life, has important bearing on the development of educational thought in the East. 'The fact we should never forget is that Gotama was born and brought up and lived and died a Hindu. On the whole, he was regarded by the Hindus of that time as a Hindu. Without the intellectual work of his predecessors, his own work, however original would have been impossible. He was the greatest and wisest and best of the Hindus and throughout his career, a characteristic Indian.'[5] It is because Buddhism was a natural transition from the Hindu philosophy of life, that we believe that there is every possibility of an amalgamation of Hindu way of life with Buddhist conceptions, forming the spiritual conopy of Asia. *The educational philosophy of the East cannot ignore the tremendous potentiality of such significant fusion in the years to come.*

We shall not examine the special Buddhist scheme of life by means of which it developed its social and educational organizations for the advancement and diffusion of its particular truths, the ideals of thought and life for which it stood. The Buddha unravelled the speculations of each of the schools of thought known to his age and reached a result which he embodied in his own doctrine. 'It is a doctrine for those whose wants are few, not for those whose wants are many.'[6] Misinterpretation of Buddha's way of life seems inevitable in a world where wants are multiplied, where self-expression and endless quest after the material pursuits continue unabated. Buddha's teaching of self-naughting, that whoever would be free must deny himself, is not an easy task in the modern world.

The main purpose of his mission was to find a solution for the alleviation of human suffering. The problem of evil, that is, of the corruptibility of all things born, composite, and mutable, their liability to suffering, disease, and death concerned him; it has a cause, and cessation from it is possible if we walk in the way of the 'Brahma'. Thus, in short, state the four sacred Truths of Causal origination—'this being so, that becomes; this not being so, that does not become', is the simple religious formula enunciated by the Buddha. 'From being one he becomes many, from being many he becomes one.' (*Dhammapada I. 212*).

'In the cycle of "becoming"... (bhava-cakka, samsara) the instability and finiteness of whatever has had a beginning is inevitable. Life or "becoming" is a function of sensibility, of desire and ignorance (*avijja*-delusion)...Everything becomes, everything flows like a river; there is nothing of which it can be said that it is (*sabbe samkhara anicca*). All that becomes is mortal; therefore to be immortal, it is necessary to put a stop to "becoming". This intimately concerns ourselves; the most dangerous aspect of ignorance—"the original sin"—is that which leads us to pin our faith that we, you and I—are this or that and that we can survive from moment to moment, day to day, or life to life, as an identity.'[7]

It is generally stated that Buddha taught that there is no Self. 'What is actually denied is the reality of the mutable Ego or psycho-physical "individuality".' 'Monks, I am the result of my own deeds, heir to deeds, having deeds for matrix...... Whatever deed I do, whether good or evil, I shall become its heir.' (*Anguttara-Nikaya III. 74-5*). 'The individual is indeed responsible for and will inherit the consequences of his actions, for so long as he thinks of "himself" as the agent; and no one is more reprehensible than the man who says "I am not the doer", while he is still actually involved in activity...The question of the real existence of a personal agent is one that cannot be answered by a simple "yes" or "no", but only according to the Middle Way, in terms of causal origination...Entities that originate causally are "not my-self"; in this ultimate sense, a man is not the agent. It is *only* when this has been realized and verified that a man can dare deny that his actions are his own; until then there are things he ought and things he ought not to do.'

> "But they who know essence as essence,
> They go on to essence—The essence of moral habit,
> Contemplation, Wisdom, and the essence of Freedom."
>
> (*Dhammapada II. 12*)

The doctrine of the causal effect of actions in Buddhism is in common agreement with the belief of Hindus and Christians in the orderly sequence of events. 'Time implies motion and duration involves mutation or becoming. The ego is an unreality because of its mutability. This self is always self-assertive and it is only when the true nature of the inconstant self has been realized that a man will set out in earnest to overcome his own worst enemy and make him a servant and ally.'[8]

It is in this sense that St. Thomas Aquinas said, 'A man out of charity, ought to love himself more than any other person, more than his neighbour.' (*Sum. Theol. II.-ii. 26.4*). Man's duty is to work out his own salvation—from himself.

Buddha expounds the three types of mastery—mastery of the worlds, mastery of *Dhamma* (Truth), and mastery of self. 'He having obtained mastery of the worlds, abandons wrong, makes right become; he guards the pure Self.'

> "The Self, O man, knows what of thee is true or false,
> ...Truth-finders see the fool walking unevenly in the world;
> Wherefore let the 'master of himself' walk recollectedly,
> The 'master of the worlds' heedfully, contemplative,
> The 'master of Dhamma' fails not of the goal."
>
> (*Anguttara-Nikaya i. 147-50*)

Nirvana is a Buddhist key word; 'Striving for Nirvana, strength came to me.' 'It is something which must be immediately experienced to be known. Therefore it must be a factor in the aesthetic continuum of immediate experience; and since it is not a determinate sensed or introspected factor, nothing remains but for Nirvana to be the undifferentiated or indeterminate aesthetic continuum.'[9]

The Buddha expressly 'holds nothing back', and he bade his disciples look to the Dhamma as the ultimate authority. The votary is asked to have faith in the Way enunciated by Him until he can experience it, until faith is replaced by knowledge. 'Faith is most conducive to knowledge.' (*Samyutta-Nikaya IV. 298*). The Buddha's authority rests upon his own immediate experience. He tells his disciples nothing of which he has not personally seen and verified and they too can see and verify the truth if only they will follow the Way. The Buddha identifies himself with *'Dhamma'* the Lex Aeterna, synonymous with Truth. 'He who sees the Dhamma sees me, and he who sees me sees the Dhamma.' (*Samyutta-Nikaya III. 120*). *'Dhammapada'* or the 'Footprints of the Law', is the guide for those who walk in the way of the Law, in other words, in the path of Brahma. Is it any wonder, therefore, that this Buddhist guide was the backbone of the Buddhist Educational System?

'The Buddha is not only a transcendent principle—Eternal Law and Truth—but also universally immanent as the "Man in this man".' 'Whoever would nurse me, let him nurse the sick'[10] (*Vinaya-Pitaka I. 302*) echoes Christ's 'in as much as ye have done it unto one of the least of these my brethren ye have done it unto me.' The perfect man is described as 'having made the Self become.' This 'making become' of the Self is an indispensable part of the Buddhist Pilgrim's Progress and equally important is the opposite task of putting a stop to all 'becoming' and so 'build we up the being that we are'. This factor of 'becoming' is an important question for the philosopher in education. The 'becoming' that is merely a haphazard process of mechanical growth is entirely different to the 'making become' which implies careful guidance and directed activity.

Education, according to the Buddhist way of life, therefore, should concern itself with selective cultivation. The man who is liberated is one who is no more becoming. Merely to have become a scholar or a mendicant is not the final goal. It may be a tremendous achievement for man to have probed into the earth's outer space, but it is not the be-all and end-all of his existence. *Buddha's message that Man's significant efforts should be directed to the pursuit of Truth and to the practice of moral virtues has tremendous significance to education today.*

The distinction between the real Self and the ego gives rise to tensions. It is our conscience, in other words, the Socratic Daimon who cares only for truth. Buddhism emphasizes the need for purity, that purity which transcends belief and knowledge, and also stresses again and again that while moral training is indispensable, it does not by itself involve perfection. Buddha's Gospel is one of Love, piety, tenderness, and impartiality. Annie Besant says, 'that it has been a religion of love for the last twenty-three centuries and it cannot be a religion of anything but love and peace in the future.'[11] An all-embracing love towards all living things permeates Buddha's teachings. 'Freedom of heart that is love, will lead to charity, kind words, and doing a good turn; and treating all alike as each deserves,' (*Dhammapada iii. 152*).

Impartiality is a state of detachment or patience, having the same significance as the term *'Ahimsa'*. Thus only man can attain liberation, the essence of freedom. The procedure is ethical and is based on the fundamental assumption that the training of the will is of sovereign value and precedes in importance the training of the body or intellect. On this foundation has been built up the Buddhist Educational philosophy. Eastern Educational Ends and Means derive from this source their greatest potency.

REFERENCES

1. Nyanatiloka Thero, *The Word of the Buddha*, Bradbury, Agnew, London, 1914.
2. F.S.C. Northrop, *The Meeting of East and West*, p. 380.
3. De La Vallee Poussin, *Buddhism*, O.U.P., 1937, p. 162.
4. R.K. Mookerji, *Buddhist Education*, Part II, Macmillan, London, 1947, p. 376.
5. Rhys Davids, *American Lectures*, pp. 116-17.

6. *The Living Thoughts of Gotama the Buddha*, presented by Ananda K. Coomaraswamy and I.B. Horner, Jaico, p. 22.

7. (a) AR.S. Copleston, *Buddhism Primitive and Present in Magadha and Ceylon*, Longmans, 1908.

   (b) Rene Guenon, *Man and His Becoming*, Luzac, 1945.

   (c) Ananda K. Coomaraswamy and I. B. Horner, *Gotama the Buddha*, Jaico, pp. 24-6.

8. Ananda K. Coomaraswamy and I.B. Horner, *Gotama the Buddha*, Jaico, p. 29.

9. F.S.C. Northrop, *The Meeting of East and West*, p. 350.

10. Ibid. p. 39.

11. Annie Besant, *Buddhist Popular Lectures*, 1907, p. 8.

9

Buddhist Educational System

The Vedic Religion and Buddhism

The Brahmanical system of education, as has been indicated in previous chapters, became one of the integral parts of national life. Indian education bore the essential mark of Brahmanical education even after the advent and spread of Buddhism. Buddhism, as a matter of fact, was not conceived as some thing different from Hinduism. Several of the principal and basic tenets of Hinduism were preserved in Buddhism intact. Ascendency of Buddhism can well be attributed in certain weaknesses and flaws vitiating Hinduism. Hence Buddhism can be regarded essentially as a product of circumstances. Hinduism long before the advent of Buddhism, had been affected by a superficial vanity; the spirit was fast disappearing. On the other hand, merely formal aspect survived. Inordinate immolation of animals was rampant in the name of the performance of the Yajna. Asceticism came to be identified with and limited to mere wandering in the forests having renounced the family and various inconceivably harsh austerities and meaningless penances had been invented in the name of means of the *Tapas* (asceticism). Buddha regarded all this as futile and purposeless. He, therefore, formulated such religious principles as might, through an analytical study of fundamental problems of life, mould religion in a novel form. Lord Buddha understood well that life was fraught with sorrow and pain, hence it was the aim of human life to attain Salvation (*Nirvana*) by renouncing the world. All the same, doctrines of Atman, sorrow, Deliverance or Emancipation of Karma, and Metempsychosis are common to both the religious creeds. In this way, as a consequence of the mingling of both Hinduism and Buddhism a new phase of Indian religious thought appeared. Buddhism has provided in its own way an answer to the pre-existing philosophic question, 'How to attain Salvation?' One of the many means suggested by Lord Buddha, Nirvana should also be regarded as one of them.

Buddhism can thus rightly be regarded as one of the phases of multi-faceted Hinduism. Whatever little difference seems to underly both the religions, is based on Lord Buddha's certain opinions concerning Religion. For example, he preached that if sacrifices involved violence to animals as well as inordinate expenditure of money, let them be stopped and forbidden. Secondly, if the Vedas had no claim of being of divine character, let them be regarded as no better than other books. Besides, he preached that it was nothing short of stupidity to consume the entire youth in learning things by rote, and that if Hindu gods and goddesses were no more than mere symbols or names, let us look for something that was real and not imaginary. In addition to these, he forbade the practice of mortification of flesh in the name of penances (*Tapas*) and preached renunciation of the family life and worldly pleasures and indulgences.

Thus we find that to a great extent Buddhism drew its inspiration from Brahminism. There is an essential internal concord in spite of external discord between both the creeds. Buddha would respect and revere the Brahmins. In his early life, he received education from the Brahmins. *Lalit Vistara* asserts that mostly a Brahman or a Kshatriya can be a Buddhist and not a Chandala or Sudra. Though Buddhism did not recognise caste distinctions, yet from amongst the so-called low castes, only those who were possessed of desire and curiosity to learn and commensurate Brahmanical intellectual powers, could be admitted to the Buddhist Fraternity, or *Samgha*. Buddha was opposed to the idea of recognising a person as Brahman only by birth. He organised an Order of monks living a pure and simple life and who, having renounced their homes in their early childhood, aimed at attaining *Nirvana* (Salvation), by knowledge acquired through education and a life of austere simplicity. This system can well be likened to the various *Asramas* (Life-stages) called Brahmacharya or Vanaprastha or Sanyasa of the Brahmanical system. Only the life-stage of *Grahastha* (family-life) was forbidden by Buddhism. All these factors

was regarded as having attained the status of full-fledged member of the Order in direct contrast to the Vedic system of education according to which the *brahmachari* was permitted to be a settled householder after being *Snataka* or a graduate. The Buddhist *Upasampada* converted the *Sramana* (novitiate) into a perfect Monk having no relation with his family or the world. *Pabbajja* was transitory in nature; but *Upasampada* (final ordination) exercised life-long binding upon the Monk. It is true that the Brahmanical education adduces the examples of life-long Brahmacharis (*Neshthikas*); but they were few and far between. Buddhism, on the other hand, imposed, as a matter of rule, life-long *brahmacharya* upon the monks. In course of time, when women too were admitted to the Order of Monkhood, this discipline was imposed upon them as well.

According to *Pabbajja* ceremony, child would go to his preceptor and with folded hands utter these words, "You are my preceptor"; and thus one-sided relation was established. But *Upasampada*, on the contrary, was performed before all the monks there in the form of a function. The method of its performance was thoroughly democratic in character and could be performed with the consent of the majority. The Sramana having dressed himself as a monk, with the alms-bowl in hand and upper robe covering only one shoulder, sat down in squatting posture bowing down to other monks. In this way he chose his preceptor (*Upajjhay* or *Upadhyaya*) and the ceremony of the *Upasampada* would come to a close. If any monk, on the other hand, wanted to withdraw himself from the *Saṁgha*, the procedure was simple and easy. Any monk under the circumstances of breaking the solemn pledge or falling a victim to worldly temptations, was liable to be expelled from the Holy Order. He had to make a declaration of his weakness before a witness not necessarily a monk.

Pupil-Preceptor Relations: Piety of relations between the disciple and the preceptor in the Buddhist system of education was the same as during the Vedic period. The pupil was called by another name too, *i.e.* '*Saddhiviharika*'. He acquired knowledge by serving his *Upadhyaya*. Like the Vedic pupil, *Saddhiviharika* too would get up earlier and go to bed later than his preceptor. Early in the morning, the pupil had to give water, clay, and teeth-cleanser to his preceptor, provide a seat and serve rice-milk for him. In *Mahāvagga* we get a detailed account of the relations between the pupil and the preceptor: "O! Bhikkhus, *Saddhiviharika* should behave his Upadhyaya well; he should rise early, cleanse the shoes and placing the *Uttarasanga* (upper robe) on one shoulder, should give the teeth-cleanser; he should provide water to wash hands and face and a seat to sit on; besides, he should serve milk-rice to his preceptor. He is to sweep and clean the room; he should go for begging with his preceptor, etc." In addition to these, keeping distance while following his preceptor, begging alms for him, washing feet and clothes of *Upadhyaya* and attending on him in sickness were some of the essential duties of the *Saddhiviharika*.

Further, we find the responsibilities and duties of the *Upadhyaya* towards his pupils. The preceptor had to treat the pupil as his own son. In emergency, he provided bowl and clothes to the pupil. When he fell sick, the preceptor served his pupil as he himself was served by him. It was the highest and most sacred duty of the teacher to impart intellectual and spiritual education of a higher order to his disciples.

We find thus, that the relations between the pupil and the preceptor were extremely cordial and harmonious. It was in accordance with ancient Indian tradition. The teacher put an ideal before his pupils by the simple and pure mode of life. He had but few wants. The great teachers of Nalanda would get only three times as much to spend as ordinary pupils would do. The preceptor considered it to be his privilege in a sense to receive services from his pupils. If any pupil ignored to respect his preceptor, he was deemed unfit and consequently was expelled from the Order. The teacher too put forth the ideal of high learning, excellent moral character, self-possession and spiritualism before his pupils to compel inherent high respect from them. It is quite evident from the writings of Hiuen Tsang that in the *Viharas* like Nalanda, there were profound scholars who put forth a living example before the pupils.

Residence of the pupils: There were no *Gurukulas* under the Buddhist system of education as they had been during the Vedic age. Pupils lived in the monasteries or *Viharas* as Sramana or full-fledged monks. The individual *Viharas* were like the links of the chain of the entire Buddhist religion. All these monasteries were organised together to form chapters, *i.e.* the orders were constituted by the amalgamation of a number of educational centres or monasteries (*Viharas*). The pupils and the *Upadhyaya* would live together in those monasteries. There was no dearth of accommodation in them. The ancient relics of Nalanda indicate that it accommodated thousands of students.

In the earlier stages of the spread and propagation of Buddhism, the monks lived in the woods, in grottoes or caves and beneath the trees; but they were allowed by Buddha to live in the *Viharas* (monasteries). This permission was valid under special circumstances, *i.e.* to ward of scorching heat, snowfall, hailstorm or rainfall. There were *Varshavasas* (rain-retreats) built by rich people of the society for the sake of providing shelter in rainy season. The Buddhist monasteries were palatial in structure, beauty, symmetry and comfort. There is a reference to a palace having been caused to be built by King Bimbisara. Many a Chinese traveller has provided us with a detailed and picturesque description of these *Viharas*. One of the most famous *Viharas* of that time is the Jetavana Vihara constructed by the merchant prince Anathapindika. There were separate chambers and halls well equipped and well-decorated, for different purposes: cooking-chamber, bathroom, dormitory, study, hall for discussion and guest house etc. Besides this, there were some other important and famous Viharas as Yashtivana, Venuvana, and Sitavana at Rajagriha.

These Buddhist *Viharas* were the educational centres used not only for religious learning but also as the centres of secular arts and crafts. Technical education in various arts and crafts such as painting, sculpture and architecture etc. was also imparted in these *Viharas*.

Further, there were certain such students as would not live with their preceptor in these *Viharas* but reside at their own houses and go to the *Viharas* for the sake of education. The Jatakas refer to some such story about Juñha, a prince of Benaras. Big universities had hostels for the accommodation of the residential students.

Meals: The Buddhist monk usually took very simple meals. The *Sramanas* would go about to the neighbouring villages with their *Upadhyaya* for the sake of begging alms and subsisted on whatever they could get thereby. Begging food more than they needed was strictly forbidden. Occasionally the students and monks were invited to meals by the citizens. Their food usually consisted of fruits, milk, milk-rice, curd as well as jaggery and sugar cane etc.

Curriculum

The Buddhist education was spiritual in essence. It was thoroughly saturated with religion, since its chief ideal was the attainment of *Nirvana* or Salvation. The Buddhist monks studied mainly religious books alone. Their life was steeped in religion. The chief subjects of their study were *Suttanta*, the *Vinaya*, and *Dhamma*.

This should not, however, lead us to infer that study of religion predominated the entire society and that there was a total lack of practical and technical education. In fact, it was not so. In Indian history the Maurya and Gupta periods are regarded as the golden ages when India had marked a high water-level of development in literature, philosophy, arts, commerce, agriculture and the methods of warfare. From economic point of view, India was considerably prosperous and well off. This disproves the fact that there was no education in secular sciences and arts at that time; because it is evident that without these sciences, an all round material development of the country would be an impossibility. The main subjects of Buddhist education were, as we shall see later on, spinning and weaving, printing of the cloth, tailoring, Lekham, Ganana (Accountancy), painting and sketching, Ayurveda or medicine, Salya or Surgery, coinage, etc.

Education was categorised into two heads: (i) Primary, and (ii) Higher Education. Primary education aimed at teaching, reading, writing and arithmetic.[1] Higher education comprised teaching in religion, philosophy, medicine, military science and the like. Caste distinction did not stand much in the way of choosing the subjects. Students would come flocking to Taxila for the sake of education from far and wide. The Vedas were also studied for the sake of acquiring comparative knowledge; nevertheless the Atharvaveda was not included in the curriculum up to the Jataka period. The vogue of learning the Vedas by rote was rampant in this period also. Bodhisatva himself had acquired knowledge of the Vedas.

We do not find any description about sciences, fine arts and crafts in the Jatakas; yet the Milinda Pañha refers to nineteen *Sippas* or *Shilpas* (Arts) which formed an essential part of the curriculum. We come across the mention of the following arts which were taught in the different institutions of Taxila; Elephant Lore (*Hathi-sutta*), magic charms, spells, hunting, spell for understanding the cries of all the creatures, Archery (Issatthasippa), the Arts of Prognostication, *Sarpa-Vidya* (Art of snake charming), medicine, etc. Students could specialize in any one of the above-mentioned arts. The theoretical as well as practical aspects of education in these arts were equally emphasized. The arrangement for practical training in surgery was a usual aspect of these colleges. It is evident from the story of Jivaka's education that he had received practical training in surgery. This explains his efficiency in the said science which stood him in good stead in performing two very successful operations of desperate cases just after the expiry of his academic career as a medical student. Journey and foreign travel were regarded as possessing the practical educative value. Besides these, nature-study, Law and Military science formed essential ingredients of the curriculum. Taxila was the centre of education in these arts and sciences.

According to the evidence of the *Milinda-Pañha,* the Brahmanical education too was in existence during the Buddhist period. As a matter of fact, both these systems of education are complementary to each other. Subjects of the Vedic education such as the four Vedas, Itihasa, Purana, Poetry, Etymology, Vyakarana (Grammar), Jyotisha (Astronomy), Vedangas, the Arts of Prognostication, Sankhya Yoga, Sakuna-Vidya (Science of Divination), the Nyaya, the Vesaishika, Music, Medical science, and spells were taught in different universities of the Buddhist period. Fa-Hion, a Chinese traveller has written that the Brahmanical system of education was popular in the fifth century A.D. The Vinaya literature was the main study of the Buddhist monks. Knowledge of Sanskrita was indispensable for higher education. Fa-Hion himself had acquired knowledge in Sanskrita by remaining at Pataliputra for three years. Besides this, Pali and other regional languages had also been popular and common. Well-nigh all the important Buddhist works have been written in Pali. In the seventh century A.D. Hiuen-Tsang too bore testimony to the popularity of the Brahmanical education. Study of the four Vedas was obligatory. Describing the curriculum of Buddhist education he has observed that education was imparted by the Upadhyayas and Acharyas in the monasteries. Primary education consisted of the elementary knowledge of the three R's and principles of Buddhism. Knowledge of grammar was essential. The child was primarily educated in the knowledge of the alphabet, vowels, *Samdhis* or rules of combination, *Samasa* and other grammatical propositions. In this way we find that primary education was a harmonious combination of both secular and spiritual aspects of education.

As regards higher education, Hiuen Tsang has quoted the example of Nalanda where Buddhist philosophy, the *Vinaya* Literature, the Yoga and other spiritual sciences were taught. The institution at Vikramasila was reputed for imparting education in Logic (*Tarkasastra*) and Jurisprudence (*Nyaya-Sastra*). Another Chinese traveller of seventh century A.D. named I-Tsing too has made a mention of these curricula and subjects of study. He has also referred to the study of the *Tripiṭaka* as that of the Vedas by the Buddhist monks.

Professional Education: Though the Buddhist education was religious in character and its aim was to educate the monks belonging to the Chapter and also those persons who bore sympathy towards the Order, yet at the same time we find that it had not ignored occupational and technical aspects of it as well. The *Mahavagga* bears testimony to such crafts as spinning, weaving and sewing. The monks in the monasteries were allowed to learn these arts and crafts. Reference to 19 *sippas* has already been made above. Besides these, the Ayurveda (medical science) and surgery made appreciable progress in this age. Jivaka Komarabhachcha, a student of Taxila, as referred to above, was a great doctor and surgeon of that age. Having studied medical science for a period of seven years, he had acquired a considerable knowledge of various herbs by travelling far and wide. He then undertook a country-wide tour as a reputed physician. He was invited to Ujjeni for medical consultation. Also, there is reference to his skill in the operation of brain and intestines. Charaka, rightly known as 'the father of Ayurveda' was a product of this age. Taxila was the centre of education in medical science; students from distant places as Rajagriha would go there for medical education. We find in the Milinda Pañha reference to certain reputed physician, viz. Narada, Dhanvantari, Angarika, Kapila, Atula, Pubba

Kachchayana, etc. Besides surgery, a miraculous progress was made by the science of snake-bite cure. There is reference to the destruction of the effect of poison with the help of antidotes, as well as catching the snakes and causing them to suck their venom out of the body.

Besides Ayurveda there were other useful crafts and arts, architecture being the most important and useful one. The Universities of Nalanda and Vikramasila and their palatial buildings, painting and sculpture of that age, the Buddhist Viharas, Stupas and Chaityas are glorious examples in case. The masses were trained in vocational occupations as agriculture, commerce, cottage industry and animal husbandry in this period in the same way as the people of the Vedic period received facilities to be trained in these arts and crafts.

Method of Education: The art of writing had considerably advanced in the Buddhist period, but it had not reached the masses as regards its practical use. The method of the Buddhist education was, therefore, oral as it was during the Vedic age. The *Saddhiviharikas* memorised roots and conjugations of grammar by rote. The *Acharya* (preceptor) and *Saddhiviharikas* (pupils) dwelt in the monasteries together. Hence the teacher had recourse to direct method in teaching. He would suggest a lesson to them, and they, on their part, learnt it by heart. The preceptor would proceed further only after having ascertained the thorough comprehension of the lesson by the pupils. The persons having sympathies with Buddhism, were called the *'Upasaka'*. These people listened to sermons of Buddhist monks by inviting them to their houses. In Viharas and monastic schools, *Hetu-Vidya* or Inductive method was adopted and the intellect of the pupils was trained through it. This method was held in great importance in the education system. Discussions and argumentations on different religious and philosophical subjects were daily held in the monasteries. Vikramasila was the most outstanding centre in this respect. The Buddhist monks engaged themselves in hair-splitting disputations while criticising Hinduism or Jainism. Followers of different religions held occasional discussions; hence students were trained in the art of debating from the beginning of their academic career. Sometimes authorities and celebrities on religion and philosophy were invited to deliver talks on different topics for the intellectual benefit of the students. Thus addresses and philosophic disputations had carved an important niche in the general scheme of education. These factors helped develop the mental faculties of the students. His mental horizon was widened considerably and a practical interest and zest for life was generated in his mind. He developed clarity of vision through discussions on different problems of life. In course of time this method became so rampant that ultimately it degenerated into a creed of "discussion for discussion's sake". It dealt, thus, a fatal blow to the acquisition of substantial knowledge and pofundity of learning. Such pedantic disputants developed only shallow verbosity.

Besides, there were certain special peripatetic teachers such as Sariputta, Mahamuggallan, Anuruddha, Ananda and Rahula who would go round journeying in the country on teaching mission. There was prevalent the custom of undertaking journey by the students at the end of their student-career in order to give a realistic and practical shape to what they had learnt at the monastic schools. This rendered their knowledge complete, solid and practical. The example of Jivaka has already been adduced in this respect. Periodical gatherings were organised for the purpose of debate and monks from different monasteries discussed and delivered talks on philosophical and religious topics. Students were provided ample opportunities to participate in these meetings whereby they increased their knowledge appreciably. There were some Buddhist monks who dwelt in solitude of forests and realized Supreme Knowledge through meditation, but there was no such system for the ordinary students.

The teaching method in regard to technical education in Secular science, Arts and Crafts was identical, *mutatis mutandis*, with that of Brahmanical education, *i.e.* students were given education through both theoretical and practical methods. As regards Arts and Crafts, the students served a term of apprenticeship under some expert artisans and thus picked up knowledge by and by. Spinning, weaving, sewing, stone-masonry and other similar crafts were learnt by the above-mentioned methods.

Female Education: According to the principles of Buddhist religion women were regarded as inferior to men and hence objects to be shunned by the religionists. The monk would take the vow of lifelong celibacy (*Neshṭhika Brahmacharya*). They feared to come in close contact with women. But it was impracticable in daily life specially in view of their necessity of going on their daily round for begging food from the householders in companionship of their disciples. Consequently Buddha had allowed them to be admitted to the chapter, and thus women monks (*Bhikshuni*) lived in the same monasteries and were supposed to lead a very holy and chaste life. During the initial stage of Buddhist education, much encouragement was given to women-education and separate monastic schools were established for this purpose. But in fourth century A.D. decline of the order of Buddhist Nuns commenced because the Viharas had assumed such an importance from educational point of view that ultimately they had attained to international level. Women, therefore, could not derive any benefit from those institutions. It should, however, be noted that whatsoever education had been imparted, it not only helped raise the standard of women's character and intellect generally but also produced a number of learned women of high calibre who guided the society in the fields of religion and philosophy. There are examples of some women who were philosophers and poetesses of a higher order. Some of them were renowned social reformers and specialised in social welfare. There are, in Buddhist period, sundry references to women religious missionaries who had gone to foreign countries in order to propagate their religion. For example, Saṁghamitra, sister of Asoka the great, had gone to Ceylone to spread Buddhist religion. Besides, there are examples of women-monks, viz. Subha, Anupama, Sumedha, etc. who had taken the vow of life-long celibacy. Highly educated women undertook teaching work and were known as Upadhyayas. Panini has referred to women dormitories for the women students. We have examples of high poetic talents of such illustrious women as Silabhattarika, Prabhudevi, Vijayanka, etc. The poetic powers of Vijayanka have been regarded as second to none but to those of Kalidasa. Political science, however, was not precluded from the curriculum of study for women. Queens succeeding their husbands after their death, undertook and conducted administrative duties efficiently. There are examples of many an empire being conducted by women effectively. For example, Nayanika of Satavahana dynasty, Prabhavatigupta of Vakataka dynasty (fourth century A.D.) and Badami (Vijaya Maharika) of Chalukya dynasty are famous in the history for their efficient administration. This goes to prove the fact that women were given theoretical and practical education in politics. Besides, they studied Criticism, Mimamsa, Vedanta, Ayurveda and Literature of higher order. The wife of Maṅḍana Misra had acted as Judge in a Philosophical disputation between her husband and Saṁkaracharya. This is sufficient to illustrate to what extent the intellectual faculties of women-folk had developed.

Now it has been quite evident that women got ample opportunities for their self development; but at the same time it will have to be remembered that higher education was limited only to women belonging to higher strata of society. Women-education was, it seems, inadequate in the wider sense of the term "Education" as it is regarded today. It had not spread and reached the house of such common masses as peasants, labourers, artisans, craftsmen and ordinary traders. Importance of the *Upanayana* ceremony which was compulsory for women under the Vedic system of education had considerably declined or almost disappeared. The natural consequence of this was that the level of the age of women's marriage was sufficiently lowered and they began to be married even during their childhood. It consequently dealt a serious blow to their education. The situation assumed a serious aspect in ninth and tenth centuries A.D. Girls were married at the age of ten or eleven. During this period the social and religious status of women fell to a considerable extent. This naturally proved very much detrimental to women education.

Contrast Between Buddhist and Brahmanical Education

Under the system of Buddhist education the students began their studies early in the morning. At some places a crow was domesticated to indicate time to the students by crowing. The daily routine of the students under the Buddhist system of education was well nigh the same as during the Vedic period. As a matter of fact, entire educational system during the two periods was fundamentally indentical. The only difference discernible between the two systems lay in the fact that while during the Vedic period pupils were taught in the Gurukulas in a homely atmosphere, there were, under the Buddhist system of education, established monastic schools and organised centres for the purpose. Under the former system, attention was devoted to 'individual' whereas under the latter system, the individual was regarded as a unit of the group and hence education was imparted collectively. Household life formed an important aspect under the Vedic education; renunciation of family life, on the other hand, was the very basis of the other system. Thus, under the Buddhist system of education, an order of Brotherhood was established by breaking tender and natural ties of family relations. A Buddhist would usually depend upon the charity of his fraternity which itself, in its turn, would depend upon that of the laity or the *Upasakas*. Consequently, it circumscribed the scope for personal ambition, ability, efficiency and activities on the part of an individual.

Second point of difference between the two systems lies in the fact that under the Brahmanical system of education the pupil had to observe strict physical and mental discipline. He was to treat pleasure and its agencies as taboo. Student life was fraught with austerities. They were required to act upon the principle, "*Sukharithinah Kuto Vidya, nasti Vidya, nasti Vidyarithinah Sukham.*"[2] But according to the Buddhist system "the body is to be decently draped, cleansed and massaged, regularly fed, sheltered in the rainy season, rested during the noon day heat, and medically treated when ailing by the best physician of the country."[3]

Further, it should be noted that while the Brahmanical system was founded on monarchical principles, the Buddhist system on the other hand, was democratic in character. In other words, under the former system, seniority and pre-eminence of the preceptor would always remain an established fact, while the pupil, under the Buddhist system would accomplish the right to vote in the deliberations of the Samgha after his admission to it. The only difference between the pupil and the preceptor was merely spiritual superiority of the latter to the former.

In the end, under the Brahmanical system of education, only that person could lead the life of an ascetic or hermit who was deemed fit and eligible to it from every point of view. Under the Buddhist system only those persons who possessed unimpeachable morality, were admitted to the *Samgha* (Order), but in course of time, certain drawbacks and weaknesses crept into it. Democratic principles were abused and the monks and nuns fell victim to moral turpitude and corruption. The authority of central organisation grew lax owing to the establishment of a number of independent local Saṃghas. As a natural consequence, Buddhism declined gradually in India and the Brahmanical system came into ascendency anew through the efforts of such religious thinkers and philosophers as Saṁkaracharya and Madhavacharya.

Demerits of Buddhism: Buddhist education was not altogether immune from defects. Not unlike vedic education, it was also dominated by religion, so much so that Arts and Crafts, in the last phase of it, came to be looked down upon by the members of higher classes and ultimately they gave them up completely. Besides this, the ratio of mass education decreased during the Buddhist period considerably in comparison to the Vedic age. The greatest defect of this system lay in the fact that democratic principle of freedom degenerated into license with the result that monasteries were converted into mere play haunts for the monks and nuns owing to the laxity of central organisation. The establishment of the system of *Samgha* (order) which was regarded as the veritable forte of Buddhist religion, ultimately proved to be the sole cause of its downfall. Moreover, military art and science, art of manufacturing arms and weapons and the art of warfare could not develop much under the Buddhist system of education. The reason for it is to be sought in its being founded on the principles of non-violence and renunciation of the world. According to Buddhist religion the world is full of sorrow. Therefore, the sole aim of life was considered to be the attainment of salvation *(Nirvana)* by renouncing the world. It naturally resulted in artificiality in the mode of life and the external life of the monks was dominated by mere formalities. The meaning of the 'struggle of life' was confined to mere metaphysical speculation. This dealt a serious blow to the all-round progress and development of life. At length, when the foreigners invaded our country, she could not resist them with her poor military skill and organisation. Still it is to be acknowledged that merits of Buddhist system of education far outweigh the defects and flaws, though it was through its short-comings that its downfall was so sudden and sure and in its stead the Brahmanical system of education was re-established in the country.

Conclusion

In short, we can affirm that Buddhist education laid the foundation stone of a high culture. It introduced certain innovations and alterations in the *modus vivandi* of Aryans. Though Indian attitude towards life had always tended to be characterised by piety and sanctity, yet the Buddhist education intensified and elevated it still more. Monastic life of the Sramanas and monks had always been exemplary for the Indians so much so that the educational institutions during the Buddhist period attracted students and scholars from distant parts of the world, such as China, Japan, Korea, Java, Burma, Ceylon, Tibet and other countries. The foreign students made a very profound study of Indian religion, literature and system of education and disseminated the seeds of Indian culture in their own lands. In the Buddhist monasteries, all differences of caste and social status which had taken deep roots under the Brahmanical education, had been removed. The sacred portals of the Buddhist institutions were open to all where all the students without difference were provided with equal opportunities for the development of their character according to their capacity and aptitudes. Along with religious and philosophical aspects of the Buddhist education, secular education formed an essential part of it. This system gave birth to such international institutions as Nalanda, Taxila and Vikramasila, which were the centres of both religious and secular education. The material and spiritual superiority of the country of that age is traceable to the then educational system. Education was closely wedded to the various problems of life and it aimed at finding out concrete solutions thereof. It was purely Indian having been evolved by the Indian educationists under conditions peculiar to our country. This is why that educational system was immensely suited to time and place. Mass education, it should be noted, was also in vogue at that time and female education received a prominent attention in the general educational set-up of the country. Besides this, there was an elaborate provision for the general education of laity having sympathy towards Buddhism because they were regarded as the rich and potential heritage and it was from amongst these *Upasakas* that Buddhist monks and preceptors were elected.

In the end we may say that in the sphere of morals and discipline the Buddhist system of education enriched human life considerably. The preceptor and pupils led a very disciplined mode of life. Any contact with women folk was strictly forbidden. But it is worthy of note that Buddhism did not believe in the mortification of flesh and undergoing severe penances. Certain Chinese travellers such as Fa-Hien, Hiuen-Tsang and I-Tsing have given a very vivid description of Buddhist monasteries based on personal experience and observation indicating the glory and grandeur of Buddhist system of education. It is largely through the long-standing traditional background of Buddhist education that we are still able to continue our harmonious cultural, political and economic relations with the far Eastern countries such as China, Japan, Korea, Shiam and Indonesia.

REFERENCES

1. The three R's.
2. Neither a pleasure-seeker get knowledge nor a student is fated for pleasure.
3. Dr. Radha Kumud Mookerjee: *Ancient Indian Education;* p. 469.

10

The Middle Way and Buddhist Education

"Dhamma is truth—the way to Brahma—attainment."

Buddhist ethical procedures in which the notion of oneself and others is involved are only a part of the 'walking with God' (*Brahma*). They are the means—these good works. There remains the life of *Jhāna*, (Dhyāna), as the Buddhist understands it, or *'Yoga'* as the Hindu recognizes it. *'Nirvana'* is the beatific state of mind. It is a higher state of human existence, producing in the mind a feeling of freedom and directing its undisturbed attention to higher things. To make this clear, the Buddha propounds the doctrine of the Middle Way. 'It is as Platonic, Aristotelian, and Scholastic as much as it is Brahmanical and Buddhist.'[1] The true 'walking with God' is the Middle Way. 'He teaches the Mean by the principle of causality.'[2] It is desire that goads us to renewed becoming and it is only as a follower of the Middle Path that we can lead the good life (*Suttanipata 1042*), just as for Plato it is only by holding on to the golden thread of the common Law that man can avoid the unregulated pulls of life (*Laws 644*).

Now which is the Middle Path that leads to insight and wisdom? It is the holy Eightfold Path. It consists of eight great truths, each one of which applies to human life, each one of which is intended to shape human destiny; and taken one by one, and understood and practised, human progress would be rapid and secure. The first of these great truths is Right Knowledge; the second, Right Thought or Aspiration; then the third and fourth are Right Speech and Right Activity; then follows Right Means of Livelihood and Right Endeavour; then Right Contemplation. These are the eight steps of the Path—these eight great truths for the guidance of human life.

'Buddha was essentially practical and sought to provide mankind with a way of living rather than of speculation. With an almost modern insistence upon the law of cause and effect, he inculcated a method of removing passion, a technique of detachment which he called the "Noble Eightfold Path". For him, sane moderation was the Middle Path to be followed.'[3]

In order to teach the cardinal principles of the Middle Way, Buddha challenged the tenets of orthodox philosophy. He accepted the world as it was and repudiated the notion of castes, the divinity of the scriptures, and sacrifices and rituals. The faith in love and charity with 'Ahimsa' as its basis appealed to the human heart. Buddhism not only introduced an important change in the educational administration, but also presented India with a new ideal in education. Through its monasteries it evolved an educational system which was independent of the state. It became the duty of the Buddhist torch-bearers, as of the medieval Christian friars, to educate the masses. 'The Buddhists thus became the pioneers of mass education and founders of great universities like Taxila and Nalanda and the disseminators of learning through their monasteries and preachers who scoured the country to popularize its tenets.'[4] This cultural democracy which consisted in bringing such truths to the common man has been the permanent contribution of Buddhism.

Ananda, what is the Marvel of Teaching?

Buddha appealed to man's reason and verification of knowledge. 'And what is the marvel of teaching? Indeed, Ananda, a certain one teaches thus: "Reason thus and not thus. Apply your mind thus and not thus. Abandon this state, and acquire that state, and abide in it".' (*Anguttara-Nikaya 1. 170*).[5] He proceeded from the known to the unknown and preferred the inductive to the deductive method. The touchstone of Buddha's teaching was Reason; his goal was Truth. He preached to a people in an age, which put religion above reason. Buddhism prepared and popularized a new code of morals which was as revolutionary to the established order as it was thorough and penetrating in its effects upon every individual life, from that of the king to that of the peasant. It broke down the dead wall of privilege and superstition in the same manner as the Reformation in Europe swept away the privileges of the Church.

Buddha's teachings enlarge the bounds of human thought and extend the compass of human action. This globe is only a part of the universe, one in which human actions neither begin nor end, but which offers a splendid field for the display of one's faculties. 'The great thinkers and social reformers of India grasped firmly one of the eternal verities, generally ignored in Western politics, that ideas whether good or evil, are more potent than armaments—for the spirit survives when the body is destroyed. It is therefore no less important for the State to purge the body politic of evil thinking than it is to stay an epidemic or provide efficient means of national self defence. For that reason, the philosophical debating halls in which king and commoner met on terms of equality, always played a more important part in Indo-Aryan politics than councils of war, Royal Edicts and for the same reason the political education of the Indian masses in the Dark Ages of European history was probably far better than that which obtained in most European countries in the twentieth century.'[6]

Thus we see that the ideals of equality of man and universal brotherhood proclaimed by Buddha emancipated man from the thraldom of conservatism. This in turn determined the fundamental aims of education from the sixth century B.C. right down to the seventh century A.D.—the Golden Age of Buddhism in India. Buddhism gave the east the fundamental inspiration for social synthesis. Education in Brahmanical societies had an astonishing fidelity in sustaining the flavour of a continuous culture by a highly informal, irregular, and oral instruction. Buddhism introduced for the first time the element of organization in education. In Buddhism there is an appeal to the moral experience of man for the verification of truth. We recall the noble 'fourfold' Truth, viz. Truth about suffering—Truth about the cause of suffering—Truth of the cure of suffering and Truth of the way to effect the cure—an adjustment of means to end, resulting in the 'Eightfold Path'. 'Never I suppose has a religion set out its case with so complete an appeal to human rational powers and empirical judgment as Buddhism.'[7]

J.B. Bury says, 'That man is the architect of his life and that he has reason to be confident in his energies when he recollects from what point he has set out, and to what heights he has been capable of elevating himself, has become the dominant trend of progress in the modern world only from the time of the French Revolution.'[8]

Buddhism has always emphasized the people's power of self-help and self-reliance and infinitely widened the horizon of their service. To live and teach how to live a chaste, temperate, and kindly life of moderation by the aid of the inner light was its objective; this basic aim has continued to inspire Buddhist education throughout the twenty-three centuries.

Christianity and Buddhism agree that human misery is the resultant effect of human selfishness. That selfishness is the root cause of all human misery has been the main theme of the Bhagavad Gita too. Self-control is the central touchstone of Buddha's teaching and there can be no difference of opinion on this elementary truth between eastern and western religious thought. The opposition is not so much between Indian thought and the New Testament, for both of them teach that bliss is attainable. 'The fundamental contrast is rather between both Indian and New Testament on the one hand and on the other, the rooted conviction of the European races that this world is all important. This conviction finds expression not only in the avowed pursuits of pleasure and ambition, but in such sayings as that the best religion is the one which does most good, and such ideals as self perfection or the full development of one's nature and powers.'[9]

Education necessarily follows the lead given by the fundamental beliefs of the people. Each particular human group admires a special type of ideal human being. Dr. K.J. Saunders in his 'Ideals of East and West', develops this theme and attributes the gentleman ideal to the British, the handsome and virtuous man to the Greeks, the disciplined warrior to the Romans, the ascetic ideal to the Indians, and the saint to the Christians. True it is that Buddhism extols the life of '*dhyana*' (contemplation) to achieve its ideal of a self-controlled, wise man. It does not mean inactivity or renunciation of the world.

In the world of men, there are those who are introspective and self-analytical. They find that all men run after happiness and nobody finds it. Happiness is as elusive as the blowing wind. Such a man begins to analyze the cause of man's happiness or unhappiness in life. When he pursues his research, he finds that it is the mind which is the cause of joy and misery. It is the way in which a man reacts to external circumstances that gives him joy or misery. So in order to get real happiness, one should take care of the mind. If one can control the mind, one can control the whole world. If you aim control over the whole of the outside world, through control of the mind, it can no longer mar your happiness or affect your inner life.

Buddhism conceives the last of the steps on the 'Eightfold Path'—Contemplation, as a strenuous mental discipline and a state of enhanced vitality, which the educative process in any country cannot ignore. There is a hierarchy of contemplative states—a kind of ladder by which one can ascend from lower to higher states of being, but the final goal of liberation lies beyond all. 'By right contemplation, he bends his mind for the realization by super-knowledge, so that he attains to being a witness in whatever faculty it may be. The meditator who in contemplation, is skilled in contemplation, and who is skilled in the attainment of contemplation—he is the supreme, the most excellent.' (*Samyutta-Nikaya iii. 263-4*).

Plato held with Buddha that meditation brings the soul into contact with ethereal regions. He says, 'As then the mind of the deity is nourished by intelligence and pure science, so the mind of every soul that is about to receive what properly belongs to it, when it sees after a long time that which is, is delighted and by contemplating the truth is nourished and thrives until the revolution of the heaven brings it round again to the same point.'[10] Contemplation tends to compose and concentrate the mind upon the object in view. 'Mental states always precede action of which they are the determining factors' (*Dhammapada 1.1*). That the highest freedom of the spirit is given only to those who have undergone the preparatory stage of body and mental purification and are prepared to engage in deep meditation which concentrates the mind and enlarges its vision, is also expressed by the English poet, William Wordsworth in *Tintern Abbey*.

That serene, that blessed mood,
In which the affections gently lead us on,
Until the breath of this corporeal frame
And even the motion of our human blood
Almost suspended, we are laid asleep

In body, and become a living soul;
While with an eye made quiet by the power
Of harmony, and the deep power of joy,
We see into the life of things.

"Dhamma is truth, restraint is Brahma-faring,
The Middle Way pursuing, the way to Brahma-attainment,"

embodies the abiding spirit of Buddhism which we have first to understand, if we are to appreciate the development of education in the East. 'The sum total of Buddha's teaching was epitomized by the Emperor Asoka in his edicts, in which he exhorted his people to exert to their utmost, practise piety and be compassionate to all sentient beings.'[11]

We have described at length the underlying ethical principles of Buddhism because of its deep influence in modern thought, more especially in the countries of the East. The educational philosophy of the East will largely draw its strength and inspiration from its fountain source. Unquestionably the religious impulse in its powerful representatives, lifts personality into a region where the wall of moral isolation between man and man wear thin. The philosopher is the best friend of the educationist, for in his hunger after spiritual insight, he tries to reflect his knowledge and beliefs in his life and deeds. It cannot be denied that educational practice is shaped by the fundamental beliefs of the people, and educational thought is an instrument of educational practice.

REFERENCES

1. Ananda K. Coomaraswamy and I. B. Horner, *Gotama the Buddha*, Jaico, p. 49.
2. Ibid. p. 50.
3. A.C. Bouquet, *Comparative Religion*, Pelican, p. 161.
4. Sir Hari Singh Gour, *The Spirit of Buddhism*. Luzac, 1929, p. 416. *See* also H.D. Sankalia, *The University of Nalanda*, B.G. Paul, Madras.
5. *Note*. Quotations taken from Ananda K. Coomaraswamy and I. B. Horner, *The Living Thoughts of Gotama the Buddha*, The Living Thoughts Library, 1948.
6. E.B. Havell, *The History of Aryan Rule in India*. Introduction, pp. xiii-xiv.

7. W.E. Hocking, *Living Religions and a World Faith*, Allen & Unwin, 1940, p. 94.
8. *See* J.B. Bury, *The Idea of Progress*, Ch. X, 192-201.
9. Sir C. Eliot, *Hinduism and Buddhism*, Vol. I, Introduction, pp. LX-LXI.
10. Plato, *Phaedrus* 58.1.
11. Sir Hari Singh Gour, *The Spirit of Buddhism*, Luzac, 1929, p. 484.

11

Indian Ideals in Education

We are to seek for the Indian Ideals which flowered into the National Life; for every country has its own ideals, and according to the nature of the Thought, which is the generating Seed, so is the nature of the National Life which grows up therefrom, and sends forth the branches and bursts into the blossoms which are the products of the National Activity.

The Secret of India's Immortal Youth

Says the Upanishad: "Man is created by Thought, and what a man thinks upon that he becomes; therefore think upon Brahman."[1] So also with Nations, since there is no creative Thought other than that of Brahman in manifestation; and because there were so many in India who ever thought of that Supreme, therefore did India flower out into a civilization unrivalled in the depth of its Philosophy, in the spirituality of its Religion, and in the perfection of its Dharma of orderly and graded Individual and National Life, expressing as none other has ever done that balance, that equilibrium, which is Yoga; that which saved her, when all the contemporaries of her splendid Nationality have been carried away by Time's tremendous rapids, and scattered as wrecks over the far horizon of the boundless Ocean of the Past. She shares their Past, but they do not share her Future, for not theirs the secret of her immortal Youth.

And what is that secret? It lays hidden in her Education and her Culture, or rather in the Ideals which created these; for the Idea is prior to the form, and if today men think that her strength is dissipated, her energy outworn, it is because she has for a moment—for what is a century and a half but a moment in her millennial life? —sold her birthright, as her Mother's first-born child, for a mess of western pottage. Let her turn again to her Ideals, and she shall renew her strength. For Ideals are the generating Life which unfolds through many incarnations, embodies itself in many a successive form, but remains ever true to type. We, who believe in India's Immortality, do not need to reproduce the bodies, the forms, of the past; but we need that life, the life of the Mother Immortal, shall embody itself in new forms, but that it shall be Her life, and not another's.

Education and Culture

Let us distinguish between Education and Culture. Education is the drawing out and training of inborn capacities and powers—brought over from former lives and developed in the *Svargic* or *Deva* world—which lie as germs in the *Vijnânamayakosha,* the intellectual aspect of the re-incarnating Self, the triple-faced *Jivâtma,* or *Ātmâ-Buddhi-Manas.* These germs, ready to sprout forth and to grow, germs of the qualities which are to manifest through the *Manomayakosha,* are as it were, sown in that stage of the consciousness which we call the Lower Manas, for the expression of which, with the emotions, the *Manomayakosha* is framed. First, the preparatory stage of re-incarnation begins in which this kosha, the sheath of the mind and the emotions, is formed; then followed the *Prânamayakosha,* that of passions and life-energy; and then the *Annamayakosha,* the sheath formed by food, the dense physical body. These three are new with each rebirth, and education has not only to draw out and distribute the germs through each sheath, but to develop them, train, and make the sheath sensitive and responsive to the impacts from the external world, accurate in recording them, and in sending them on to the mind, which connects the impression with the object causing it, and thus establishes relations between itself and the outer world, these relations and the action of the mind upon them being Knowledge. Observation by the sense-organs in the physical body; the effects of these on the sense-centres, as sensations; the perception by and the action of the mind on these by memory, analysis, comparison, classification, inter-relations (causes and effects), reasoning on them, anticipation, all these form the field of Knowledge which is tilled by Education.

Culture is the result on the mind of certain forms of knowledge, and is based on these; but it differs from Education in that it is not the drawing out and training of faculty, but is the result of the exercise of faculties on subjects which arouse sympathetic emotion and imagination, broadening the mind, eliminating personal, local and racial prejudices, acquiring an understanding of human nature in its many aspects, and contacting the life-side rather than the form-side of creatures ; hence the quick internal response to other lives, and the intuition of the unity of life beneath the diversity of life-expressions. The difference between Education and Culture is symbolised by the condition of entry into the School of Pythagoras, acquaintance with "Mathematics and Music"— the capacity to use the Intellect—Higher Manas, or Manas in the *Vijnânamayakosha*—by synthesising the products of the mind and discovering the laws producing them, and by the purifying of the emotions by Beauty. Literature and Art are the instruments of Culture. Science and the "clear cold light" of reason are the area and the guide of Education. The Life in Nature and the intellectual intuition, which recognises truth by its harmony with his own nature—"whose nature is Knowledge"—are the area and the guide of Culture. If these are completely separated during the plastic period of youth, Science tends to hardness, and, in over-specialisation, to narrowmindedness and intolerance ; Culture tends, when exaggerated, to false sentiment and fastidiousness in non-essentials. The training of the instruments of knowledge and the storing of the memory with facts is the work of Education by others in youth, and their application to new facts and conditions is the self-education which continues during life. Culture in youth consists in the unconscious development and refinement of passions into emotions amid beautiful surroundings, for the contact with beautiful objects and the evoking and the control of the emotions in response to them, and the moulding of these by Literature and the Arts, develop the discrimination which is an element in self-culture, the critical faculty which manifests as a balanced judgment, not as mere fault-finding, and lends poise, dignity and gentleness to the attitude towards life. We shall see in a few moments how Beauty was an essential feature of the Indian Ideal of Education and Culture, and the necessity for the revival of this Ideal in modern life.

Educational Systems: Ancient and Modern

But let us first realize two fundamental differences between Ancient and Modern Systems of Education in their relation to the State, one of them prevailing alike in India and in Britain, and the other peculiar to India.

In the Ancient System of India, Education and Culture were self-controlled, and while the State, the organized Nation, profited by them and from them drew its dignity, its religion, its morality, its effectiveness, and its consequent efficiency, the Legislative and Executive Departments of its Government exercised over them no control, and did not interfere with their management. Kings built Universities and bestowed on them wealth, but claimed in them no authority. A Monarch might enter into the Convocation of a university, but no one rose to greet him and he took his seat like any other visitor; but on the entrance of its Head, the "Venerable of Venerables," all rose and turned their faces towards him and in silence awaited his words. The university was the Temple of Learning and the learned were its only Hierophants. When Learning visited Royalty, when a Wise One entered a Court, even Shri Krishna descended from His throne and bowed at the feet of the Sage.

In the Modern System, education is under the control of a government department, the Legislature makes laws for it, the Executive appoints its Directors or the Ministers, who are really its Masters, sends its Inspectors into its Schools and Colleges, and puts the educators into a steel-frame, which it mis-names efficiency. This is now alike in East and West. But in India, where Kings had been its nursing fathers and had poured out their treasures at its feet, the foreign governments ignored the ancient system, and, as its rule spread, education and culture died of starvation in the Kingdoms which became Provinces. The splendid inheritance from the Indian past—Hindu, Buddhist and Muslim—disappeared, leaving only the Schools of Pandits, maintained by Indian Princes or by the reverent charity of the Hindus, till but one University, that of Nadiya, survived; the Temple and Musjid schools remained for a while and the muffasal village school—that which the East India Company, on being compelled by the British Parliament to spend a lakh on education, called in 1814, "this venerable and benevolent institution of the Hindus, "[2] after the testimony of Sir Thomas Munro in 1813, that there were "schools established in every village".[3] The East India Company ascribed to these the "general intelligence of the natives as scribes and accountants."[4] Dr. John Matthai, in his *Village Administration in British India*, says that "when the British took possession of the country," they found in most parts of the country (except western and central India) that "there existed a widespread system of national education".[5] Even in 1838, Adam's Reports show a similar state of things in Bengal. He reports the results of an enquiry, held in 1835-1838, made in typical districts of the Presidency, and found both *Toles* and *Madrasahs* (High Schools) and *Pathashalas* and *Maktabs* (schools attached to Temples and Musjids). Colleges were found, he writes, "in all the large villages as in the towns. The age of the scholars was from about five or six to sixteen. The curriculum included reading, writing, the composition of letters, and elementary arithmetic and accounts, either commercial, or agricultural, or both." I may add that in the village schools "Elementary Arithmetic" included multiplication tables not of only 12 x 12, but up to 20 x 20. The schools however continued to diminish in number. The *Quinquennial Review* for 1907-1912, shows 2,051 *Madrasahs* in 1907 against 1,446 in 1912, and 10,504 Musjid Schools in 1907 against 8,288 in 1912.

Let us pause for a moment on the age of the scholars mentioned above. In the old days, the education of the child up to the age of seven seems to have been more in the home than in the school. From seven to sixteen, the boy was to be taught and trained in school, and then to pass on to the University. The stage of infancy ends at seven, and up to that age the body should be the first care, and lessons should be in the form of play, and great freedom of choice should be given to the little ones. No care in later life can restore the stamina of the body ill-nourished, or unwisely nourished, during those first seven years of life. With the joint family system there were children enough in the household, including those of the dependents, to make a society for the children, in which they learned unconsciously lessons of kindness, of courtesy, of gentle manners and refined speech, of little sacrifices born of love, of mutual helpfulness and mutual service. With the narrowing of the home circle, the playing school is in many ways better and the children are happier in the merry games and the gay company of their little comrades. But the school must be well-chosen, the teachers tender the helpful; songs, stories and play that exercises and trains the senses, the hand and the eye, and teaches graceful harmonious movements, are enough.

From seven to fourteen are the years for training the memory and the emotions, for the stories of heroism and of virtue that inspire, drawn from the history of the motherland, and great man and women; stories, too, of other countries, of all that can arouse enthusiasm and inspire to service. Thus will the children have their minds and emotions so trained as to fit them to cross in safety the perilous bridge between childhood and youth. Form fourteen to twenty-one is the time for hard mental study. By sixteen, the special capacities will have shown themselves, and will mark out the best avocation for the future life, and specialised Education may safely begin. This is but the barest indication of the broad stages in the preparation for manhood and womanhood, the Ideal of the Student Order of the well-regulated life.[6] But the knell of popular education was struck in 1854, when Sir Charles Wood tried, and the Government supported, the singular experiment of teaching the people in a foreign tongue, with the result that after seventy years only 3.4 per cent of the people received primary education. So we have three stages in education in India in relation to the State: I. Lavish help from rulers and complete liberty of education, paid for by the wealthy and free to the poor, who, in exchange, served their teachers and performed household duties; II. Entire neglect for 97 years, with an interval when a lakh a year was spent on it; III. The Government English-speaking Schools and Colleges, and later Universities with, of recent years, partial and grudging introduction of the vernaculars.

Education and the State

How shall we apply the Indian Ideals to the salvation of Modern Education and Culture in India ? That is the question which Indian universities alone can solve, and before they can answer it, nay, before they can even begin the task, the old relationship must be recreated between the State and the Universities. Learning must again be inspired with the Ancient Ideals, and these will be embodied in new forms. And in order that these new forms shall be expressions of India's life, and not strait-jackets to confine her, the old freedom must be restored to Education and Culture. Governments should assign to educational and cultural institutions the material means for their support, gifts of land, grants of money for buildings, and for the necessary equipment, so that they may be able to give to the nation the priceless assets of learned and skilled men and women of high character, to carry on the work in every department of national life. Money given to education by the nation is not a gift, but an investment. It returns high interest to the nation as well as power and happiness to the individual. Learned men produce literature which raises the nation in the eyes of the world and, far more important, spreads knowledge over the earth, literature which ennobles and inspires not only contemporaries, but generations yet unborn. Science makes discoveries which add to human knowledge, increase man's power over the forces of nature, and—if it tread only righteous paths—will preserve, uplift and strengthen human life and human happiness. Only by education and culture of man's spiritual, intellectual, emotional and physical nature can be lifted from the savage to the sage and the saint, can poverty be abolished, can society be made fraternal instead of barbarous, can crime, the fruit of ignorance, be gotten rid of, and international and social peace replace war and the strife of classes. Avidya is the mother of poverty, of sorrow, of misery. It is the darkness which the Sun of Vidya must chase away.

A generation of really educated people, with a proportion of the cultured, will change the face of India. Japan educated her people in forty years. As rapid as was the destruction may be the recovery, and each successive generation will show an improved result. Already[7] Indian Ministers have made Primary Education free in seven provinces and compulsory in three, compulsion to be introduced as rapidly as possible in the other four. When India gains her own political freedom, may she be wise enough to restore Freedom to Education and Culture, and, once more, the highest Honour to Learning.

The Place of Mother-tongues

After freedom in the Educational and Cultural field is won, for it is not possible until this freedom is possessed, the very first thing must be the restoration of the mother-tongues of India to their proper place in that field. Nothing so denationalises a people as the imposition upon them of a foreign tongue. dominating their life and thought. When Germany, Russia and Austria rent Poland into three fragments, each banned the Polish tongue in the schools and imposed its own. Macaulay, with the most generous feeling and the most utter ignorance, urged the substitution of the English language, literature and civilization for those which he regarded as heathen and superstitious. The mother-tongues were despised, and a gulf was dug between the English-educated minority and the learned in the ancient mother-language and the middle classes educated in tongues derived from it. The free universities will use the languages of the country throughout all schools and colleges, with English as a second language, and probably other tongues as well. So far, the universities have given little culture that has been gained by individuals for themselves. But free universities will have curricula which shall give both education and culture. Students will, as of old, be surrounded with beauty in the schools, the colleges and the Universities.

The Place of Religion in Education

The second basic difference between the Ancient System and the Modern English one, as imposed on India, is the absence of religious and moral education. In Britain itself, the religion of the country and the morality based on it are taught in the schools as an integral part of education; lately, as Nonconformity and Free Thought spread, a conscience clause has been introduced exempting children, whose parents objected to the Anglican form of Christianity or to Christianity itself, from compulsory attendance at the religious services and lessons. But when the rule of the East India Company spread, and English education was introduced into India, the government schools dropped religious and moral teaching, since, on the one hand, a Christian government could not teach heathen religions, and, on the other, as there were several religions in India, the government must treat them all equally, and therefore, remain neutral in regard to them. Thus Indians must pay the taxes which keep up government and other schools, and must further send their children to these, or to missionary schools where an alien religion is taught, or open their own schools and teach any religion they belong to government giving them grants-in-aid.

Modern education in India has practically confined itself to the training of the mental and intellectual nature, and has ignored the unfolding of the spiritual nature, the evoking and training of the emotional nature, and, until lately, the development and training of the physical body to a high state of efficiency. The result has been, in the older generations, the over-strain of the nervous system, the enfeebling of the physical health, the shortening of the period of vigorous maturity, often a sudden breakdown, or, at best, the premature appearance of debility and old age. Further, the exclusive development of the intelligence and the neglect of the emotions has overstimulated the self-regarding instincts, and has largely destroyed the feeling of social and national *Dharma,* of duty to society and to the Nation; hence the decay of public spirit, of social service, of responsibility and of sacrifice for the common weal, which characterize the good *citizen* as distinguished from the good *man*. These were prominent in the results of the Ancient System ; as Shri Krishna said:

> Janaka and others indeed attained to perfection by action; having an eye to the welfare of the world, thou also shouldst perform action. Whatsoever a great man doeth, that other men also do: the standard he setteth up, by that the people go...As the ignorant act from attachment to action, O Bharata, so should the wise act without attachment, desiring the welfare of the world...He who on earth doth not follow the wheel thus revolving, sinful of life and rejoicing in the senses, he, O Partha, liveth in vain.[8]

Vocational Education

This brings us to a very serious question, which has to be decided before you can settle the grading of your education and culture; that which in the West is called "Vocational Education." This is founded on the realization of the fact that in modern days society is no longer a cosmos, but has fallen into chaos, into anarchy, and that this disorder must be remedied if modern civilization is to survive. As society in the ancient Indian Ideal was a community of rational beings, not a fortuitous concourse of atoms, it was regarded as an organism, a body politic with definite organs, each discharging a definite function, for the benefit and health of the whole community. This system was called Caste, and it was necessarily built up by Caste Education. The qualities of each pupil point to his natural avocation in the Nation. The lad who loves the open air and the care of animals, should not be an accountant, or a clerk in a city office. Nor should be quiet youth who seeks study and loves figures be sent off to a farm or a market gardener's. This is recognized in the "learned professions": Law, Medicine, Engineering, demand and have separate instruction. A sturdy athletic lad, fond of games, is not tied down to a stool in a Bank, but is made an Engineer, to plan out railways, or enters some other active occupation. A budding philosopher must not be sent to a factory, nor a poet to a coalmine. While a general level of education and culture should be reached, so that mingling of different types should be useful and agreeable, specialization is necessary after this is attained. At Takshasila, it was not thought unreasonable that a poor student with an aptitude for some branch of learning, should meet the cost of his board and lodging by cutting firewood and helping in domestic affairs. In studying he was on equal terms with a student whose father paid one thousand pieces for his education. No student was allowed to have any money, and a King's son was as poor as the son of a Brahmana peasant.

Students there were taught according to their caste. The Brahmana followed literature as a rule, while the Kshatriya learned less literature, but became skilled in the use of arms. Medicine and Surgery and Anatomy were there for the future physician, Mathematics for the astronomer. The courses include so much that to follow them all was manifestly impossible.

As most progressive people, hypnotized by words, object to Caste, because it has been abused, if you wish to avoid prejudice, you can drop the word and call it Vocation. But, as Shri Krishna pointed out:

> The four castes were emanated by Me, by the different distribution of qualities and actions.[9]

This is the essence of Caste; the utilization of physical heredity to provide bodies suitable for the manifestation of the qualities was an advantage, but unessential, and could only be secured by the co-operation of Devas with men, the men following the Dharma laid down for each caste and thus preserving a sub-type of physical body, to which the Devas guided the appropriate egos, *i.e.* the egos who had evolved the given "distribution of qualities." The group of qualities was that which fitted the ego to discharge one of the functions of one of the fundamental organs of the body politic :

Education, spiritual, intellectual, moral, physical; Government; Organisation of Production and Distribution; Production. In each there are many subdivisions, as Government would include Kings, Assemblies, Judges, Lawyers, Police, etc. These are the predominant and essential groupings of qualities, whether they are called Castes or Vocations. In the Aryan race, the four great groups were called Castes, and caste was a scientific system of social service, according to the inborn qualities of the individual, birth being a convenient, but not essential, concomitant. While it remained on these lines it was honoured. It became a matter of national and social privilege, and is now therefore resented and, in its present form, it is doomed to disappear. Sub-castes arose sometimes from guilds of artisans, like goldsmiths, who now form a fairly powerful sub-caste in Southern India. Families carrying on the same occupation tended to live together in a particular area in a village, and made a "cheri," of their own. Others arose on religious points, or different customs. But those connected with occupations were the most numerous. Under the ancient system, youths were trained for their future functions, national and social, and this is reappearing in the West, as specialised and vocational training, no longer confined to the learned professions, such as Law and Medicine, but extending over all avocations, commercial, trading, industrial and manual, turning the unskilled into the skilled, and thus increasing the value of each to the nation, each with his own vocation, necessary and honourable, because a function of the organized national life.

It is remarkable that John Ruskin, with his far-reaching vision as artist and poet, as well as Auguste Comte, with his encyclopaedic knowledge and keen and lucid intelligence, both recognized the necessity of rescuing Europe from its anarchic social condition, if it were to survive. John Ruskin, in his *Unto This Last*, says:

Five great intellectual professions, relating to daily necessities of life, have hitherto existed in every civilized Nation:

The Soldier's profession is to *defend* it.
The Pastor's to *teach* it.
The Physician's to *keep it in health*.
The Lawyer's to *enforce justice* in it.
The Merchant's to *provide* for it.
And the duty of all these men is, on due occasion, to *die* for it.

> "On due occasion," namely:
> The Soldier, rather than leave his post in battle.
> The Physician, rather than leave his post in plague.
> The Pastor, rather than teach Falsehood.
> The Lawyer, rather than countenance Injustice.
> The Merchant—what is his "due occasion" of death ?
>
> It is the main question for the Merchant, as for all of us. For, truly, the man who does not know how to die, does not know how to live.[10]

Ruskin then proceeds to discuss the Ideal Merchant, and, doubtless quite unconsciously, he describes the Ideal Vaishya. But I must not follow him further on this line, as it would lead me away from education.

Auguste Comte's classification is not so good, as it is based on a separation of Capital and Labour, and on a rigid barrier of birth instead of on a distribution of qualities.

It is, however, worthy of note that two thinkers, one purely intellectual, the other artistic, should both revert to what is supposed to be an outworn superstition, and that the intuition of the artist has carried him to the truth of the existence of a law of nature of essential importance to society, the disregard of which is menacing civilization. The law unites length of days and general prosperity with the assignment of human beings to the national function for which their qualities fit them. For the proper discharge of that function they must also be fitted by a suitable education.

India must once more have an Ideal whereby to shape an education suited to her needs, and to her coming lofty position among the nations of the world. Can she find a loftier Ideal than that which was her Pole Star in the past, and which preserved her through an antiquity the history of which remains alone in the "Memory of Nature," in the archives of her Rishis, in her own literature, an antiquity which cannot be checked by what is called history, for so far none exists earlier than her own, and archaeological researches extend it ever further and further back, and so far tend to confirm her claim to an immense antiquity. All we can say is that history as recognized in Europe, shews nothing contrary to it, and that Europe-recognized history has never known her save as learned, wealthy, prosperous, great in her commerce, her trade, her arts and her crafts, go a long way to prove that Buddhism was but a modified form of the vast Hinduism.

Buddhism came into existence about 600 B.C. The main educational centres of Buddhism were Monasteries or *Vihāras*. As a matter of fact, the history of Buddhist system of education is but the history of the Buddhist Fraternity. The entire educational scheme was controlled and supervised by the monks. It comprised both religious as well as secular types of education. Like the Vedic educational system, the ceremony of initiation formed an essential part of Buddhist education.

Pabbajja (First Ordination): *Prabrajya* or *Pabbajja* was the first preparatory ordination for education. At an early age, the boy after the performance of the ceremony of *Pabbajja*, would enter the monastery as a '*Sramana*'. Prior to the admission to the Order, the novice had to pledge oath of 'Three Refuges': *Buddhaṁ saranaṁ gachhami'* (I take refuge with the Buddha); '*Dhammaṁ saranaṁ gachhami'* (I take refuge with the Religion); *'Sanghaṁ saranaṁ gachhami'* (I take refuge with the Order). Caste distinction did not come in the way of admission as far as possible. Lord Buddha himself held that just as all the rivers by merging into the ocean became one with it, in the similar way, different castes became one after being admitted to the Order. The child had to undergo the ceremony of '*Pabbajja*' at the age of eight whereafter the disciplinary regulations of monastery were applicable to him, and he had to live under the guidance of his preceptor having left his home. A *Sramaṇa* was strictly forbidden to commit violence, speak untruth, take intoxicants and meat and indulge in dances or music. It should, however, be remembered that a child was ineligible to his admissibility to the Order without the consent of his parents. The ceremony of first Ordination (*Pabbajja*) was forbidden to a novice suffering from such infectious diseases as leprosy, itches or consumption and the like. In addition to these, strict restriction was imposed upon the admission to the Order, of the slaves, criminals and government servants especially soldiers.

Upasampada (Final Ordination): *Upasampada* is the second and final ordination in Buddhist system. This ceremony could not be performed before the age of twenty years. After this the monk in the magnificence of her courts and the skill of her artificers and her agriculturists, her people brave and gentle, courteous and hospitable to strangers, until the interlude of which the charter signed by Elizabeth of England was the embryo, and which will close when she is again Mistress in her own household.

I have spoken of the honour paid to learning in India; whether it was Ancient, Middle or Modern India, whether in the Hindu, Buddhist, or Muslim period. Learning was sought for its own sake as the mark of the highest human development, that of man, the thinker, short only of the supreme achievement of the Paravidya, SELF-REALIZATION. Even to that, Jnâna was one of the paths.

The Ashrama Ideal

It is worthy of notice that, in India, education spread downwards; it was not built up from below. Indian Civilization was a product of the country not of the town, of the forest not of the city. Greek Civilization evolved in her cities and reached its highest point in the City-State. But as Rabindranath Tagore has said:

> A most wonderful thing that we notice in India is that here the forest, not the town, is the fountain-head of all its civilization...It is the forest that has nurtured the two great Ancient Ages of India, the Vaidic and the Buddhistic. As did the Vaidic Rishis, Lord Buddha also showered His teaching in many woods of India. The royal palace had no room for Him, it is the forest that took Him into its lap. The current of civilization that flowed from its forests inundated the whole of India.[11]

Here is an Indian Ideal that it would be well to revive, for this planting of Universities in the midst of great cities is European, not Indian. Oxford and Cambridge alone in England have kept the tradition of their Aryan forefathers. The modern "Civic Universities," as they are called, are planted in the midst of the most tumultuous, hurrying, noisy cities in England. Not from them will come sublime philosophies or artistic masterpieces; but they will, doubtless, produce men of inventive genius, miracles of machinery, new ways of annihilating space. But for a country in which a man is valued for what he is, not for what he has, in which a man's life consisteth not in the abundance of the things which he possesseth, the Indian ideal is the more suitable. The essence of that ideal is not the forest as such, but the being in close touch with nature; to let her harmonies permeate the consciousness, and her calm soothe the restlessness of the mind. Hence, it was the forest, which best suited the type and the object of the instruction in the days which evolved Rishis; instruction which aimed at profound rather than at swift and alert thought; which cared not for lucid exposition by the teacher, but presented to the pupil a kernel of truth in a hard shell, which he must crack unassisted with his own strong teeth if he would enjoy the kernel; if he could not break the shell, he could go without the fruit; instruction which thought less of an accumulation of facts poured out into the pupil's memory than of the drawing out in him the faculty which could discover a truth, hidden beneath a mass of irrelevancies. Of such fruitful study the Hindu Ashrama in the forest is the symbol. It must have a few representatives, at least, in India, if she is to rise to her former level in supreme intellectual and spiritual achievement ; some places in which the three *Margas* may be taught and Yoga may be practised, until the Yogi is fit, as of old, to go out into the world of human activity, as the Wise Man who lives that which the *Bhagavad-Gita* teaches. This was learnt by some of the adults in the Ashrama and the Vihâra, where also under the then conditions the youth of the nation could be trained in any of the *Vijjas* (branches of learning) and the *Shilpas* (Arts and Crafts) without sharing in the studies of the elders and the ascetics, yet sharing in the atmosphere they created, which radiated from them. A few "forests" should exist in India for those who seek the Paravidya, that She may again become the spiritual Teacher of the World.

The Buddhist Vihâra obtained similar results by founding the university in a spot of natural beauty, and enclosing a huge space with a high wall, pierced as in Nalanda with but one gate, in Vikramasila by six, in all cases carefully guarded by a *Dvâra Pandita*. Within were not only splendid buildings—"Towers, domes, and pavilions stood amidst a paradise of trees, gardens and fountains." There were flower-strewn lakes and blossom-laden shrubs. Well was understood the influence of natural beauty. The sacred books of Hindus and Buddhists were studied; the curriculum included anatomy and medicine, and it will be remembered that Ashoka in the third century B.C., established hospitals both for men and animals, and Mr. Dutt speaks of these being "established all over the country." One list of the subjects studied gives the five *Siddhantas*, Logic,

Grammar, Philosophy and Metaphysics, History, Arithmetic, Geometry, Astronomy, Sanskrit, Pali, Music and Tantric medicine. Mr. Macdonnell states that in Science, Phonetics, Grammar, Mathematics, Anatomy, Medicine and Law, the attainment of Indians was far in advance of what was achieved by the Greeks.

In the *Chhandogyopanishat* we read how Nârada returned to the Lord Sanat Kumâra, and prayed to be instructed by Him, and He asked what he knew already. And Nârada gives a list which reminds one of the curricula of the Universities which we know, and which evidently existed in the Ancient Hindu Age. For Nârada replied:

> O Lord, I have read the Rig Veda, the Yajur Veda, the Sama Veda, fourth the Athârva Veda, fifth the Ithihasa-Purâna, Grammar, Rituals, the Science of Numbers, Physics, Chronology, Logic, Polity, Technology, the Sciences cognate to the Vedas, the Science of Bhutas, Archery, Astronomy, the Science of Antidotes, and the fine arts. Shankara annotates the last as the Science of making essences of dancing, singing, music, architecture, painting, etc. (Shilpa)......Unto him said Sanat Kumara: "All these that you have learned are merely nominal."
>
> And then He leads him on step by step.
> Thus "did the Lord Sanat Kumâra explain what is beyond darkness."[12]

The lists given may avail to shew why men remained in the forest, or in a monastery which was also a University for Youth, into quite late maturity.

The Ideal of Brahmacharya

During the whole course in School as in College, strict Brahmacharya was enjoined. Here, again, is an Ideal which must be restored. The rule of Manu for the student was strictly observed : simple dress, plain food, hard bed, the vow of the Brahmachari. There were no exceptions—Prince, noble, commoner—all were treated alike. Not in Ancient, as in Modern, India were young Princes allowed to live softly, luxuriously, and they lived to a healthy old age. Now, we have boys at school who are fathers, and the seeds are sown of premature old age.

Nor must we forget how the lack of Brahmacharya in the student reacts on the child-wife. Happily now young men are demanding educated brides, and hence the period of education is being prolonged. I am not going to argue as to the orthodox view of pre-puberty marriage, Pandits find texts for and against; but this I say: if you will look at the registered death rates at different ages, you will find that the curve of the death rate of married girls shoots up suddenly at the age of 15; silent but terrible witness to the superstition which cuts short the thread of girl-life, and sacrifices the fairest and sweetest women in the world on the altar of child-marriage.

I have not found in connection with the Buddhist Universities the same attention to physical exercises as one reads of in the *Jatakas* in relation to Takshasila. There students practised archery, the use of the sword, and the javelin, and there were military, medical and law schools. We read also that young nobles, trained in Arts and crafts, used to visit on their travels, after leaving the university, artists and craftsmen, to see that a high level was maintained. Thus the university re-acted on the villages, and preserved the artistic capacities and traditions of the people.

In the Muslim period, there was a remarkable development of Architecture, an art in which the Musalmans excelled, as Arabia, Spain and India testify. The Courts of the Musalman Rulers were sanctuaries of learned men, of painters, poets and musicians. Their use of jewels in architecture was extraordinarily skilful, giving richness without being meretricious. As with the Hindus and their Temples, schools were attached to the Musjids, giving primary education, while Madrasahs accorded the higher education. Whether in Hinduism, Buddhism or Islam we find a similar care for Vocational Education among the higher social classes, supplying the nation with the professions necessary for the healthy functioning of the national life, maintaining the high level of Literature and the Arts, as well as the training of the Statesman, the Minister, the military and civil organization and administration. The manual labour classes were equally well provided for by general instruction in reading, writing, arithmetic, accountancy, and careful training in the simple and more artistic crafts, the first for home use, the second for sale to local and export merchants. The teaching of religion and morality was universal, and much was done for the adult culture of villagers by the wandering Sanyasis who travelled on foot from village to village, and in the evenings related stories from sacred books and chanted *stotras* and legends.

Taking a bird's eye-view, we may perhaps say that the Ashramas were dominated by Philosophy and Metaphysics, while not neglecting the Sciences and the Arts; the Vihâras, were dominated by Science, while again not neglecting Philosophy and Arts; the Madrasahs were dominated by Art, with a divided allegiance to Science. Such classification are, however, somewhat arbitrary, and all poured rich knowledge into the national life. To the people all were closely related for they spread that love and reverence for learning which shed abroad, by the stimulating force of example, the superiority of learning to Wealth, the value of Voluntary Poverty and of Sacrifice consecrated to Social Service, a Social Order which conduced to mutual usefulness and a beauty which, as in Japan to-day, is said by Mr. E.B. Havell to be "not a luxury for the rich, but the basis of National Education." He goes on:

> Poetry has done as much for National Culture in Japan as it did formerly in Greece, and until the nineteenth century, in India also. Poetical tournaments are still a favourite form of popular entertainment in Japan, and even among the poorest classes any occasion of domestic importance, either joyful or sad, is marked by poems composed by the people themselves. In the spring mornings in Japan the working classes, the poorest of the poor, and not only the well-to-do, will rise by hundreds to watch the opening of the lotus flowers; the flowering of the plum and cherry trees in the early summer are days of national rejoicing. India need not cease to take delight in Beauty, and to have faith in the inspiration of Nature which her ancient Rishis taught, because she has become poor. It is far worse to be poor in spirit than to be poor in worldly goods. Modern science and English education are not sufficient substitutes for Art. It will not profit India to gain the whole world and lose her own soul.[13]

The disappearance of Indian Ideals was as sudden as it was disastrous: invasions and even the establishment of a foreign empire and foreign kingdoms previous to the invasion and triumph of the East India Company in 1757, had not touched the soul or the spirit of India. She had been invaded, but she had assimilated the invaders, and had enriched her own culture by theirs. Portions of her land had been conquered and occupied, but she turned the conquerors into Indians. But the East India Company not only drained her of her accumulated wealth and reduced her to poverty, but despised her Learning and her Art, crushed her with ignorance, and filled the palaces of her Princes with Brummagen imitations and glass-legged sofas and chairs. It destroyed her self-respect and jeered at her religion and her traditions. It consummated her degradation by imposing on her an education in a foreign language, till her educated people talked it better than their mother-tongue. Having destroyed the schools which had given it clerks and accountants, it wanted English-knowing men to fill the lower ranks of its administration, so introduced its new system. It got them, but the corollaries thereof were unexpected and disconcerting. It taught them English history and they became interested in English struggles for Liberty. It gave them the masterpieces of English literature, and they studied Milton's *Areopagitica*, and declaimed Shelley's Masque of Anarchy. They admired the ideals held up, and desired to find liberty among the "blessings of British Rule." They found it not, and thirty years after the introduction of Sir Charles Wood's educational measure, they met in Madras and decided to create an Indian National Congress.

Forty years later, having revived Indian religions and started Musalman and Hindu Colleges and Schools, and having meanwhile studied Indian history and assimilated its lessons, we have resolved to revive the ancient ideals of Indian education and Indian culture, to teach our children in their mother-tongue, to make Indian ideals the basis of Indian civilization, renouncing the hybrid and sterile ideals of anglicized-Indianism, and adapting them to a new form, instinct with the ancient life, and moulding it into a glorious new body for the ancient spirit. India will then lead the world into a new Era of Literature and Beauty, Brotherhood and Peace.

—*Kamala Lectures*

REFERENCES

1. Chhandogyop., III, xiv, 1.
2. *Village Administration in British India*, Chap. II, para v. p.43.
3. Evidence Before the Two Houses of Parliament, March and April, 1813, See Note D in James Mill's *History of British India*, Vol. I. p. 371, 5th edition.
4. Matthai, *Loc. cit.*

5. *Loc. cit.*, p. 42.
6. *Ancient Indian Education*, Rev. F.E. Keay, pp. 145, 146.
7. In 1925. (Ed.)
8. *Bhagavad-Gita, iii, 20, 21, 25, 16.*
9. *Loc. cit.*, iv. 13.
10. *Loc. cit.*, pp. 37, 38.
11. *Visva-Bharati Quarterly*, April 1924, p. 64.
12. *Loc. cit.*, VII, i. 1-3; xxvi, 2.
13. *Artistic and Industrial Revival in India*, by E.B. Havell, pp. 65, 66.

12

The Ideal Teacher[1]

Our educational lives must be full of our own life, of first-hand life, and not of second-hand life or of third or fourth-hand life. Emphatically has the teacher to be himself to the utmost of his power, even though he must need to live within the confinement of a system. The best he can give to his pupils is himself, not someone else, is what he himself says, not what someone else says. The teacher must be positive, definite, eager, full of ideals, full of endeavour to bring them down into the actual. This is why the vocation of the teacher is so onerous. He must be worth sharing with his pupils. There must be in him the power to inspire his pupils to become all that they will desire to be. There must be nothing small about him, nothing dead, nothing indifferent, nothing automatic or machine-like, nothing of hopelessness or despair, everything of joy, of assurance. He must be a fire so that his pupils may catch fire.

The Object of Education

Education is to the end that the individual may shine more and more abundantly. Our subjects of the curriculum, all our elaborate paraphernalia and methods and plans and systems, all our technique, whatever it may be, our examinations, our orthodoxies and conventions—all are fundamentally to this end. To this exalted end I would venture to demand much from the teacher, even though I know full well that all too little is given to him. I demand in the first place Truth. I demand that he shall be true to himself above all else. I demand that he shall not be a slave but a master. I demand that he shall stand upon his own feet fair and square, and not lean upon others, whoever those others may be. If he do so stand, if thus he be true, then my next demand will of a surety be satisfied. I demand that, knowing his own truth, he realises in immeasurable intensity that a teacher's supreme gift, if one can call it a gift, to his pupils is abundant facility to discover their own truths for themselves and to rejoice in them. The teacher's truth by no means necessarily fits his pupils, is the truth for them, their truth: and the true teacher is well aware of this fact.

I demand that the teacher shall fully realize that every part of the material of education is a means to Truth, is a step in the direction of Truth and *nothing more*. History, Geography, Mathematics, Science, Literature, Philosophy, and all other aspects of the great evolutionary process, are not, as we have them, the last word, are in many cases little more than a lisp, are all inadequate and partial, are more or less untrue, or at best are but aspects, shadows, of the Truth. We must not declare them to be ultimate Truth. No science dogmatises. Hence the dogmatic must be left out of education, for it interferes with the Truth.

Freedom From Systems

I know well the part systems have to play in educational life. We cannot altogether do without them. But let us ever be on the alert to subordinate the system to the end, to subordinate the form to the life, ever to honour independence, originality, freedom, above all that is slavish, unfree, subservient. I infinitely prefer intractability, provided it be constructive and original, to weak-kneed fawning docility. We may be committed to mass-production, but let us be more than thankful when something tears itself away from the mass and develops to its own exclusive, and, I would hope, revolutionary, pattern. Nay more. Let us be watchful for any material which shows signs of departing from the beaten track, however, it departs and, I will venture to add, whatever the havoc it creates by the abandonment of the broad road that leads so very slowly to salvation.

Education is not a standard to which pupils have to conform but an inspiration to which it is hoped they will react. And please note the word "inspiration." I demand that pupils shall inspire, and to this end they must surely be inspired.

We must never lose sight of the fact, the supreme fact above all other facts, that our educative process is to help our pupils to find their own truths whatever these may be, however different these may be from conventional truths, from the truths which are ordinarily current in the world of men and women.

For this, I demand that the teacher shall take infinite pains to relate every subject of education to the pupil himself. There is no subject which is not related to the pupil, which does not form a part of his own individual growth which sooner or later he will not need. History, Geography, Science, Religion, Philosophy, Mathematics, all are intimately connected with him, help him—as part of his very being—to discover himself. And this is their splendid and wonderful value.

No Failure

There is no failure where a pupil walks steadily forward, no matter how, to his supreme Self. He may walk through what the world may call failure, defeat, disaster. Yet if he is walking to Himself there is triumph at every step. The object of education is not to shield from difficulty and trouble, from defeat and failure, but to vitalize in all possible ways the will to walk forward at whatever cost.

Coercion is the absolute negation of education, as is punishment, as are orders. Rules, yes. And I leave to the thoughtful the task, which need not be so very difficult of reconciling the absence of coercion *et hoc genus omne* with the need for rules and certain limitations. In other words, I leave to the thoughtful the duty of recognizing the truth that order and freedom are complementary terms.

Regard for Both Body and Soul

I demand that he shall recognise with the fullest possible implications that his pupil is an immortal soul, with a past of perhaps infinite magnitude stretching behind him, with a present leading to a future the glorious nature of which we can but dimly apprehend. The child is not a child save in body. Let the teacher be above all else, the friend of the soul and the adjustor of the body to the requirements of the soul, if he has the intuition to be able to find these out. Let us by all means have regard for the age of the body, but let us have equal regard for the age of the soul. And let us realize that the body is but a vehicle for the soul, a means to the soul's great ends. The teacher thus becomes the link, the most important link, between the age-old soul and the vehicle which take the soul once more into this outer world. He is the soul's ambassador, the soul's friend and comrade; and because he is this he may have sometimes to annoy the body for the sake of the soul, provided he knows the soul, and takes care that he is not annoying the body for the sake of his own soul, to force it into line with his own standards of rectitude. We talk of freedom in education. There is only one true freedom—the freedom of the soul, which is the purpose, as I understand it of evolution. The freedom of the body—it would, of course, be a false freedom. It may well be the imprisonment of the soul.

I demand that the teacher shall not hesitate to encourage his pupils to set out on a voyage of discovery both as to their Whence and as to their Whither. Let imagination, intuition, reason, all help. If education and the teacher cannot offer a suggestion or two, through the medium of the material at their disposal, as to the way in which the nature of the Whence and the Whither may be sought, just as they lead us to a knowledge of the Now, they fall lamentably short of their duty.

Examinations

Examinations, professions, careers, difficulties, obstacles, defeats, disasters, the cramping effect of the inevitable planning of the educational system to fit an average size of pupil, with the result that there must be more misfits than fits—all these we must, I fear take in our stride. They must not be ends. When they are ends, they are mischievous. When they are means they may perchance be helpful.

Mind and Emotion

If education were for living and not merely for livelihood, if education were for joy and happiness and not merely for temporal success, if education were for self-expression and not so exclusively for imitation, if education were as much for eternity as it is for time, if education were as much for service as it is for self-seeking, if education were as much for wisdom and truth as it is for so-called facts, if education were as much for the soul as it is supposed to be for the mind, then indeed would the younger generation be well-equipped for Life. By reason of the fact that this is an age of Mind, education, concentrating on the mind, has practically forgotten, if it ever knew the emotions, and is only now remembering the physical body. The right education of the emotions is the direct route to brotherliness, to the spirit of unity, to all that makes for generosity and compassion, to happiness and peace. Without the co-operation of the emotions the mind becomes hard and narrow, just as without the co-operation of the mind the emotions tend to become aimless and uncontrolled.

Education in India

No more splendid background is there in the world for education than India, where is the true home of education, where the deepest principles of education lie imbedded in her eternity for those to find who seek for the Real in religions eternal rather than in regions of time. I see everywhere problems, everywhere plans and methods, schemes and projects. I see education extending sway over the pre-natal, delving into psychological temperament, penetrating almost up to the very soul itself, specifically in the works of Mr. Edmond Holmes. But is it not all largely tinkering? Is it not all largely taking the child as he is, as a child, as an emptiness, more as a vase to be filled than, as Madame Montessori so truly wishes him to be, a spark to be fanned into a flame? How little do we realize that education is everywhere, is the universal process of Life, is the very expression of Life itself, and that there is no isolation in education, that education at one point affects education at all points, that education here or there is affecting education everywhere.

What an opportunity you have here in India, an opportunity that I am afraid the existence of an alien spirit in education causes us most terribly to miss. In very truth you have but to lift up your eyes unto the hills whence cometh all help to know of what nature Indian education should be. I am guilty of no flight of fancy when I say that in the glorious Himalayas, the root base of eternal India, we have the keynote to the whole of Indian life, and therefore to the soul of Indian education. Does not India draw from these mighty mountain Beings much of the faith in which a large majority of her people live? Does she not draw from them almost her whole science of art and of beauty? Does she not draw from them her protection? Does she not draw down from them much, very much of her material wellbeing? True, we have among us our Musalman brethren whose life immediately came from Arabia, where their great prophet stood out in such unique magnificence. True, we have our Parsi brethren whose life is more immediately traceable to Persia, and our Christian brethren who come as it were from Palestine. We have our Buddhist brethren, but they are of our own land. We need not look, let us not look, to the West for power in our education, for unity in our education, for lofty purpose in our education, for truth in our education. Let us cease to believe that education of the West is the ideal for the East. Far from it. For some parts of the *Body* of our education we may well go to the West. But for the *Soul* never.

Indian Ideals

But if great things are to be done in the educational field in India there must be, I am sure you will all agree, unrestricted freedom. Under a foreign system of education no youth of any land can truly grow. Only with an education full of Indian ideals, full of Indian spirit, full of Indian power, full of Indian unity, full of Indian simplicity, full of Indian purpose, full, that is, of Indian life, can Indian youth grow into Indian manhood, can India be herself. You ask: "Where are these Indian ideals, where is this Indian spirit, where is this Indian unity, where is this Indian purpose, where is this Indian life?" I say it is everywhere; overlaid by foreigndom, but there. And I say that you have but to look up to the Himalayas, the Guardians of India, to know that all these things still live, are at the worst asleep, are to awake once more to the glory of the Mother of all lands and to the peace and happiness of the world.

For the moment we may only be able to aspire, to hope, to dream. Perchance a shadow from our dreaming shall bring somewhat of the future down into the very present.

—(*New India*, 8 November 1928).

By George S. Arundale

REFERENCES

1. From the Presidential Address to the Fourth Session of the All-India Federation of Teachers.

13

The Ideal School

A life which is well-ordered from beginning to end—that is what is implied in the phrase, "the Four *Āshramas.*" Two of them—namely that of the student and that of the householder—may be said to represent in the life of an individual that outward going energy which carries the Jiva into what we call the *Pravritti Mârga*—that great path of action along which the world rolls, and which each individual man treads within the limit of a life in his own little way. The life of the student and the life of the householder, these form the *Pravritti Mârga* of the individual. The two later stages—the life of the *Vanaprastha* and that of the Sannyasi—these are the stages of withdrawal from the world, and may be said to represent the *Nivritti Mârga* in the life of the individual. It is well to recognize this, so as to have an orderly view of life. So wisely did the ancient ones mark out the road along which a man should tread, that any man who takes this plan of life, divided into four stages, will find his outgoing and indrawing energies rightly balanced. First, the student stage, properly lived and worthily carried out; then the householder stage, with all its busy activity in every direction of worldly business; then the gradual withdrawal from activity, the turning inward, the life of comparative seclusion, of prayer and of meditation, of the giving of wise counsel to the younger generation engaged in worldly activities; and then, for some at least, the life of complete renunciation. Any man who takes this plan of life and lives it out will find that he cannot have a life which should be more wisely ordered, which should be made better than that, in which to spend his days from birth to death. This is not an ideal for one nation only, but for all nations, not for one time but for all times; one half of the life active and stirring, the other half, quiet, self-contained. In the East and in the West alike this ancient ideal of a well-ordered life might well be revived, might well be again practised; and then we should not see on the one hand the pitiable spectacle of boys thrown into the life of the householder before their time has come; and on the other, the equally pitiable spectacle of the old man, whose heart should be turned to the higher life, still grasping money and power, until death wrenches away what he will not voluntarily loose.

Education in Ancient India

Let us take the four stages in order, and consider each. First the student life. What was the ideal of the past? That you may read in detail in your books; here I shall outline it only. The boy was placed in the hands of his teacher to be trained and educated on every side of his nature. The education given to him was one which drew out his powers in the four great factors which form the human constitution. First, we always read of boys that they were versed in the Vedas. The boys were taught religion; they were trained in the sacred literature of their faith, and in the actual daily practice of their religious ceremonies. Thus we find that Râmachandra was not only thoroughly trained in the knowledge of the Scriptures, but also that He performed his Sandhya morning and evening; and was thus trained in the outer religious duties, as well as in sacred learning, both being necessary for the evolution of spirituality. You know how under the wise hands of His teacher, He learned the great Science of the Self, the secret of Peace; how His religious nature was trained and developed—He who needed no education, save for the instruction that His example might give as to how the young should be trained. That is the first note of ancient education.

The next point is, that the boys were trained in morality. The moral nature was trained as well as the spiritual. They were taught to be obedient, reverent, truthful, brave, courteous, to love and respect their parents and teachers, to be unselfish, to concern themselves with the welfare of those around them. "He was intent on the welfare of others." That is given as the crown of the moral education of the boy.

In the third place, the intellect was trained. The boys were taught the different branches of science and instructed in various kinds of theoretical and practical knowledge. Intelligence, the third part of human nature, received its proper training along with the spiritual and the moral.

Lastly, the body was trained. The physical part received due attention. They were taught games and manly exercises, to ride, to drive, to manage their own bodies, and the bodies of the animals who serve the needs of man.

Thus the education given was an all-round education. Every part of man's nature received its proper training. The result was, that when the boys went out into the world, they went out ready to play their parts as members of a great state, as citizens of a great nation—highly pious, moral, learned and strong. These four great characteristics marked the result of education in ancient India.

Modern Indian Education

What do we find in modern India? An education directed to one part of the boy's nature only, developing the intelligence, training the intellect, but leaving entirely on one side of the spiritual nature, and the moral or emotional nature disregarded. The education as now given disregards for the most part the physical nature also, centering itself on the growth of intelligence, on the development of intellect alone. Even that, I may say in passing, is not done in the best possible way.

Such an education as that can never build up a true man of the world, able to discharge his duties in the world. Only one part of him has been developed, only one quarter of his whole nature has been trained; moral character has been neglected, spirituality has been ignored, body has been left weak, overstrained, overworked. What sort of a nation can you have where the education given to its young is but one quarter of what it should be—one-fourth only given, and that too imperfectly and inadequately? What is the result? You get plenty of clever men, but for the most part they are selfish, thinking only of their own aims, each man fighting for his own hand, careless of the welfare of the nation as a whole, gaining for himself or for his family, caring not how others suffer provided that he succeeds, looking on with cold and indifferent eyes at all wrongs perpetrated around him, his heart not moved with sympathy for the trouble and the misery of the people.

He is a man developed in intelligence but lacking in character, in self-respect, in public spirit, in straightforward speaking of truth, in uprightness of words and life. That is the result we see around us, the result of the neglect of religion and of morality.

How many men today are "intent upon the welfare of others," forgetful of their own success? How many realise that no man can truly succeed, unless he raises others with him at the same time? How many remember that there is only One Life, that the man who tries to wrench himself away from it, in selfishness and indifference, only succeeds in shutting out much of the life from himself, and that the wall that he builds to exclude his neighbour from himself excludes himself from the life that flows around him?

All-round Education in the West

What are we then to do—to do practically and not in theory only, not leaving the work for the future, that work which must be done now? As you know, the attempt to bring back the ancient ideal is already being made in your midst. This very College (the Central Hindu College), in the hall of which I am speaking, is the work of those who are vowed to the restoration of the ancient type of education, of that fourfold training of the nature which alone can build up the India of the future, though not seeking to reproduce entirely the old models. It is the ideal that we must see, and that we must reproduce in modern garb, adapting it to the times. Would it surprise you to know that in the English nation this fourfold education is even now being given, in the Public Schools and Universities? If you go to any English public school, you will find that it begins its work every day with the worship of God and the reading of the Christian scriptures. Every boy is taught to worship, and is trained in definite moral ideals. You will find that not only is religion thus taught along with morality, but that a good physical teaching is also given, and insisted upon in the great public schools. Every boy is made to play, to exercise his body, to work his limbs, and strengthen his muscles. And if you go to Harrow, Eton, Rugby or Winchester, you will find the fourfold education there, though of course on Christian lines. The old ideal is being worked out there in principle, and the fundamental ground-plan of education is right and sound, and it makes patriots as well as all-round developed men. While they nourish love of religion, they nourish patriotism at the same time. If you go to Harrow School Chapel, you will find its walls decorated with brass plates, bearing the names of old Harrow boys who have served their country well. So that when the boys worship God, they see before their eyes the names of the old Harrow boys who once sat where they sit, who as men have given up their lives in times of need for Crown and Country, who have died for Fatherland, and who have held the name of England high among the nations. No boy can worship in that Chapel without receiving some inspiration to heroic living, without welding his love of country into his religion. The boys' ideals are moulded in this way, and they grow up country-loving, patriotic, proud of their land, and so worthy to be citizens of their country. We must revive this education here.

Brahmacharya

With regard to this education I have somewhat more to say; and here comes a point for which I ask your careful, your thoughtful, attention. I find, when I read the old scriptures, that during the period of student life, the student was always under the vow of Brahmacharya. I find every student was under that vow of virginity, of absolute celibacy; and until the student period was over, he was not permitted to enter the household life. Thirty-six, eighteen, or nine years—these are the periods given for the student life. During that period given for the student life. During that period absolute celibacy was imposed upon the student. Until that period was over, he was not allowed to take a wife, and we often read of a man as a warrior, before he become a husband. What has become of that old ideal in modern India? Boys in school are found to be fathers of children; boys who have not yet even passed into college are found with a baby at home, a child the son of a child. It is utterly against the old ideals. It is destructive of India's life. What is the result? That a boy, at the end of his college life, is often weak in body, his nervous system is weakened, his brain-power is exhausted, and he is a wreck physically when he ought to be in the full flush and vigour of manhood.

The pressure of modern education puts a heavy strain upon him, and then, added to that, are the duties of the husband, the responsibility of the father. My brothers, it is not right. It means the ruin of India. You find yourselves old, when you ought to be but of middle age. Do you not see that you are not what you should be? Do you not see that the brain does not and cannot bear the tremendous strain put upon it? Do you not see that the stature of Indians is growing less? Where the marriages are the earliest, there the stature is the lowest, and it is getting worse and worse. Is that a part of India's life, as it was meant to be moulded by the great Gods who gave Their laws through ancient legislators?

This is a question the answer to which is in your own hands. The difficulty we know well enough. For a man who dares to act according to the ancient ideals will find himself surrounded by hundreds of unkind critics, men who have not the courage to act, although in their hearts often longing for and desiring change. How many fathers have told me: "Yes, we know that it is necessary;" but how few have the courage to act upon their opinion, and face the social difficulties that action would bring. Yet only by such courage are great changes made, and nations redeemed. We have come down through cowardice, we must mount through courage. We have become degraded through ignorance, we must rise again by education and restoring the old ideals. If some of you have the courage to say: "We will not act against the ancient rules; we will not do that which we know to be wrong morally and to be evil physically," and if you will therefore make the marriage period later, no matter who may oppose, then you will begin to take the first practical step towards the training of a stronger, manlier and more vigorous race. I am not asking you to throw off the old customs and to adopt new ones, as some others have advised. I am asking you to restore the old.......We cannot make the full change back to the old ideal at once, but I do trust that we may be able gradually to work towards the ancient ideal, and thus may set an example which all lovers of India will venture to follow, that we may strike the key-note of a better physical future of India, and build up a stronger manhood.

—*Ancient Ideals in Modern Life*

—*By Annie Besant*

14

Important Ancient Seats of Learning

One of the special features of ancient education in India was the deep spiritual relationship between the pupil and the preceptor. In connection with the Brahmanical system of education we have seen how the pupil would receive education by dwelling at the house of his preceptor. Gurukulas functioned as educational institutions. Personal attention was devoted to the development of a student's personality. It is, however, to be remembered that spiritual and philosophical advancement being the chief objective of ancient education, it was thought to be essential to aim at the internal or psychical progress of the students. Owing to this educational system, regular institutions such as we find in the Buddhist or modern period could not be established, though even during that age some hermitages and pilgrimage centres had come into being. But mass prayers were not organised at such places. These places could not be regarded as the educational centres. Nevertheless, it should be accepted that during the Vedic period, Samghas (Chapters), Parishads (Conferences), Charana, monasteries, and Gurukulas had certainly been established. In Vedic and Upanishadic literature we find references to Samghas and Parishads where scholars and philosophers would gather from distant parts of the country for the sake of philosophical and theological disputations. Wherever the Gurukulas had been established, education was imparted there to the pupils according to group system. These institutions were established mainly in villages. Some of them existed in the forests. But these institutions were not conducted as regularly and systematically as the Buddhist monastic institutions later on. It is an indisputable fact that Hindus by coming into contact with Buddhist religion, followed their example in founding well-established, regular educational institutions; and big shrines and hermitages began to function as so many schools. Large and benevolent endowments were conferred upon such shrines by Hindu kings and subjects for the sake of the spread of education. These places consequently assumed the form of institutions imparting primary and higher education to pupils systematically. There were certain places for special training; for example, the princes would go to Taxila to learn Āyurveda, Dhanurveda and Law from distant parts of the country. Ujjeni and Kasi were the famous centres of philosophy and music respectively. Besides these, there were certain educational centres in southern India; for instance, there was a big Sanskrit institution at Salotgi, a village in the district of Bijapur. In course of time, it made such a marked progress that as many as twenty-seven big hostels had to be constructed for the residence of the students. There was another centre of Hindu education at Ennayaram founded in eleventh century A.D. Tirumukkudala, Malakapurama, Dhar and Pondicheri were other seats of learning. Here mention should be made of important centres of Hindu education, viz. the 'Agrahara' villages, which were founded by Hindu kings in southern India in the form of colonies for scholarly Brahmanas. In this context, the 'Tols' of Bengal are also worth mention. It is, however, worth remembering that these institutions had been founded on the pattern of Buddhist educational centres.

Organised Institutions

Such institutions originated during the Buddhist period. Buddhism had been founded on republican principles according to which 'Dhamma' was preached to the masses in their own language. Therefore educational institutions to teach Pali and Sanskrit for primary and higher education respectively, were established. Buddha felt the need of institutions for the education of the *Upasakas* or sympathisers too. This brought monastic schools into being. Monasteries assumed, later on, the form of big Viharas for education. The monks, nuns and laity were provided facilities and opportunities for education at these centres. Students belonging to different ranks and classes and coming from distant *Janapadas* or republics received education free of charge. Not only that, these centres attracted students from abroad, i.e. China, Japan, Tibet and other countries of South East Asia. They would learn Buddhism and carried with them

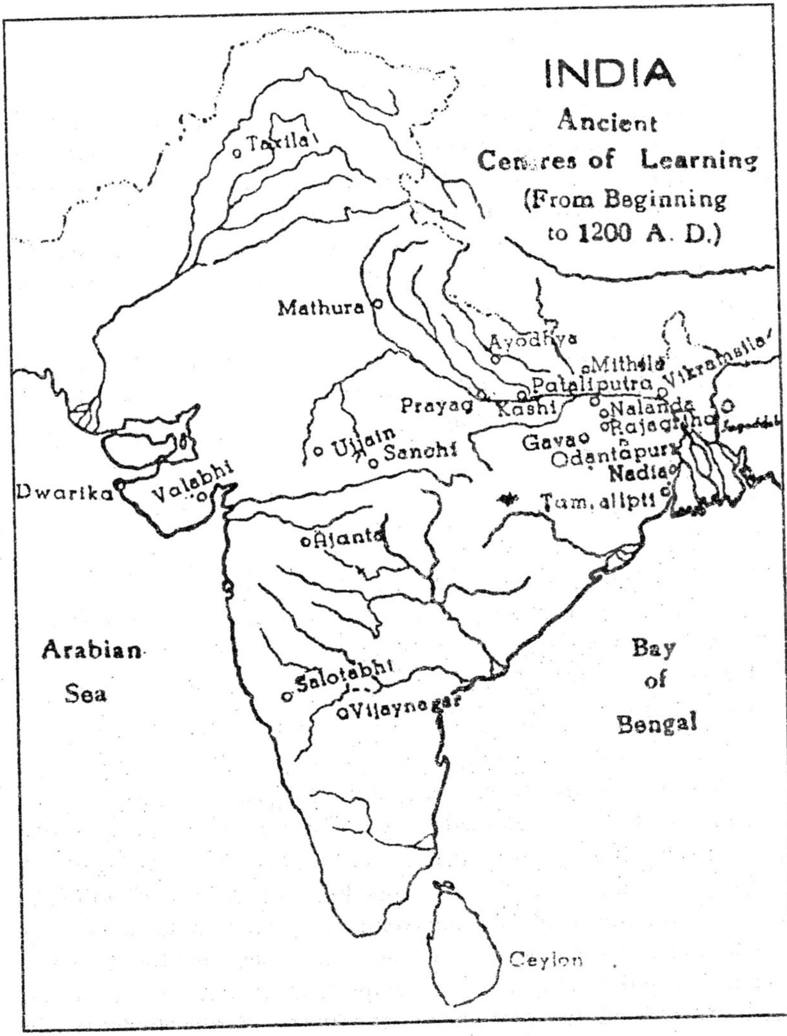

translated works from the original ones. Nalanda and Taxila rose to the status of universities. The administration of Buddhist educational centres was conducted on democratic principle. Usually some learned monk would act as the head of institution. There were different Heads for different departments such as Admission, Examination, Curriculum, Hostels, Boarding, Construction of buildings, Medicine,

Library and other branches of studies. There is the example of a monk-student of 9th century A.D. belonging to Jalalabad who had come on pilgrimage to Bihar and was appointed the Chancellor of the University of Nalanda. It goes to prove that people did not observe either local or provincial distinction as regards education. These organised institutions in the form of monasteries, Viharas and Universities formed the spinal chord of culture of the country. Hence much credit for the cultural relations existing still between India and other Asiatic countries goes rightly to these various educational centres.

Now we shall mention in short certain important centres of learning of Buddhist period. Of these institutions, Taxilā, Nalandā, Valabhi, Vikramasila, Odantapuri, Nadiā, Mithilā and Jagaddala deserve special reference.

Taxilā

From times immemorial Taxilā had been an important centre of Brahmanical education. During the Buddhist period, its fame continued in Northern India. But when Fa-Hian visited it in fifth century A.D., there was no sign of university there and Hiuen-Tsang, when he visited it in seventh century, was very much disappointed to see the last relics of this important educational centre.

Taxilā was the metropolis of Gandhar province in ancient times. But the history of its foundation is still more antique. The Rāmāyana mentions that it was founded by king Bharata who named it after his son 'Taksha'. It was constantly overwhelmed with foreign invasions owing to its situation on the north-western frontiers of India. Hence politically it underwent many vicissitudes as a result of occasional invasions. The Persians, the Greeks and the Kushanas attacked it and established their empires from time to time. It can easily be inferred that with change of empires, its educational system too must have continued to change.

In fact there was no organised institution or university at Taxila. Education rested mainly on domestic system. Many learned and erudite preceptors imparted education to the students separately. Hence it had become a very big educational centre of northern India. We find references in the Jatakas to the going of students from

Benaras, Mithila and Rajgriha to Taxila for education. Taxilā was mainly the centre of higher education. Usually, students having attained the age of sixteen years would go to Taxilā. Here the chief branches and subjects of study were *Vedatrayi* (Three vedas), *Vedanta, Vyakarana, Ayurveda,* eighteen *sippas* (crafts), Military education, Astronomy, Agriculture, Commerce, Snake-bite cure, etc. Panini, the 'Father of *Vyakarana* (Grammar), and *Jivaka,* an expert in surgery and medicine were the product of Taxilā. No caste distinction was observed as regards the training in these sciences, a fact which can well be testified to by the example of a Brāhman boy who went there to learn military art and science. Taxilā had been influenced by Greek culture also. Some preceptors taught Greek there. Training in Greek Military art was also conducted at that place. As a matter of fact, Taxilā was very famous as a centre of training in Indian military science. The study of medicine took a period of seven years which can be borne out by Jivaka's residence at Taxilā for a number of seven years. Kautilya, the famous author of *'Arthasastra'* had received his higher education here.

Thus for several centuries Taxilā served as the beacon-light to the country in educational sphere. This light of learning continued to burn undimmed in spite of vicissitudes of fortune and stormy cataclysmic changes. At length it was overwhelmed by the barbaric Hūns who extinguished this light for ever, never to shine anew.

Nalanda

In the province of Bihar, situated at a distance of forty miles south-west of Patna and seven miles north of Rajgriha, Nalanda was a famous cultural and educational centre of northern India. In the beginning it was but a small village having nothing to boast of its educational importance. But by and by its importance grew in magnitude. It enjoyed a considerable degree of fame and importance for Buddhist monks owing to its being the birth place of Sariputta, a favourite disciple of Lord Buddha. When Asoka the Great visited the place in connection with seeing the Chaitya of Sariputta, he got a Vihara to be constructed there. "In this way the first founder of the Nalanda Vihara was Asoka". This place began to grow in importance since the rise of Mahayana branch of Buddhism in the first century A.D. By the beginning of fourth century A.D., it became educationally important and famous. Two important Buddhist celebrities named Nagarjuna and his disciple Ārya Deva, who were probably born about fourth century A.D. had lived at Nalanda which indicates the importance of the place growing fast. But up to the fifth century, Nalanda had not achieved paramount educational importance in India because when in the year 410 A.D. Fa-Hian visited this place, he found that Nalanda had not much educational significance. Its real importance begins with the year 450 A.D. For the next three centuries, it remained at the zenith of its fame and importance which fact is evidenced by the writings of Hiuen-Tsang who came here in seventh century A.D. He has given us vivid description of the glory and magnitude of this ancient seat of culture and learning.

Nalanda reached its zenith of progress at the hands of the kings of Gupta dynasty. Kumargupta First (414-445 A.D.) built a monastery there. Following him afterwards, Tathagatagupta, Narasinghgupta, Baladitya, Buddhagupta, Bajra and Harsha too established monasteries at the same place. Thus owing to the construction of these monasteries, the area of Nalanda expanded considerably. These monasteries formed the main part of the university buildings. The entire university area was marked off by a big and strong enclosing wall having only one gate-way. At this gate, there lived a teacher designated as Dwar Pandit who was incharge of the test for admission to the university. The gate opened into eight big Halls where students were delivered addresses *en masse*. These halls stood in the middle of *'Saṁgharama'* that comprised the main building of the Vihara. Besides these, there were three hundred study-chambers where students were taught by the preceptors. The architectural design of the university buildings was of a supreme order. The arts of sculpture and architecture of India were unique in that period; it is conspicuously reflected in the *Vihāras* of Nalanda. The main building was so lofty that "the row of monasteries (*Viharavali*) had their series of summits (Sikhara-Sṛeṇi) embracing the clouds (*ambudhara*)."[1] These buildings had many storeys and their turrets and domes were in fact very high. The entire buildings were constructed according to a well-arranged plan. Even today the ruins of Nalanda present an eloquent testimony to the height which had been attained in the science and art of engineering during that period; Besides these buildings, down below, the area was dotted with beautiful and spacious tanks bearing on their bosoms the blue lotus intermingled with *Kanaka* (golden) flowers which enhanced their beauty. I-Tsing gives us an account of more than ten water tanks wherein students displayed their aquatic feats. Besides, there was a very big library building of nine storeys in the same area. This library had three departments known as *'Ratna Sagar'*, *'Ratnodadhi'*, and *'Ratna-Ranjaka'*. The library as a whole was called *Dharmaganja* (Abode of Religion). It had a collection of rare works about all religions, subjects, Arts, Sciences and Crafts.

There was an elaborate arrangement for the residence of the students of Nalanda University; they used to live in hostels. There were thirteen monasteries for the purpose, comprising a number of chambers for the residence of the students. These rooms had stone-benches for sleeping, separate niches for placing lamp and books. Each courtyard had a well in its corner. There were big kitchens of messing purpose where cooks and common servants were provided by the Vihara. Their ruins have been excavated by the Archaeological Department.

At Nalanda university, the students were provided with food, clothes, education and medicine free of charge. We are simply amazed at the provision of free education of ten thousand students at Nalanda in ancient times when we compare the inordinate expenditure involved in the modern university education. In ancient times, verily, the responsibility of education was shouldered both by the state and the people, who would make huge benefactions for the cause of education. The kings of many generations had made an endowment of 200 villages to the university whereby the huge expenditure of it was managed. Besides this, kings had been supplying buildings, land and food in their individual capacity from time to time.

I-Tsing, a Chinese traveller who had stayed at Nalanda for a period of ten years, has given us a vivid account of the system of education and curriculum of Nalanda university. Nalanda, despite being the centre of *Mahāyāna* Buddhism, provided education in *Hināyana*, Jainism and Vedic religion also. A comparative study of all religions was *sine qua non* of victory in philosophical discussions. Formal disputations formed an integral part of the system of education. It was essential for a genuine philosophical investigator to have made a profound study in well-nigh all the religions prior to embarking upon any research work. All the facilities for this purpose were available there. Besides these, students would learn the Vedas, Vedangas, Vyakarana, Astronomy, Philosophy, Puranas and Medical science. Thus Nalanda can veritably be called the centre of philosophical learning.

The monks, Ācharyas (Preceptors) and students led a very disciplined and pure life in the Viharas. The students of this university were held in high esteem everywhere in the country. Students hailing not only from different parts of India, but from foreign lands also sought admission to the university. It attracted innumerable students from distant countries such as China, Japan, Korea, Tibet, Ṣumatra, Java and Ceylon for the sake of receiving education in Buddhism. There were as many as 1500 learned professors in the university. Special attention was devoted to the development of students' personality. The system of education was almost identical with that of Brahmanical period. The art of writing had developed to a considerable measure in the Buddhist period. Along with reading books, the students increased their knowledge by listening to the learned lectures of philosopher scholars. Reference has already been made to the system of formal discussions. There was the arrangement of one hundred lectures daily and it was obligatory on the part of the students to attend these talks. The fame of the teachers was widely spread. Hiuen-Tsang has mentioned the name of certain teachers of outstanding merits, i.e., Chandrapala, Dharmapala, Gunamati, Sthiramati, Prabhamitra, Jnanchandra Silabhadra, etc. It is a point worth marking that being impressed by the repute of this university, Balaputradeva, the king of Java, had built a monastery at Nalanda.

It is evident thus that Nalanda was an eminent centre of learning and illuminated our country for centuries to come with its undimmed light of knowledge. It has made unique contributions to the evolution, expansion and solidification of Indian culture. Nalanda, the unique symbol of Indian philosophy, arts and civilization, after a glorious carrier of well-nigh eight hundred years, fell a prey to barbarism of the Mohammedan conqueror named Bakhtiar Khilazi towards the end of Twelfth century A.D. The magnificent buildings and invaluable libraries were consigned to the burning flames and the innocent monks and students were ruthlessly massacred. Thus the light of learning which had been kept aglow through ages with the fuel of all that is spiritual, pious and noble in human life, was extinguished never to shine again.

Valabhi

Another important educational centre of Buddhist period was Valabhi. It was capital seat of the Maitrala Kings between 475 and 775 A.D. It can aptly be regarded as the rival of Nalanda from the viewpoint of fame and educational importance. There were several Viharas and monasteries at Valabhi. When Hiuen-Tsang had visited the place, there were some hundred Samgharamas established at this centre of learning. Like Hiuen-Tsang, I-Tsing too had found Valabhi in the western side of India as glorious as Nalanda and students from every part of India would flock there for education. These students having finished their higher education, were appointed in the courts on high and responsible posts. This clearly indicates that Valabhi was the centre not so much of religious education as of other secular subjects such as *Arthasastra* (Economics), Law, Politics and Medical Science, whereas Nalanda was a centre for Mahayana branch of Buddhist religion, Valabhi was the centre for Hinayana.

By the seventh century A.D. Valabhi had accomplished appreciable fame as regards its education. Still prior to this period it was an important commercial centre carrying on sea-borne trade. It was the dwelling place of many a wealthy merchant. These wealthy merchants patronised education at Valabhi. The Maitraka Kings made large benefactions to the university especially for the library. In this way this university continued to function upon twelfth century disseminating the seeds of learning in the country. Afterwards it met no better fate than her sister institutions at the hands of vandalism and ultimately was wiped out of existence.

Vikramasila

This Vihara had been founded by the King Dharamapala in the eighth century. Its site lay on a hillock on the bank of the Ganges in Magadha. From the viewpoint of architectural design, the Vihara of Vikramasila was a unique thing. It was enclosed on all sides by a strong wall. In the centre was erected a temple adorned with the images of Mahabodhi and in addition to this there were one hundred and eight other temples.[2] King Dharmapala had erected many a grand chamber at Vikramasila where teaching work was conducted. Their walls were adorned with beautiful paintings.

Vikramasila, surprising though it may seem, soon rose in eminence. The teachers here were very learned and philosophers of higher order. Its fame spread up to Tibet. Almost for four centuries students from Tibet continued to come to Vikramasila for the sake of education. These students translated several religious works in Sanskrit into their native Tibetan language and thus propagated Indian culture in their own country. Dipamkara Sri Jnana, a famous scholar of Vikramasila had gone to Tibet as a missionary to spread religion there.

Administration of the university of Vikramasila belonged to a very high order. The teaching work was under the control of a Board of eminent scholars. It is stated that Nalanda too was administered by the same Board. The Head of the Administrative Board was by the same Board. The Head of the Administrative Board was usually a learned monk. Different departments of educational system were under the superintendence of separate Heads. A Pre-admission test was held at the time of admission to the university. In all the directions of the main building there were gate-ways kept and guarded by the (*Dvara-Punditas*). Preceptors responsible for the examination to admit students to the university. Dr. Radha Kumud Mookerji has made mention of the Dvara-Pundits between the years 955-983 as follows:[3]

1. *Ratnakarasanti,* East Gate.
2. *Vagisvarakirti* of Benaras, West Gate.
3. *Naropa,* North Gate.
4. *Prajnakaramati,* South Gate.
5. *Ratnavajra* of Kashmir, First Central Gate.
6. *Jnanasrimitra* of Gauda, Second Gate.

Besides this, as regards the historical account of Vikramasila, we are enabled to glean some information from the writings of

Tibetan alumni and those of I-Tsing's. Here mainly secular education was imparted. The main subjects of study were Vyakarana, Logic, Tantra and Philosophy. The most interesting thing about this university is the conferring of Degrees on the successful candidates in the examination and this practice was conspicuous in other contemporary universities by its absence. It clearly indicates that this university was conducted on sound administrative and academic basis.

In this way we find that for a considerably long period Vikramasila was regarded as the queen of educational institutions. In the beginning of the thirteenth century A.D. Bakhtiar Khilazi, mistaking it for some military fort attacked it. Nearly all the monks and Brahmins were murdered ruthlessly. All the books were burnt collectively. Before consigning the books to fire, they were made to be read; subsequently the vandals came to realize that it was but a centre of learning. The monk Sribhadra, the head of the institution, reached Tibet having passed through Jagaddula and started his mission of propagating religion. Thus fell a mighty educational centre under the barbarism of the Mohammedans.

Odantapuri

This university had been established long before the kings of Pala dynasty came into power in Magadha. The Pala kings expanded it all the more by the endowment of a big library containing many works on Brahmanism and Buddhism. Odantapuri could not attain to that level of fame and repute which either Nalanda or Vikramasila had accomplished. Still nearly 1000 monks and students resided and received education there. Odantapuri had contributed its share in spreading the tenets of Buddhism. It attracted students from Tibet too. The monastery erected at Odantapuri served as a model for the establishment of First Buddhist monastery in Tibet.

Mithila

In Ancient times, Mithila was called by the name 'Videha'. From times immemorial, it had been the centre of Brahmanical learning. During the Upanishadic age, King Janaka held philosophical disputations with learned scholars gathering there from distant parts of the country. Mithila preserved this tradition even during the

Buddhist age. Jagaddhara, a famous scholar, wrote commentaries on several texts such as those of Gīta, Deva-Mahatmya, Meghadūta, Gīta-Govinda, Malati Madhava and the like. Mithila has the honour of producing an eminent poet named Vidyapati who has been the source of inspiration to the poets of Bengal and Bihara by virtue of his lyric poetry even today. Beginning from 12th century right up to fifteenth century A.D. Mithila had been an important educational and cultural centre. Along with literature and fine arts, education was imparted in different branches of science also. There was a famous Law College at Mithila. Gangesha Upadhyaya founded a school of New Logic (*Navya-Nyaya*). It was here that his epoch-making work named *'Tatva-Chintamani'* had been written. Mithila produced a number of other scholars and literary celebrities. Even up to the period of Moghul Emperor Akbar, it continued to flourish as an important centre of education and culture credited with country-wide repute. It was famous especially for its *Nyaya* (jurisprudence) and *Tarka Sastra* (Logic). Mithila had instituted a peculiar examination known as *S'alaka-parīksha* which the students would take at the completion of their education. Success in this examination alone could entitle the students to the diploma of graduation of the University.

Nadia

Nadia or Navadvipa had been founded in the eleventh century A.D. by the kings of Sena dynasty of Bengal. Its site lay at the confluence of the Bhagirathi and the Jalamgi in beautiful natural surroundings. We can see its ruins which present to us the dumb history of its past glory. It had produced innumerable scholars from time to time. The lyrics of *Gita-Govinda* by Jayadeva still reverberate in the ears of the people. Poems composed by *Umapati* and *'Smriti-Viveka'* written by Sulapani are immortal works. Even during the period of the Mohammedan rule, Nadia enjoyed popularity and fame as an important centre of education, especially for such branches of learning as Logic, Vyakarana (Grammar), Politics and Law. The importance of Nadia grew still more as a result of the downfall of Nalanda and Vikramasila and it began to be regarded as an eminent centre of Hindu culture and education. A school of Logic (*Tarka-Sastra*) owed its existence to Raghunatha Siromani. There runs the story of a famous student named Vasudeva Sarvabhauma who had gone to Mithila with a view to specializing in the *Nyaya* (jurisprudence) and Logic and had commitied the whole of Tatva-Chintamani to memory because there was a rigid tradition that no student was permitted to copy the texts taught or translate the original works. Later on this scholar Vasudeva Sarvabhauma was responsible for the establishment of an Acedemy of New Logic at Nadia. Afterwards, Raghunatha Siromani, one of his learned disciples introduced a new trend of thought in the Nyaya which has been referred to above.

In this way we find that Nadia contributed much to the spread and propagation of education and culture in the country. In medieval period, its fame did not dwindle. Even today, education is imparted through the Tol-system there. In 1836 there were said to be 46 schools and 380 pupils. But in 1818, Ward estimated 31 schools only, but as many as 747 students...............................of the 31 school which Ward found, 17 studied logic, 11 studied law and the other three poetry, astronomy and grammar respectively."[4]

Jagaddala

In the beginning of eleventh century, Ramapala, a king of Bengal had founded a town named Ranavati on the banks of the Ganges and which he equipped with Vihara called Jagaddala. It remained a famous centre of Buddhist education for a period of hundred years. It was destroyed by the Mohammedans in the year 1203 A.D. Students hailing from Tibet translated the Sanskrit works here. It was noted for its famous teachers, Mahapanditas, Upadhyayas and Acharyas. Of all these scholars, Vibhutichandra, Dana-Sila Subhakarak and Mohakaragupta are the most outstanding names. Like other centres of education Jagaddala too is well known for its Logic and Tantra-Sastra.

Besides these famous educational centres, there were other small centres in the country flourishing during the Buddhist period. Some famous Chinese travellers like Hiuen-Tsang and I-Tsing made wide tours in northern India and discovered monasteries and Viharas established at different places. These monasteries were the centres of Buddhist education and were scattered throughout the country Bihar and Bengal being the main regions thereof.

REFERENCES

1. यस्यामम्बुधरावलेहि शिखर श्रेणी विहारावली।
मालेवोर्ध्व विराजिनो विरचिता धात्रा मनोज्ञाभुवः

(Quoted by A. S. Altekar: in *Ancient Education in India* from: 'Epigraphia Indica').

2. Dr. Radha Kumud Mookherji: *Ancient Indian Education;* p. 587 (1947).

3. Dr. Radha Kumud Mookerji: *Ancient Indian Education;* p. 588 (1947).

4. F. E. Keay: *Indian Education in Ancient and Later Times.* pp. 146-47 (1942).

15

Educational System and Literature

The Ancient Indian educational system as recorded in the Vedic texts with the residential hermitage of the seer serving as a school remained the same for a long time. It was only in the Gupta period that the foundation was laid for big centres of learning like the modern universities with their different faculties, extensive buildings, libraries and facilities for communication. The curriculum of studies was, however, modified in post-Vedic times. It was no longer purely ritualistic but was broad-based and included subjects like grammar, philosophy and those of a secular nature. The type of students from the different strata of society could have a wider choice in the selection of subjects, many of which had a utilitarian value. Educational planning was, thus, in conformity with the needs of the people. The house of the teacher, no doubt, continued for a long time to be the seat of learning. Knowledge was also diffused through wandering teachers popularly known as *charakas*, and also through *parishads* or assemblies of intellectuals, similar to the modern seminar. Specialisation centres gradually arose and it was the fame of the savant which drew aspiring students to hear him. Education to a certain extent was caste-oriented, for instance, a Brahman boy was interested only in the Vedic education necessary for his professional duties like the performance of sacrifices and teaching. A Kshatriya boy, on the other hand, was interested in practical training in the use of arms, besides literary and Vedic studies as well as in state-craft, as this was helpful to him in his future career. The Vaisya had to be well-up in commercial subjects. It may, therefore, be proposed that education was fast becoming job-oriented. It might as well be mentioned that the pursuit of knowledge was not merely for the sake of knowledge alone. In fact, it was extremely difficult for anyone to attain proficiency in all subjects. One had to be selective to complete one's education within the required period of time so as to prepare oneself for the life of a householder. There were, nevertheless, a few people who were interested in a longer period of study, even up to the age of 35, but such instances appear to be rare.

A review of the ancient Indian educational system may now be made here with particular reference to the objects of study, place and time, curriculum, methods, pupil-preceptor relations, different kinds of teachers and schools of learning, fees, women's education, writing, diffusion of learning and vocational education. All these aspects need consideration in a chronological manner so as to heighten the educational approach in different periods, and also record changes, if any. The contributions of writers in the various disciplines, forming the mass of literature of the ancient period in Sanskrit, Pali and Prakrit, both religious and secular, would, however, require a separate study in this chapter.

Objects of Study

The purpose of study according to the ancient educational system is the training of the mind as an instrument of knowledge, and not simply to fill it with extraneous matter. The individual as a base (*adhara*), as such, receives cosmic energy (*prakriti*) which pervades the world, and it is through education and the attainment of knowledge that infinite energy of a divine character is stored in him which helps him in developing his personality. Thus, knowledge provides the vital force in him. It is supposed to be useful throughout his life. Further, real knowledge helps him to distinguish the self from the non-self appearing in various forms. The seeker after the highest knowledge, says the *Brihadaranyaka* Upanishad, should not seek merely the knowledge of books, for that is mere weariness of the tongue. Similarly the *Katha* Upanishad points out, 'Not by the study of the Vedas is the *Atman* attained, nor by intelligence, nor by much book learning. The Mind has to be prepared through *sravana* or listening, *manana* or concentration and *nidhidhyasana* or meditation.' These were possible only under an enlightened and accomplished teacher who himself had attained perfection or *siddhi*.

Away from the crowd in his lonely hermitage the ancient Indian teacher provided an ideal atmosphere and environment suitable for the pupil to attain knowledge through different methods. Compressing his knowledge in *sutras* or aphorisms the teacher conveyed it to his pupil orally and the latter concentrated on it till he reached the highest stage of meditation. The entire learning process was motivated not without a desire to attain state of perfection. So much for the Brahman. A Kshatriya had in addition to be secular in approach and his educational needs were different. The object of education appears to be varied in that its value in later life depended on the vocation of the person. The common feature, however, was the attainment of that knowledge which was useful for spiritual advancement. The Brahman was the custodian of the Vedas. Grammatical study was helpful to him in grasping the etymology of words, their formation, inflections and modifications. The entire span of Vedic studies helped him in obtaining religious felicity and even in establishing communion with God, as they say. It, therefore, appears that education had fundamentally a religious and philosophical basis, though its utilisation value was not completely lost, as one can see in the nature of the curriculum.

Initiation and Subjects of Study

The initiation of a Brahman boy started at the age of seven after the performance of the sacred thread ceremony. The boy was placed in charge of a Brahman preceptor. This was quite a normal feature in the educational system of the Hindus. It continued for a long time, as late as the seventh century A.D. We find reference to Bana, the famous author of *Harshacharita*, staying with his teacher and returning home when he was about fourteen years of age. So, also, the Brahman Mayurasarman, who founded the Kadamba dynasty in the south, had entered a *ghatika*, very probably an institution supported by the state but run by him, until he took up the role of a warrior. For a Brahman boy the study during his stay in the household of his teacher consisted of the three Vedas along with other subjects. The method of teaching was simple. The preceptor made the boy repeat the hymns till he could get them by heart (*uggahati*). After several repetitions he committed them to memory and could intone them correctly, understand their meaning and fix the right place of each verse, finally grasping the mysteries behind them. The study thus gave an insight into the Vedas and the pupil became conversant with Vedic lexicography (*nighantu*), rituals (*ketubha*), phonology and legends. This curriculum was prescribed for a Brahman boy, according to the *Milindapanha*, and is in conformity with another more or less contemporary works. It appears that the course was condensed to a certain extent. Two centuries earlier, in the time of Patanjali, the pupil was expected to study all the four Vedas, six *Angas* and their mystical (secret) treatises, the *Sakhas* of Yajurveda, the Samaveda and its thousand *pathas*, he sacred traditions of the Bahuvrichas, the Atharva Veda and its nine branches, treatises on dialogues, the science of logic (*vakovakyam*), the epics, historical legends (*itihasa*), the Puranas and the science of medicine (*vaidyakam*). There are also references to the study of metrics (*Chandasastra*) and *Dharmasastra*. There was also provision for studying lighter subjects. Juristic studies could as well be undertaken. Grammar in the time of Patanjali was not receiving adequate attention, hence he wrote his commentary.

The *Divyavadana* (fourth century A.D.), however, prescribes a different method of initiation for a Brahman boy and also suggests an elementary course of study. This study, according to it, did not commence with the Vedas, but with the first lessons in reading and writing at the teacher's house who had many other students as well (*prabhutadarakah*). The course of study started with the lesson *siddham*, culminating in accomplishments in writing (*lipyam*), *arithmetic* (*sankhyam*), accounting (*ganana*) and even in rules relating to coinage and exchange. The Smriti authorities mention a sacrament called *vidhyarambha* or *akshara-svikriti* (the beginning of education or learning of the alphabets). The boy started with a primer called *Matrika-nyasa*. Sometimes, rich householders employed resident tutors for their children. as mentioned by Kshemendra (11th century). Besides these subjects of a general nature, the pupil studied rules of asceticism (*irya*), mendicancy (*charya*), ceremonial purity (*saucham*), good social form (*samudachara*), the proper mode of address (*bhoskara*), and all the four Vedas. It, therefore, appears that several other subjects dealing with grammar, philology, logic, etc., were not in the course of study or were optional. After completing his formal education. the pupil could participate in ceremonial practices. It was possible for a Brahman boy to commence his studies with general subjects such as a study of letters (*aksharas*) and writing (*lipyam*) with the elementary teacher (*darakacharya*) or confine his attention only to Vedic studies as a *manavaka*. This depended on the aptitude and the ability of the boy as all Brahmans were not conversant with the Vedas. Learned Brahmans were expected to have studied all four Vedas, the six Vedangas, the Puranas, Nyaya Mimamsa, and the *Dharmasastras* thus covering the ritualistic, legalistic, juristic, historical and philosophical aspects.

The records of the Gupta period show that the fourteen (or eighteen) subjects, popularly known as *vidyas*, were regarded as within the scope of learned Brahmans. The legal texts, for instance that of Brihaspati, give a long list of subjects and the year of commencement of each by the aspiring student. Some of these concern fine arts like painting, sooth-saying, chiromancy, the science of policies, astronomy, grammar, mathematics, and philosophy. The Chinese pilgrim Hiuen-Tsang in the seventh century A.D. observes that the children after finishing a work called 'The Twelve Chapters' are introduced in their seventh year to five sciences, viz., the science of sounds or grammar, that relating to arts and crafts, the science of medicine, the science of reasoning and finally the science of internal discipline. Elsewhere he refers to the grammatical treatises in use in his time, namely Panini's *Sutras* and its abridgment, and certain special ones. Later on, I-Tsing, his junior contemporary, provides us with a schedule of study. The children, according to him, began with the *Siddha* composition in their sixth year and mastered it in six months. In the eighth year they took up Panini's *Sutras* and the verbal appendix, which they completed in eight months' time. A good grounding in grammar took another five years, the student taking up the commentaries in his fifteenth year. After attaining mastery in grammar, the student studied logic (*hetuvidya*), metaphysics (*abhidharma*) and other allied disciplines. Courses for higher studies were provided at advanced centres of learning.

Rajasekhara, a contemporary of the Pratiharas, mentions a list of subjects which seem to be appropriate for a Brahman pupil. These include the Vedas studied in the order of *Rig, Yajur, Sama* and *Atharva;* the four *Upavedas, Itihasa, Dhanur, Gandharva, Ayur* (medicine) and *Geya* (music); the six *Vedangas*, dealing with articulation and pronunciation of the Vedic texts, *Kalpa*, pointing to *mantras* in different *sakhas* of the Veda, *vyakarana* or grammar, *nirukta* or etymology, *chanda* or poetics, and *alankara* or embellishments. These subjects had to be mastered by one aspiring to be a poet. It appears that during this period, proficiency in grammar was necessary for studying other subjects, but it could be done for its own sake; for instance Dadda, father of the poet Madhava noted in the Khajuraho inscription of the Chandella ruler Dhanga, was learned in grammar (*sabdanusasana*) alone.

The education of a Kashatriya boy was martial in character. No age of initiation nor period of study was proposed for him. According to Gautam, a legalist, a Kshatriya generally commenced his education in his eleventh year and a Vaisya in his twelfth. According to some writers, the initiation (*savitri*) of a Brahman pupil did not occur till the tenth year, and for a Kshatriya till the twentieth. The Kshatriya princes, according to the *Milindapanha,* were educated in eighteen major and minor subjects including systems of philosophy—*Yoga*, *Nyaya* and *Vaiseshika*) arithmetic (*Sankhya*), music, the Puranas, history (*itihasa*), astronomy (*jyotisha*), magic (*maya*), causation (*hetu*), spells (*mantana*), the art of warfare (*yuddha*), poetry (*chandas*), conveyancing and holy and traditional law. King Milinda was accomplished in these disciplines. The same work refers to training in archery and also describes the process of training—handling of different kinds of bows at the training ground, using a firm grip, bending the fingers, planting the feet firmly, lifting the arrow and placing it on a string, drawing the string back, holding it, aiming at the mark and finally hitting the target—a man of straw (*tina-purusha*). Another work mentions a few additional subjects like the knowledge of ceremonies (*kriyakalpa*), political economy (*arthavidya*), poetry (*kavya*), pantomime (*rupa*), the art of decoration (*rupakarmani*), playing on the vina, dancing (*nritya*), singing (*gita*), dramatics (*natya*) and a study of different types of persons and animals.

The epics also convey fairly good information on the education of a Kshatriya prince which included the *Dhanurveda* or Veda of the bow, the Nitisara or Science of Polity, and the art (*siksha*) of elephants, besides, writing and numbers (*lekhyasainkhya*) and the fine arts (*gandharvavidya*). The princes were expected to be men of culture and not of religion alone. The prose romances of the Gupta period occasionally provide glimpses of the education of a young prince. The subjects for study included all scripts and languages, the Vedas with their auxiliaries, poetry and dramatic art, law, grammar, astrology, logic, *mimamsa,* politics, music and poetry, besides the art of war. These disciplines provided a proper and balanced education for the young prince equipping him to shoulder the responsibilities of being crown prince and later on of ruler. The study of gambling, thieving and such other crooked arts have hardly any relevance except for understanding the tricks of cheats. There are references to rulers attaining proficiency in numerous subjects, in the last phase of ancient India. The Jodhpur inscription of Bauka, a Pratihara ruler, refers to Kakka possessing a knowledge of prosody (*chanda*), grammar (*vyakarana*), logic (*tarka*), astronomy (*jyotisha*) and the attendant arts, and poetry in all languages. There are references to kings as authors and others well up in poetry. These include Harsha the author of *Priyadarsika,* and *Nagananda,* and Samudragupta who shone in the company of poets; so also Bhoja, the Paramara ruler, Somesvara I, and Ballalasena. The enlightened rulers, not only patronised poets and writers as suggested by Rajasekhara, a contemporary of the Pratiharas, but were themselves men of literary talent. This writer also gives a list of subjects of study and mentions three types of students—*buddhiman,* intelligent and hears but once; *aharyabuddhi,* mediocre and learns by practice; and *durbuddhi,* devoid of skill either by birth or training.

The education of a Vaisya boy was more practical-oriented. He received instructions in writing (*lipi*), arithmetic (*sankhya*), according (*ganana*), handling different types of money (*mudra*), laws and rules relating to debts (*udhara*), deposits (*nyasa*), and trusts (*nikshepa*) and eight kinds of examination of goods (*ashtapariksha*), though only two, *vastupariksha* and *ratnapariksha,* are mentioned. This was necessary as the goods were viewed before purchase. According to the *Mahavagga,* an earlier Pali work (B.C. 4 or 5th cent.), the education of a Vaisya boy was confined to writing (*lekha*), counting of money (*ganana*) and examination (*rupa*) of different types of money in circulation in the countries visited by merchants. The Vaisya boy thus received practical education and became conversant with the rules relating to debts and deposits as well. The age of initiation for him was generally fixed at 12 but one whose ambition in life was the attainment of longevity and prosperity in agriculture and other pursuits was advised to perform his *upanayana* at the age of 14. Education for a Vaisya thus began later and was shorter in length.

On the basis of the information culled from ancient Indian literary sources, it appears that a comprehensive curriculum of studies was laid down for the *dvijas* or 'twice-born', belonging to the first three castes. The Sudra could not study the Vedas but could otherwise benefit from the Vedic texts. The 'saving knowledge', as it is called, is not denied him. It is conveyed to him through easier works like the *Mahabharata* and the *Puranas,* sometimes called the fifth Veda. There are examples of Sudras, like Vidura and Dharmavyadha, attaining highest knowledge. In historical times there are references to Sudra princes and rulers like the Palas of Bengal and the Kakatiyas of Warangal, and it is highly unlikely that they denied themselves the privilege of a good education or participation in sacrifices.

Place, Period and Method of Study

The place, period and method of study varied according to the circumstances and nature of the work. The teacher's house or the *gurukula* was generally the palce of study and the pupils were under the canopy of the preceptor. Yajnavalkya enjoins a *naishtika* Brahman (a celibate all his life) to live with his teacher and, in the absence of the latter, with his son, or wife, or even with fire. These boarders were known as *antevasin,* and the teacher providing them with food and lodging was called *ante-guru. Danda* or a staff was the common mark of pupilage, indicating the school which was the *alma mater.* Sometimes this mark was associated with a region as with the pupils from Panchala (*Panchalamanavakas*). The fame of the teacher attracted eager students from different places. A teacher approached from a distance of a hundred *yojanas* was known as *yaujana-satiko-guru.* In later times, advanced centres of learning like Nalanda and Vikramasila attracted students from distant countries as Korea and China. Besides these boarders, there were also day-scholars (*darakas*), young boys who went home from school for their meals (*bhojana vela*). A school for day-scholars was known as *lekhasala* or *lipisala* which suggests that writing was the most important part of the curriculum there. Writing was done on a tablet (*lipiphalaka*) made of *ugrasara-chandana,* with pen (*tiraka*) and ink (*masipinda*). Pencils were also in use. Besides writing, counting (*ganana*) was an important item of study. This was done at the place of the finger with the seal ring (*mudrasthani*). According to the *Milindapanha*, calculation was done by using the joints of the fingers.

The method of study, particularly in arithmetic and even in the art of writing, was clumsy, but one could acquire proficiency with attention and practice. There are references to tests in writing and calligraphy. The *Lalitavistara* refers to sixty-four kinds of scripts, but the *Mahavastu* mentions a modest number, ten. These include *Brahmi*, Kharoshthi, Greek (*Yavanani*), a flowery script (*pushpalipi*), *Kutalipi*, *Lekhalipi* and *Mudralipi* or seal writing, and a few others. The first three are definitely known to be in use in inscriptions and coins. The procedure for Vedic students, known as *manavakas*, was different. They studied religious scriptures with an *acharya*. The preceptor sometimes imparted instruction to as many as five hundred pupils at a time. The pupils committed the *mantras* to memory. The *manavakas* also received training in ritual and could deputise for their preceptor if necessary. When the pupil had acquired mastery of the three Vedas (in content, intonation and underlying mysteries) he was put to a test by his father. He repeated his lessons for the last time before his teacher. This was preceded by a sacred bath and a farewell ceremony, known as *samavartana*.

As a rule students studied in the day, but there are references to studious pupils working at night as well. Sometimes the earnest one studied in a quiet place after shielding the light from the wind. Dried cowdung (*karisha*) was burnt for light and it was necessary to sit in a quiet corner, lest the strong wind set the hut on fire. The householders used lamps, but it is doubtful if the pupils could afford to pay for the oil. This night-time study must have been only in disciplines in which texts had to be consulted, otherwise the rote method employed in Vedic instruction did not demand studying in a quiet corner. The *Srotriyas* committed to memory the *chandas* or Vedas. They had to recite aloud the *mantras* and the *richas* of Vedas and sacred scriptures. The Vedic scholar began his recitation after uttering the syllable *om*. Possessing a firm grounding in grammar, the pupil could follow Vedic recensions in the light of the preceptor's comments. Recitation, popularly known as *nipatha*, was done in the company (*vyatipatha*) of others. Doubts, if any, were removed by the commentary or interpretation of the teacher whose ruling was binding. Emphasis was laid on pronunciation and recitation (*vadavada*). Those reading clearly were called *sadhvadhyayin,* but others, rather slow, were known as *vilambitadhyayin.* Some recited with a sweet voice like an Indian cuckoo. The preceptor taught his pupils in a congenial atmosphere but there are references to slapping (*chapetam dadati*) of the young pupil for wrong pronunciation. This must have been done when the students were very young.

There are also references to examination in the Vedic texts. In fact the *kasika,* a commentary on Panini's grammar, classifies students on the basis of errors committed in recitation at the time of examination, for instance *aikanyika, avaiyanyika,* and *traiyanyika,* i.e. committing one, two or three mistakes in pronunciation respectively. Some committed as many as twelve. Students were also tested on their memory; some committed the text to memory without understanding the meaning, while others grasped the contents rather than the exact wording.

Relation Between the Preceptor and his Pupils

The relationship between the teacher and his students has always been one of prime importance in the education field. The teacher had certain obligations to his pupils which he was to discharge during the period of their stay. The latter too were enjoined to perform certain duties towards their preceptor. This mutual obligation based on the Vinaya texts are also mentioned in detail in the *Milindapanha.* This specifically refers to the life of students or monks in a Buddhist *vihara,* but they seem to have been universally practised in the ancient centres of learning. The teacher, according to these texts, was expected to conduct himself in accordance with the twenty-five virtues prescribed for him. These included keeping an eye over his pupil, telling him what to cultivate and what to avoid, when to be particularly attentive, instructions relating to bed, sickness, food and company. The teacher was expected to boost the morale of his pupil, encouraging him not to fear and to be zealous. He was to teach him nothing partially, nor keep anything secret, nor indulge in foolish talk with him, but pardon him when he noticed any defect in him, encourage him to come forward and make him strong. The preceptor was to look upon his pupil as his son and love him, share his food with him, never desert him in adversity and always befriend him.

In the same work the duties prescribed for the pupil are to feel alike pain and joy with no passion or excitement, not to go to any other teacher, guard themselves in thought and deed, delight in peace, be generous according to their capacity and hold right views on religion. According to the *Apastamba Dharmasutra,* a teacher should regard his pupils as his sons. This sort of relationship between the two is also mentioned by I-Tsing, the Chinese pilgrim. The *Dharmasastras* also stress on zealousness in study, not holding anything secret or withhold information, and pay full attention to the teaching of the sacred sciences. The *Prasna* Upanishad gives a definite injunction that the teacher was not to conceal anything from his pupils as such concealment would spell ruin for him. The older texts, like *Taittiriya-Aranyaka* and the *Satapatha Brahmana* make it incumbent on the teacher to reveal everything to his pupils and put his heart and soul in instruction. Other injunctions in these texts relate to the pupils conduct and behaviour regarding food, men and matters. Manu also suggests that the rules of purification and good conduct be endorsed by the teacher.

In addition to the above duties, their attachment to only one teacher and the performance of certain personal services, Gautama also suggests that the pupils should stay with their teacher during the period of their study, and not go anywhere else. It seems that wandering from teacher to teacher was not encouraged. The acquisition of knowledge, according to ancient Hindu canons, has always been subject to pain and suffering. In residing with the teacher, the pupil had to suppress his desires and conform to the dictates of the preceptor. The life of physical discomfort, as experienced in sleeping, living on distasteful and ordinary food, and attending on the preceptor was a real test of the student's aptitude in learning and his thirst for knowledge. Respect for the teacher was shown by standing up in his presence. Further, intimate contact between the teacher and his pupils was vital to the ancient system of education. The pupils imbibed the qualities of the teacher, his methods, the secret of his efficiency and the spirit of his life and work. The same principles were also applicable to the sphere of industrial and vocational education. The apprentice lived with the master craftsmen, learnt his secrets and assimilated his spirit and method. This would be apparent from a study of the system of vocational education.

It might be interesting to consider the relations between the pupil and the teacher's family, especially his wife, and the emoluments that had to be paid to the teacher for board and lodging and for instruction. The wife of the teacher (*upadhyayi* or *upadhyayani*) commanded the respect and attention of the pupils in the hermitage, as she had to cater to their material needs. There were several types of teachers (*acharya, guru, sikshaka* and *upadhyaya*) and a distinction was made on the basis of the type of teaching done by them. Emoluments had to be paid in cash or in the form of service. The *upadhyaya,* according to a legalist, taught only a portion and charged for it. The *acharya* had a more dignified role to play. Men of affluence generally paid in cash at the time of initiation for the entire period of stay, which could be a thousand golden pieces or coins (*suvarnas*). Others, who were poor but eager, rendered such service as desired by the preceptor and his wife, in return for food and education. The wife of the teacher naturally had some control over the pupils. With begging bowls in hand, the pupils went round to the householders for food and other necessities. These were presented to the teacher or his wife. There were also instances of delinquents, who lacked seriousness. Yajnavalkya, therefore, prescribes some fundamental qualities and requisites in a student. He should be grateful, non-hating, intelligent, pure, healthy, serious, honest, energetic, kind and should, at the end of his study, either impart knowledge or donate a sum of money. He should serve and worship the preceptor and be attentive to him. Manu prescribes service to the teacher both as a student and afterwards. A pupil running away from the house of the teacher to enter the life of a householder was condemned as *khatuarudha*—one who wanted to ascend the bed to which he was not entitled. The farewell ceremony was the concluding function after the period of studentship. The pupil took a sacred bath, paid the parting fee to his teacher, listened to his valedictory address and then took his leave to enter the new stage of life with truth (*satyam*), duty (*dharma*) and devotion without malice.

Professional and Vocational Education

Professional education, particularly in medicine and surgery, demanded special attention. It was different from the one for the Vedic texts, grammar and other disciplines. As the two branches of medical science had attained considerable importance in ancient India, it might be worthwhile noting the educational planning in these. There are references to physicians (*bhishag*) even in the Rig Veda, and Taxila was an important seat of medical science in the sixth century B.C. with Jivaka, the famous physician of Ajatsatru, receiving his education there. But there is no information regarding the pattern for imparting instruction in these two sciences till the time of Charaka and Susruta of the Christian era. Asvaghosha, a contemporary of Kanishka, refers to skilful surgeons performing delicate operations in extracting splinters lodged near the heart, while Strabo, mentions Indians as being scientific and accurate. Susruta furnishes information on the initiation of pupils in the medical sciences. The student desirous of studies in medicine, according to him, had to be a *dvija* (one of the twice-born castes) of tender years (*vayas*), belonging to a good family (*anvaya*) and gifted with qualities like a calm temper (*sila*), prowess (*saurya*), purity (*saucham*), modesty (*vinaya*), capacity and strength (*saktibala*) a clear insight into the things studied, contented frame of mind (*prasannachitta*), pleasant in speech (*vakya cheshtam*) and painstaking in efforts (*klesasaham*). Certain physical attributes, like thin lips (*tanujaushta*), teeth and tongue, were also required. One deficient in the qualities noted above or lacking in attributes was not to be admitted. A Sudra of good character and parentage could be admitted but the *mantras* usually recited were omitted. Further, a Brahman pupil was initiated by a Brahman teacher alone. The latter could as well initiate pupils of the other two castes and this process was followed in the descending order of social hierarchy, i.e., a Kshatriya could initiate one of his own caste and a Vaisya too, and a Vaisya could do so in the case of one of his caste. The address of the preceptor on this occasion is interesting and instructive. The student was required to renunciate lust, anger, greed, ignorance, vanity, egoism, envy, harshness, spite, falsehood, idleness and all those things that spoil the name of man. The student was also required to pare his nails and clip his hair. He was asked to lead the life of a truthful, self-controlled anchorite. The pupil had to adhere to the wishes of the teacher at meals and in all acts and activities in which he was engaged. Susruta prohibits visits to certain places and mentions days on which study is to be avoided. He also refers to injunctions regarding the treatment of persons like hunters, fowlers, habitual sinners and those degraded in life.

This ancient Indian surgeon describes the rules relating to general medical education. The *Milindapanha* is more specific in mentioning initiation of a student either as a physician (*bhissako,* Skt. *Bhishag*) or as a surgeon (*Salla,* Skt. *Salya*). The student first procured for himself a teacher either on payment of a fee or by the performance of services. He trained himself fully in holding the lancet, in cutting, marking or piercing with it, in extracting darts, in cleaning wounds causing these to dry up with the application of ointment and in administering emetics and purges and oily enemas (*vamana-vasana*). Only after completing his apprenticeship and becoming skilful, did he visit the sick. With his training in surgery, he could perform delicate operations.

It appears from these accounts that the training of the physician was different. He was expected to know all the diseases (*sarvavyadhi*) which were of four kinds, namely, rheumatic, choleric, phlegmatic, and those caused by a complication of the corrupted humous. The student was also to know all the drugs. Besides pharmacology, the medical syllabus also included gynaecology. The *Saddharmapundarika* refers to the throes of labour while the *Auadana Sataka* mentions the performance of a ceasarian operation (*udaram-ghatayitva*). Eminent physicians (*mahabhishaj*) were skilled in diagnosis. They could make a grievous sickness light with the aid of a strong drug. As Ayurveda had several branches of study, a student of one subject could approach the master of another for an interpretation of allied topics. A complete knowledge of medicine could not be attained by studying a single subject, but several, and a person was expected to be master of these for ensuring success in his profession. He attained proficiency both in theory and in practice (*sastra* and *karma*). These are compared to the two wings of a bird in flight or the two wheels of a chariot. A physician thoroughly groomed in texts but unskilled in the practical application of his knowledge was no good. He simply behaved like a coward at the battle-field. It is, therefore, suggested that a physician must be well read in the treatises of medicine, and equally skilled in practical work or surgery. Full of resourcefulness and originality, possessed of light touch and swift hand, clean, cheerful in spirit, of keen intellect and professional experience, devoted to truth and morality, the physician should have qualities of both head and heart. He is compared to the helmsman who can successfully handle a boat even if it lacks rudders.

Industrial Education

Admission to a cottage industry or craft was regulated. It was based on some form of contract enjoining obligations on both sides. This was done when a young man wishing to be initiated into a craft approached a master craftsman. After obtaining the permission of his relations, he proceeded to live with his new master for a fixed tenure of training or apprenticeship. He lived with the trainer who provided him board and lodging. The apprentice could not leave his master except after completing his period of stay, nor could he take up another job during this period. After completing the training, he was required to make gifts to his master according to his means and then take leave of him. The skill of the apprentice could not be for any work except that connected with his training. If the training could not be completed during the stipulated period, there could be a formal extension of the apprenticeship period with the same obligations on both sides. There are references in inscriptions to the school of sculpture at Mathura established by the master-craftsman Kunika with Naka and Gomitaka as his pupils. They carved out colossal Yaksha and Yakshi images. Guilds of different professions had made arrangements for training, and their laws and regulations governed it. The *Milindapanha* mentions *sudantevasin* or apprenticed cooks who with a piece of nutmeg could prepare a dish, treating it with various ingredients. This training was necessary for those interested in finding a place in the royal refectory, or in the houses of the affluent upper class. There are also references to some professional schools like those of actors (*sailatin*) and musicians (*mardangika*), and imparting of military instruction and the use of weapons.

Buddhist Education

The education of the Buddhist monks centred round monasteries and there is no mention in Buddhist canons and texts of other places for imparting education. All education, sacred as well as secular, was in the hands of monks. They were its custodians. The initiation ceremony of the Buddhist order and church resembled the Brahmanical pattern. The first step in Buddhist initiation, called *Pabbajja* or going forth, implied admission. The layman admitted to the order was placed under the care and discipline of a preceptor. The minimum age fixed for such initiation was eight years and the period of studentship was twelve years. Serious moral or physical defects were a bar to admission into the Buddhist Sanghs. The youth had to obtain the permission of the elders. Rules prescribed for the first ordination were simple. These included tonsuring of hair, wearing of yellow robes, followed by the oath of the Three Refuges—Buddha, Religion and Order. The young monk was administered ten commandments before he was entrusted to the care of the preceptor. There are references to two kinds of teachers—*Upadhyaya* and *Acharya*. The former was the higher authority entrusted with the duty of instructing the young Bhikkshu in the sacred texts and doctrines, while the latter assumed responsibility for his conduct. These two terms which signify the gradation of teachers are mentioned in reverse order in the Brahmanical system. The period of training for an ordinary monk was ten years but it could be reduced to five years in the case of an intelligent persons.

The Buddhist system, like the Brahmanical one, enjoined the pupil to serve his preceptor as part of his education. The *Mahavagga* and the *Milindapanha* emunerate twenty-five qualities in an ideal teacher and ten in a student which have been mentioned earlier. The *Upajjhaya* (Skt. *Upadhyaya*) or *Achariya* (*Acharya*), who had under him as many novices as he could manage, exhorted them to be particular about their health, studies, manners and morals, and spiritual progress. The curriculum of the monks included the *Sutta* (*Sutras*), *Dhamma* (*Dharma*) and *Vinaya* (rules) texts. The Buddhist study generally commenced with the Discourses (*Suttans*), followed by deeper things of the Faith (*Abhidhamma*). The intelligent pupil could proceed the other way. He was to master the whole of the *Abhidhamma* by heart with its major divisions into good (*kusala*), bad (*akusala*) and indifferent (*avyakta*), the *Dhamma-Sangam*, a compendium of psychology, the *Vibhanga*, with its eighteen chapters, the *Dhatupatha*, *Puggalapannatu*, *Kathavatthu*, *Yamaka* and the *Patthana* as well as its divisions or sections. Education in the time of these earlier Buddhist texts was mainly oral. This did not mean that the art of writing had not developed since there are references to sixty-four kinds of scripts in *Lalitavistara* (a Sanskrit Buddhist text of the 1-2 century A.D.). The oral tradition was as much the characteristic of Buddhist as of Brahmanical education. Besides regular teachers, arrangements were also made for instruction by distinguished teachers who were acknowledged authorities in their subjects, like *Upali*, a specialist in the *Vinaya*. Listening to religious discourses as a means of instruction was an important feature of Buddhist education. Stress was also laid on discussion and debates which stimulated the proselytisation activities of the Buddhist order. Periodical gatherings of monks from different monasteries in religious congregations for confessions of sins also served as forums for academic discussions.

The Buddhist system of education distinguished itself from the Brahmanical one mainly in terms of environment and congregational brotherhood. The latter was more personal in that the hermitage of the teacher served as the spiritual home of the pupil. The Buddhist vihara or monastery on the other hand had several teachers and was a bigger educational centre. The final ordination known as *upasampada* marked the end of the period of education. The period between the two ordinations was twelve years at its maximum, after which a monk attained full membership of the Sangh. A more comprehensive study of the Buddhist system of education could be undertaken with reference to advanced centres of learning like Nalanda and Vikramasila.

Women's Education

The Vedic tradition regarding the education of women continued in later times as well. There are references to Rig Vedic women *rishis* such as Ghosha, Romasa and Lopamudra, and the *Brahmavadinis* of the Smriti texts who were eligible for *upanayana* or initiation into Vedic studies. The *Mahabhashya* refers to *upadhyayi* and *upadhyayani*. They are also mentioned later on in the lexicon *Amarakosa*. The terms probably suggest a woman teacher and wife of a teacher respectively. It also refers to a young girl of the *Aupagavi* school (*Aupagan manavika*) and a Brahmani studying *Kasakritsni* doctrines. It is doubtful that *Saktiki* and *Yastiki* suggest 'female lance or spear-holder'. Even the deeper problems of philosophy were probed into by talented ladies like Gargi and Maitreyi, but this was probably discouraged in later times. The Greek ambassador to the Mauryan court, Megasthenes (fourth century B.C.), points out that the Brahmans did not communicate knowledge of philosophy to their wives lest they should desert them. The *Grihya Sutras* mention uttering of Vedic mantras by the wife at ceremonies along with her husband. She was thus fairly educated and able to participate in sacrifices. It is suggested that an educated *kumari* or maiden (*vidushi*) brings happiness and prosperity to the families of both her father and husband. She should be married to a learned husband (*manishi*). There are also references to distinguished nuns who took a prominent part in the work of the Buddhist church. Buddha regarded several talented ladies as *theris,* the most distinguished among them being Dhammadina. Other distinguished ladies included Soma, daughter of Binbisara's chaplain, Champa, Kisa Gotami, and the beautiful Sundari. Sukka was a forceful speaker, and it is said that people flocked out of the city to listen to her. Buddhist convents were open to ladies who had an aptitude for learning and culture. There are several instances of accomplished women in the Jain church. A few terms like *Sravika, Sraddhachari* and *Sishni* are noticed in records from Mathura which also mention Dina, Vasula and Balahastini as distinguished women. The women students were attached to a *Sraddhachari* though there was no bar to their ordination by a male teacher. A contemporary work, *Mahavastu,* refers to the literary accomplishments of ladies. Amara, an artisan's daughter, was endowed with literary talents.

The older Smritis (first to fourth century A.D.) denied to women Vedic study and even the recitation of mantras at the time of sacraments. This suggests that the education of women in general seems to have received a setback, but ladies from noble families did attain proficiency in learning. In fact, Vatsyayana (fourth century A.D.), the author of the famous work on erotics, the *Kamasutra*, gives a long list of sixty-four subsidiary branches of knowledge (*angavidya*) studied by women. These included riddles in wood, recitation, completing unfinished verses, and knowledge of lexicons and metres. A good wife was also fairly educated, i.e., well up in history and legends and elementary economics and accounting to help her in running her household. Girls were trained in the art of singing and dancing, as was princess Rajyasri, sister of Harsha and Malavika, the princess of Vidarbha. In the *Priyadarsika* of Harsha, singing, dancing, and instrumental music are considered as the accomplishments of a noble damsel. Rajasekhara refers to women's competence in poetical skill and mentions examples of a princess, daughters of high officials and even courtesans who were poetesses as well as adept in the sciences (*sastras*). His own wife, Avanti Sundari, from a noble family was learned and talented and her views on rhetoric are quoted by this poet-cum-dramatist a couple of times. Court ladies and even the queen's maids-in-waiting were capable of composing verses in Sanskrit and Prakrit and were equally accomplished in painting and music.

Advanced Centres of Learning

While the hermitage of the *guru* was the centre of education in earlier times, big institutions were founded in the Gutpa period. These were primarily religious centres to meet the requirements of the monks and the laity, but the curriculum of studies was fairly comprehensive and included subjects meant for the Brahmans. One such institution was Nalanda in Bihar, others were in Kathiawar and Kanchi in the south. Sakraditya, identified by some as Kumara Gupta (fifth century A.D.), was the founder of Nalanda university. The nucleus was developed by his successor and others who created endowments. When Hiuen-tsang visited it in the seventh century A.D., he found there six monasteries built by as many kings. The university area was marked off by a lofty enclosing wall with one gate opening into the great college. The buildings were majestic in size and height, with richly adorned towers. Subsequent benefactions from the Palas and even by Balaputradeva, the ruler of Suvarnabhumi (Indonesia), added to the glory of the institution which was shaping itself into a world centre with students from different countries, especially from south-east and eastern Asia. This institution was one of higher learning, noted for its specialised study. As pointed out by Hiuen-tsang, foreign students came here to put an end to their doubts. Some, according to I-Tsing, came from Mongolia, and also from distant countries like China, Korea, Tibet and Tukhora. Admission to the university was not easy. Only 20 per cent got through the entrance examination. The high standard of scholarship maintained in discussion and the experts in debates on religion were always ready with difficult problems which they posed to the students seeking admission. Things were, however, easy for admission to the secondary course.

After such a rigorous selection process, students handled and fashioned by the university were naturally of a high order. The students of Nalanda were looked upon as models throughout the country. The picture of academic life there, as drawn by Hiuen-tsang is very bright. There were thousands of brethren, all men of great ability and learning, several hundreds being highly esteemed and famous. Pre-occupied as they were, with learning and discussion, they found the day all too short. Out of the total number of 10,000 residents at Nalanda, there were 1500 teachers divided into categories according to their ability and range of knowledge. Silabhadra, unique in learning and character, was the president (*Kulapati*) of the university. There were proper arrangements for board and lodging. Rules and regulations governing life in the monastery at Nalanda were no doubt strict particularly in the spheres of intellectual and moral training of the alumni, but the task of enforcing discipline in cases of recalcitrant was left to the entire body of students. They were generally monks drawn from the different denominations of the Buddhist church and some amount of strife and discord was natural among them. The intellectual life no doubt involved animated controversies and acrimonious debates but these did not mar the peace and calm of Nalanda. There was freedom of thought, opinion and belief.

I-tsing had stayed there for ten years and fully utilised the library which was well-equipped. The range of studies was fairly wide including Brahmanical and Buddhist, sacred and secular, philosophical and practical, science and the arts. The students studied the Great Vehicle, the works belonging to the eighteen sects, and also the Vedas, logic (*hetuvidya*), the lexicon (*sabdavidya*), medicine (*chiktisavidya*), the Atharva Veda, Sankhya and Yoga systems, philosophy, Nyaya, and other sacred books of the Brahmanas.

There are references to eminent scholars and savants of Nalanda, many of whom went to foreign countries. Among the noted alumni may be mentioned Aryadeva, one of the earliest scholars, Silabhadra, Dharmapala, Chandragomin, Santarakshita, who was a pioneer in the propagation of Buddhism in Tibet in the eighth century, Padmasambhava, one of the prominent exponents of the Yogachara school of Tantrisan, Sthiramati and Buddha Kirti. They worked as missionaries in Tibet. Several scholars from Nalanda also went to China for translating Buddhist works into Chinese.

It was not a one-way traffic. Many Chinese came to India for studying at Nalanda after Hiuen-tsang and before I-tsing, as mentioned by the latter. These included Hiuan-Chao, Tao Hi, Tao-Shing, Tang, Tao-Lin and a few others from China. Tao-Shing took an Indian name, Chandradeva, as did Aryavarma and Hwui-Yieh from Korea and Tukhora. There were several scholars from other parts of India as well, for instance, the great teachers Asanga and Vasubandhu and Dinnaga from south India and Gunamati and Sthiramati from Vallabhi in western India. Dharmapala was also from the south, being a native of Kanchipura. Silabhadra was from Somatata (East Bengal), the son of a king and a Brahman by caste. People of different nationalities and from different parts of India representing varied tastes and ways of life only added to the cosmopolitan character of the university which lasted for nearly 700 years till it was destroyed at the hands of Bakhtiyar Khalzi at the beginning of the thirteenth century A.D.

The other advanced centres of learning in ancient India were Vallabhi, seat of the Maitraka kings (475-779 A.D.) of Kathiawar (western India); Vikramasila on the banks of the Ganges in northern Magadh (Bihar); Jagaddala (Varendra in East Bengal); Odantapuri (south Bihar) & Mithila (north Bihar). All these were the result of the benefactions of rulers and their size and academic stature varied as also the pattern of education. Vallabhi in the time of Hiuen-tsang had about 6000 priests in some hundred *sangharamas* and, like Nalanda, it attracted students from all parts of India. Sthiramati and Gunamati were in charge of the monastery at Vallabhi which had a good library. This seat of learning provided scope for secular studies as well, in disciplines like *Niti* (statecraft), *vritta* or prosody, and *chiktsa-sastra* or medicine. Vikramasila was set up as a result of the patronage extended by the Pala rulers of Bengal, especially Dharmapala (ninth century A.D.). It was later than Nalanda but the board of the faculty here also administered the affairs of Nalanda probably at a later stage in the time of the Pala rulers. It had six colleges and a central hall, each with a staff of the standard strength of 108 teachers. Here, too, the standard of scholarship were upheld by the most erudite scholars known as *duara-pandits*. The president of the university was always the most highly learned and religious sage. There are references to the well-known savants of this university working in Tibet. These included Acharya Buddha Jnanapada, Vairochana, a pupil of the famous Padmasambhava, Jetari, Ratnavara and the famous Dipamkara, also known as Acharya Alisa. Here too scholars came from different parts of the country. Dharmakirti was a native of Tibet who came to study. Sanskrit and later on translated many Sanskrit works into Tibetan. Sakya Sri Bhadra of Kashmir, a logician, gives an eyewitness account of the tragic destruction of Vallabhi by Muslims which is confirmed by Muslim sources. The other centres were more or less local ones and their span of life too was not more than a hundred years. Jagaddala and Odantapuri were also victims of the Muslim invasion of Bihar and Bengal. Mithila was a stronghold of Brahmanical culture and it developed into a famous school of *Nyaya*. It flourished from the twelfth to the fifteenth century A.D.

These advanced centres were in a way like the *parishads* of the later Vedic times, such as the Panchala *parishad*, patronished by the philosopher-king Pravahana Jaivali who daily drove out to attend its meetings. The rulers no doubt patronised these university centres with benefactions and patronage but seldom did they visit the place. Discussion among scholars more or less on a seminar pattern was a proper vehicle for the diffusion of learning. The old tradition of *charakas* or wandering teachers continued in a new form with the alumni visiting other countries like China and Tibet to spread the gospel of Buddhism. Eminent savants attracted pupils from near and far. A change was perceptible in the area of study and in the campus. Philosophy represented by a variety of schools in the early period was supplemented by other branches of learning, and itself had considerably advanced in scope. The hermitage of the *rishi* or the open space for discussion was replaced by huge massive buildings with ample space for lodging and lecture halls, where talented speakers held forth. The contributions of distinguished seers and savants—secular as well as religious—form a separate study, different from the one undertaken relating to ancient Indian education, but closely allied with it.

Language and Literature

The study of language and literature in ancient India was in the main, confined to the study of Sanskrit and the literature associated with it. The birth of Buddhism and Jainism witnessed a change in the use of the languages in which the scriptures of these two Sramana religions were recorded—Pali and Prakrit. Sanskrit (Samskrita)—meaning 'adorned',—is ordinarily applied to the whole ancient and sacred languages of India in its Vedic and classical forms. Vedic Sanskrit differs from the classical like the Greek of Homer from Attic Greek. The Vedic apparatus of grammatical form is much more rich and less definitely fixed than that of Sanskrit. Much of the wealth of the former is lost in the latter, and many case-forms and verbal forms of Vedic grammar disappeared in Sanskrit. In its phonetic structure the Rig Vedic language had the same sounds as classical Sanskrit. The comparison of Vedic language (and to a lesser extent Sanskrit) with the oldest form of Iranian speech, the language of the Avesta, suggests that they are dialects of one and the same language. With the passage of time there was a transition from the main Aryan language to that of the Vedas and classical Sanskrit, and later on to Pali and Prakrit. Sanskrit, however, continued to have an independent existence throughout the period of ancient India, but only as the language of the sophisticated elite or *Sishtas* as they were called. The impact of Sanskrit was felt on the regional languages and literature popularly known as the vernacular.

The study of ancient Indian literature, thus, is not confined merely to the Vedas and the religious literature. The four varieties of metrical and formula compositions known as the four Vedas in the narrower sense contain ritualistic matter or sacerdotalism. The earlier names of the four Vedas are *Richah* ('stanzas of praise'), *Yajumshi* ('liturgical stanzas and formulae'), *Saman* ('melodies') and *Atharvangirasah* ('blessings and curses'). The collection going by the name of Rig Veda contains 'stanzas of praise' and also 'blessings and curses' as well as most of the stanzas which form the melodies of the *Saman* or Samaveda. The Atharva Veda contains *richah* and *vajumshi* while the Yajurveda contains many blessings in addition to the liturgy. The Samaveda is merely a collection of a certain kind of stanzas of praise, derived from the Rig Veda with some variations and additions and set to music. The collection of these four Vedas are known as Samhitas, each one of which is handed down in various schools or recensions called *charana* or *sakha*. They sometimes differ widely from one another; for instance, the Black and White

Yajurveda had their separate schools, the Taittireyas, Maitraniyas, Kathas and Kapishthalas of the Black school being named after people in different regions.

The poetic stanzas and ritualistic formulae of the Vedas known as *mantras*, 'pious utterances' or hymns, are followed at a later period by a different type of theological treatise called Brahmans. They are bulky expositions of the sacrificial ceremonies describing it in its minute detail, its value or raison d'etre and its potency. They are written in connected prose. They were composed in schools or recensions differing widely from one another. The Rig Veda has two Brahmanas, the *Aitareya* and the *Kaushitakim* or *Sankhayana*. Sometimes the matter in the Brahmana is linked with the text of the Samhita, otherwise it is independent of the Samhita. Thus the Satapatha Brahmana or 'the Brahmana of a hundred lectures' is based on the Yajurveda. The Brahmanas of the Atharva Veda, namely Gopatha, on the other hand, has little in common with the Vedic text either in spirit or in content. Similarly, the *Panchavimsa* and the Jaiminiya Brahmanas of the Samaveda are its independent recensions.

The later development of the Brahmanas is symbolised by the Aranyakas or 'forest treatises' which are partly theosophical in character. They were either recited by sages living in forests or conveyed by the teacher to his pupils in the solitude of the forest. The two important Aranyakas are the *Aitareya* and the *Taittiriya* belonging to the two Vedic schools of that name. They are not concerned with the performance or with any explanation of the sacrifice, but with its mysticism and symbolism. Their contents are secret and of an uncanny nature. The chief interest of the Aranyakas is that they form a natural transition to the Upanishads, the oldest of which are included in or appended to them.

The Upanishads contain dialogues and philosophical speculations of the Indian sages and teachers for many centuries. The word *upanishad* originally implied seating oneself at the feet of one's teacher and listening to his words. In ordinary usage, however, it represents the doctrine communicated by the teacher or the mystical or secret doctrine in general. Its teaching is the *Vedanta,* the sum and substance of all true wisdom, the highest and most abstract teaching or knowledge by divine revelation (*sruti*). Although nothing is known about the authors of these treatises, many names of teachers who were heads of schools have been preserved. In the more ancient Upanishads the instruction is generally conveyed in the form of a dialogue, the teacher replying to questions or answering the doubts of his disciples—the unsatisfied longings of the human mind and heart. The most important as well as the oldest treatises are the *Brihadaranyaka* and the *Chandogya* Upanishads, the former being the most interesting. Its earlier chapters are Vedantic dealing with the philosophical doctrines of the *atman* as transcending the polytheistic worship of the gods. In it, meditation on the sacred symbol *OM* is stressed. The *Katha* Upanishad relates to the story of Nachiketas and the three gifts he received from the god of death. According to this Upanishad, 'higher than the senses are the material things, higher than the material things is the mind, higher than the mind is the intellect, higher than the intellect is the great Self (*atman*)'. It would thus appear that the central doctrine of the Upanishads is that the Brahman and the *atman* is one, 'one only without a second'. Only Brahman, the unknown self (*atman*), is real, the rest is unreal (*maya*).

The Sutra Literature

While the *mantra* and the Brahmana are considered as revealed knowledge (*sruti*), the rest of the Vedic tradition is called Smriti or the product of the holy men of ancient times. This form of Vedic literature, comprising the *Srauta Sutra* or manuals of Vedic ritual, the *Grihya Sutras* or *'house books'* and the *Dharmasutras* or law books, forms a class by itself. The first class of texts—the *Srauta* or *Kalpa Sutra*—deals with Vedic ritual and serves as a technical guide to Vedic sacrifices. They are named after the respective Brahmanas attached to separate Vedas. The *Grihya Sutras* or 'house books' are treatises on home life, dealing systematically with events in the everyday life of the individual and his family as pious and religious people. These manuals are distributed among the four Vedas and their schools, each manual being assigned to one of them. The *Dharmasutras* also deal to some extent with the customs of everyday life, but are for the most part confined to secular and religious laws. The legal *Sutras* are attached directly to certain Vedic schools or are supposed to have originated from one. These Dharmasastras are later in age and are written in classical Sanskrit. The *Manava*

Dharmasastra or the 'law book of Manu', which is a late work written in the early centuries preceding or following the Christian era, might have been based on the lost *Dharmasutra* of the Manava or Maitrayaniya school of the Black Yajurveda, while the 'law book of Yajnavalkya' which is more brief than Manu's law book is definitely connected with some school of the White Yajurveda. The law book of Vishnu belongs to the third century A.D. and that of Yajnavalkya to the fourth century, as the advance on Manu in order, method, and detail of legal matters of these law-writers is considerable. Narada belonged to the fifth century A.D. He provided a legal code unhampered by religious and moral teachings.

Grammatic Literature

Grammar, etymology, lexicography, prosody and rhetoric also engaged the attention of ancient Indian authors. The earliest works of an etymological and phonetic character are the *Naighantukas* and the *Nirukta* of Yaska noted for their Vedic gloss and phonetic treatises. Later on, the *Ashtadhyayi*—the eight chapters of Panini—was composed. This famous grammarian mentions several of the predecessors, among them being Sakatayana and Sakalya, Gargya and Galava. His own work, supposed to have been revealed to him by God Siva in 14 sutras, known as *Maheshvarasutrani,* consists of nearly 4000 aphorisms, each of two or three words only. This work, written in a kind of short-hand, employs single letters or syllables to indicate the names of cases, moods, persons and tenses. The rules of grammar laid down by him were applicable to the language spoken by the elite. The date of his work ranges between the sixth and the fifth centuries B.C. A supplement to his work was provided by the *Varttika* or corrective of Katyayana who discussed, annotated and added to the rules of his predecessor, thus adapting them to classical Sanskrit which was just beginning to be written. Some of the rules of Panini are thus made obsolete by Katyayana. The great commentary on the *Ashtadhyayi* incorporating the *Varttikas* of Katyayana was provided by Patanjali in his *magnum opus*—the *Mahabhashya*. He was the last sage in the triumvirate of grammarians. He wrote this work for the Brahman elite at a time when the people's interest was waning and the Sanskrit language was losing its purity. Patanjali was a contemporary of Pushyamitra Sunga (second century B.C.) whom he mentions several times in his work.

This commentator in illustrating the rules of grammar with personal examples also provides a picture of the India of his time. Grammatical studies were also undertaken by Bhartrihari (died c. 651) who commented on the *Mahabhashya* in his work the *Vakyapadiya* consisting of three books of verse. He was followed by Kaiyata, another commentator (c. Twelfth century). Jayaditya and Vamana, the authors of *Kasikavritti* commented on Panini's *Ashtadhyayi* before the arrival of I-Tsing (seventh century).

Epic Literature

The *akhyanas* or 'stories' and *itihasas* or legends narrated in the epics can be traced to the Vedas, but this is not recorded anywhere. The *Mahabharata* and the *Ramayana* are the only ones now available as literary texts. The former is a free narrative in 10,000 stanzas of four lines each, while the latter is one-fourth of the former and exhibits the beginnings of the artistic style known as *'Kavya'*. The *Mahabharata* is supposed to be the work of Vyasa, although there are numerous interpolations. The heroic story centres round the clash between the Kauravas and their cousins the Pandavas, the latter being the rightful claimants to the throne of Hastinapur. It finally ended in the eighteen days war which was, in a way, national in character as all the Indian princes took sides. It finally ended in the defeat and destruction of the Kauravas. The story is interrupted by episodes and is made the pivot around which philosophical and ethical discussions revolve at great length. The work is thus considered as an encyclopaedia of moral and religious instruction. Among the episodes, the *Bhagavad Gita* or 'The Song Celestial' is the most important and interesting. The dialogue between the wavering Arjuna and his friend, the charioteer Krishna who finally persuades him to fight as a Kshatriya devoted to his duty, took place just as the two armies arraigned against each other on the battlefield of Kurukshetra. It represents the synthesis of *Karma* (action) and *Yoga* (contemplation) with stress on *Bhakti* (devotion). The poem is couched in the spirit of eclectic Hindu philosophy or theosophy.

The *Ramayana*, extending in its present form to about 24,000 *slokas* and divided into seven books, is the work of a single author, Valmiki. The story centres around Rama, the crown prince of Ayodhya, who through the machinations of his step-mother goes into exile with his wife and younger brother, Lakshmana. The abduction of Sita by Ravana, king of Lanka, in the absence of her husband and brother-in-'aw, culminates in a war against Ravana and his consequent destruction. The return of the two brothers and Sita to the homeland at the end of the period of exile was a happy augury for all. The work in its present form is not free from digressions. Both in the use of poetical figures and in descriptive style it is nearer to the later artificial epics (*kavyas*) of which it is considered a forerunner. In fact, at least two poets, Asvaghosha (first century A.D.) and Kalidasa (fourth century) borrowed from this great epic for their themes.

The Puranas, supposed to be related in character to the great epics, are later poetic work of a cosmogonic, epic and didactic nature. They are eighteen in number and appear to be sectarian religious manuals written from the fifth century A.D. onwards to administer to the needs of worshippers of Vishnu or Siva. Brahma is referred to in a perfunctory manner. They are generally divided into five parts dealing with cosmogony or primary creation, secondary creation following the destruction of the world and its rebuilding, genealogy of the gods and patriarchs, periods of reigns of manu (*manvantaras*) and the history of the dynasties of kings. The themes are largely borrowed from the epic literature, and represent religious beliefs, practices, and legends in an exaggerated and often disorderly fashion. Here, as in the *Mahabharata,* the world is represented as consisting of seven concentric islands separated by different oceans. The central one, with Mount Meru in the middle, is Jambu-dvipa, of which Bharatavarsha or India is the main division. The oldest Purana is supposed to be the *Vayu Purana* dating from about the fourth century A.D. and closely related to the *Harivansa,* a supplementary book of the *Mahabharata.* Of the eighteen Puranas the *Vishnu Purana* dealing with five main topics is one of the best known. The *Bhagavata* and the *Siva Puranas* deal with the glorification of Bhagavata or Vishnu, and Siva respectively. The Puranas, as a piece of religious literature, have had a great impact on the Hindu people.

Poetry

The ancient Sanskrit literature is fairly rich in poetry, popularly known as *kavya* or verse set in metres. There are a good many artistic epics which are classed as *mahakavyas* or great poetic works, including lyric, poetry and didactic verse aimed at instructing the people. These artistic epics or '*mahakavyas*' are interesting from the point of view of subject matter, descriptive power and delicacy of illustration. One also notices in them the mingling of lyric, erotic and didactic elements. These gems of poetry include the *Raghuvansa* and *Kumarasambhava* of Kalidasa whose age is disputable. Some scholars place him in the second century B.C. as against the accepted view of the fourth or fifth century A.D. They argue that Kalidasa borrowed his theme of *Raghuvansa* from the *Ramayana* of Valmiki and it was he who was a model for Asvaghosha, a great poet of the second century A.D. The three have many things in common in presentation and embellishment (*alankara*). Parallels can be traced, for example, between Suddhodhana, father of Gautama, the Buddha, bemoaning his son's exit and the charioteer returning without the prince in his famous *kavya, Buddhacharita,* and Dasaratha, bereft of Rama after the latter left Ayodhya in exile for fourteen years. So also, Yasodhara's lament for the sufferings of the prince, her lord, in his new life of hardship is modelled on Sita's sorrow for her lord's sufferings in the forest. It appears that Asvaghosha was indebted to Valmiki as was Kalidasa, although both were independent of their predecessors in their approach and treatment of the subject matter. It may, therefore, be suggested that the *kavya*, poetry, may be traced to Valmiki, author of the famous epic, the *Ramayana*. There are references to *kavyas,* especially a *Vararcha kavya* in the *Mahabhashya,* and also to verses in ornate metres of the later *kavya* style which suggest that practically all the main branches of classical Sanskrit literature were in existence at that time.

The first substantial poems exhibiting the complete development of classical Sanskrit, are by a Buddhist who thought it proper and desirable to popularise Buddhism in the language of the elite, namely Sanskrit. He, therefore, wrote the life of the Master in his *kavya, Buddhacharita,* and an incident relating to the conversion of the Lord's half-brother in *Saundarananda,* as well as a Sanskrit drama *Sariputraprakarana*. The importance of the first long poem lies in the deliberate art of reducing the narrative on the lines fixed for a *kavya*. The poem opens in the *kavya* style with a description of the city, the king, and the queen, followed by the story faithfully portrayed in simple verse. Neither is the connecting thread of the story lost, nor is the reader's patience exhausted. The poet portrays the life of the Buddha in simple and faultless Sanskrit with a moderate use of *alankaras* or embellishments. At times he introduces a touch of humour; for instance, 'hearing the news of the arrival of the Tathagata in the city of Kapilavastu, some of the magnificent women in the rush to see the prince were delayed in their movements by the weight of their chariot-like hips and full breasts'. The poet compares the faces of the women peeping from the windows to lotuses on the pavilions and the city appears as paradise with its heavenly mansions full of *apsaras* or heavenly nymphs. This description is imitated by Kalidasa. The Buddhist Sanskrit poet also conforms to another principle of *Kavyadarsa* in his exposition of *Nitisastra* or statecraft by pointing out in the words of Udayin that 'denial of courtesy ill-befits one young in age and beautiful in appearance'.

The other poem relates to the conversion of the reluctant Nanda, half-brother of the Buddha. In the words of the poet, 'this ornate poem was a little honey mixed with the bitter medicine to make it palatable for those whom he wanted to win over to the faith of the Tathagata'. The poem begins with the usual description of the city of Kapilavastu and a brief account of Nanda's family. There is a description of Sundari's beauty and her union with Nanda who thus form the unmatchable couple. Then follows the whisking away of Nanda and his conversion by the Buddha, thereby causing grief to his wife Sundari. Nanda is solaced in his separation in two cantos dealing with the nature of women in general. In the words of the poet, 'flattery is on their lips and treachery in their hearts'. The pilgrimage of Nanda in the company of the Lord to Mount Himavani and the trip to Indra's paradise follow, where seeing the heavenly nymphs he forgets his beloved Sundari. Here he is bitten by the viper of love and becomes inactive. Thereupon he is advised by the Lord to acquire merit by practice of the law to obtain the heavenly nymphs. Possessing the law of holy knowledge, girding on the armour of attentiveness, and taking up his post on the chariot of the vows of discipline, Nanda finally prepares himself for victory. His wife Sundari, too, with desires turned away from the sense objects, preaches freedom from passion among women.

The *kavya* style undoubtedly attained its height in the works of Kalidasa. Skilful in the art of poetry this gem among Indian poets specialised in introducing sentiment in his poetry. The aspect dominates over ornamentation. He wrote two dramas, *Malavikagnimitra* and *Sakuntala*. The former deals with an incident in the Sunga period. The prince viceroy Agnimitra longs for Malavika, a lovely Vidarbha princess, and finally succeeds in attaining her. *Sakuntala,* the other drama, relates the romance between Dushyanta and Sakuntala, their secret marriage, their separation and finally their reunion. His other works include *Ritusamhara* or 'cycle of the seasons', *Meghaduta* or the 'cloud messenger', *Kumarasambhava* or the birth of the war-god Kumara, and above all *Raghuvansa* or the 'Race of Raghu'. The first two are the most elaborate of the lyrics. The theme of the former concerns a message sent by a Yaksha, or elf, exiled from heaven. The messenger is a passing cloud who is to report to the Yaksha's wife who longs for her husband. The 'cycle of seasons' is famous for its description of nature matched with corresponding human moods and sentiments. *Kumarasambhava* consists of seventeen cantos, the first seven of which are devoted to the courtship and wedding of the deities Siva and Parvati, the parents of the youthful god of war. The main theme of the poem is on account of the destruction of the demon Taraka, for which purpose the god was born. The *Raghuvansa,* considered as the masterpiece of Kalidasa, describes in the first nine of its nineteen cantos the life of Rama and that of his ancestors. The next six cover the story of Rama himself, on the basis of the Ramayana of Valmiki. The remaining cantos deal with the twenty-four kings who ruled as Rama's successors in Ayodhya. It appears that Kalidasa was as much at home in describing courtship scenes such as in the *Kamasutra* of Vatsyayana as he was in the description of nature. This is evident from his *Meghaduta*. He is considered as the finest master of the Indian poetic style, superior even to Asvaghosha. The breadth of his knowledge and the depth of his observations on life and nature are evident in his works.

The Later Kavyas

The subject matter of the later *kavyas* is derived from the two great epics, the *Ramayana* and the *Mahabharata*. and has more lyric, erotic and didactic elements. The post-Kalidasa poets include Bharavi, Bhatti, Kumaradasa and Magha. The *Kiratarjuniya* of Bharavi, no less gifted than Kalidasa, describes the combat between Siva in the guise of a Kirata or mountaineer, and Arjuna. The story is based on the *Mahabharata*. It was composed earlier than A.D. 634, the date of the Aihole inscription of the western Chalukya ruler, Pulakesin II, which mentions him as well as Bhatti, the author of *Ratnavali*, also styled as Bhattikavya who wrote under Sridharasena of Vallabhi (d. A.D. 641). The latter relates the story of Rama with the sole object of illustrating the forms of Sanskrit grammar. His poem is considered as a lamp in the hands of those whose eye is grammar, and a mirror in the hands of those who are blind to others.

The *Sisupalavadha* or 'Death of Sisupala' by Magha, describes how Sisupala the Chedi king was slain in combat by Krishna his cousin. This work is often described as a Maghakavya. Magha was later than Bharavi who was his model. Both borrowed the themes of their *kavyas* from the *Mahabharata*, but while Bharavi praised Siva, Magha was devoted to Vishnu. Magha is placed about the second half of the seventh century. The *Nalodaya* or 'Rise of Nala' and the *Naishadhiya* or *Naishadha-charita* deal with the story of Nala of the *Mahabharata* losing his kingdom in a wager and finally being restored to power. The lesser epic poets include Mentha or Bharatrimentha, and Bhaumaka, the author of *Ravanarjuniya* or *Aryunaravaniya* who won fame in Kashmir. Also included is another Kashmiri poet Ratnakara (ninth century). The *Raja-tarangini*, or 'River of Kings', by Kachana, a considerably later work written by the son of a minister at the court of the Hindu ruler of Kashmir, is partly an epic poem and partly history. Rendering a trust-worthy account of the history of Kashmir down to A.D. 1148, Kachana may be considered more a historian than a poet.

Mention might as well be made of the lyric and didactic poetry written in the early medieval period. The bulk of the former is in single miniature stanzas, suggesting the didactic proverb poetry. The most famous of such stanzas are those of Bhartrihari who lived in the seventh century A.D. The collection of these stanzas contain lyric, didactic and philosophical matter, number 300 and are divided into three centuries—the century of Love (*Sringarasataka*), 'the century of Wisdom' (*Niti*), and 'the century of Resignation' (*Vairaga*). The collections contain stanzas borrowed from earlier poets. The poet Bhartrihari (who was probably a courtier) was different from the grammarian of the same name who wrote *Vakyapadiya*. The Sataka opens with pictures of the beauty of women, the passion of their love which varied with the seasons and the joys of its fruition. This pleasure sought in love and beauty is contrasted with the lasting peace achieved through penance and wisdom. The poet is convinced that beauty is a delusion and a snare; woman is sweet but poisonous as a snake. While love leads only to worldly attachment, renunciation brings peace and joy leading to union with Brahma, the highest spirit, the Absolute.

Like Bhartrihari, Amaru also completed his Sataka ranging from 90 to 115 verses according to different manuscripts. His date is undecided, but he is quoted by Anandavardhana (850). He seems to be later than Bhartrihari. His *Sataka* is essentially a collection of pictures of love and the relationship of lovers. His concept of love is gay, high-spirited and delightful, ending in smiles. The maiden may be angry but she will relent. Amaru, who is noted for elegance and precision in style, appears to be an expert at depicting the moods of love, bliss and devotion, and also anger and dejection. There is a certain delicacy of feeling and expression. The lover's quarrels are treated in a light-hearted manner. 'Is not Love with his feathered arrows my companion', or, 'speak low, for my beloved dwells in my heart and he will hear you,' are some of the prettiest instances of the poet's fancy.

Bilhana and Jayadeva are two other poets who fall in line with Bhartrihari and Amaru for their contributions to lyric and didactic poetry. Bilhana is the author of *Vikramankadevacharita* and also of *Chaurapanchasikha or Chaurusuratapanchasika*—'the joys of clandestine love' of a robber with a princess. It is suggested that the story relates the experience of the poet himself who was in desperate love with his patron's daughter. He recited the stanzas while he was being led to the place of execution. The Chalukya king was enchanted. Bilhana was pardoned and also got the princess in marriage. Another poet Jayadeva (twelfth century) is noted for his *Gitagovinda* or 'cowherd's song' in which the love of Krishna and the beautiful Radha, their estrangement and final reconciliation is portrayed in a kind of lyrical monologue.

Prose Romances

The absence of early specimens of romances in prose makes it rather difficult to assess the standard of the works of Dandin, Subandhu and Bana written in the sixth and seventh centuries A.D. Dandin was earlier than the other two as might be evident from the geographical data in his *Dasakumaracharita*—'the character of ten princess'. His *Kavyadarsa*—'Mirror of the Art of Poetry'—is probably the work of his maturity. Here he is an exponent of poetic theory. In his earlier work he used prose along with poetry. It is a romance of manners, and his portrayal of reality is interesting. It has been suggested that he was the author of *Mrichchakatika*—'the little clay cart'—but this is doubtful as the work is attributed to Sudraka. Some other works are also ascribed to him. Subandhu, the author of the *Vasavadatta,* was older than Bana. He relates in his work the popular story of a princess of Ujjayini bearing that name. Despite the heavy pedantic style with its involved construction, abundance of long compounds, and fondness for detail, the work is interesting for its description of nature and its portryal of the princess' beauty. Bana's *Harsha-Charita* and *Kadambari* are equally important as romances in elegant Sanskrit prose, but here again these are written in a pedantic manner. The former is an historical romance in which the author gives some account of the life of his patron king Harshavardhana (A.D. 606-47). The latter relates the fortunes of a princess of the same name in the work. This work suffers from the grave defects of complexity and lack of proportion. One often loses sight of the plot which itself is very complicated. Scholars criticize it for its subtlety and tautology, the outrageous overloading of single words with epithets and the construction of sentences in which the solitary verb is held over for pages. His prose is considered as a jungle where progress is impossible unit the traveller cuts out a path for himself.

The later prose romances include the *Madhavanala-kamakandalakatha* and the *Tilakamanjari* by Ananda and Dhanapala respectively. The former is a well-known story of Madhavanala, a Brahman, who was deeply in love with the dancer Kamakandala whom he married after a long period of separation. The story is in simple prose interspersed with numerous verses in Sanskrit as well as in Prakrit. The *Tilakamanjari* named after the poet's daughter is a romance by Dhanapala. A contemporary of Siyaka and Vakpati of Dhara (c. 975), he draws as many parallels as possible from *Kadambari* in describing this lady's love of Samaraketu. Dhanapala also recognizes his indebtedness to Bana. To this category of prose romances may be included the *Champus*—a name of unknown sense—which has verses interspersed with prose. The earliest traces of this form are found in the *Jatakamala* of Aryasura and in the Allahabad inscription of Harishena in the time of Samudragupta (fourth century). The earliest works of this class in full *kavya* style is *Nalachampu* which describes the story of Nala, and *Madalasachampu* by the same author Trivikrama in the tenth century A.D. Another work, *Yasatilakachampu,* written by Somedeva in the time of the Rashtrakuta ruler Krishna III (c. A.D. 959), narrates the story of the legendary king Yasodhara of Ujjain in seven chapters in full *kavya* style.

Sanskrit Drama

The origin of Sanskrit drama is in obscurity. There seems to be a wide gap between is early beginnings in the dialogue hymns of the Rig Veda and the actual plays (second-fourth century A.D.) though the rude form of pantomime can be traced much earlier. The earliest reference to drama can be found in the *Mahabhashya* of Patanjali (second century B.C.) which speaks of representations of the *Kansabadha* or 'death of Kansa' and the *Bali-bandha* or 'capture of Bali'. The *Natyasastra* of Bharata is the earliest and the most authoritative treatise on Sanskrit dramaturgy. Its date is, however, uncertain, but it could be anywhere between the second century B.C. and third century A.D. Asvaghosha, the famous Buddhist poet referred to earlier and a contemporary of Kanishka (second cent. A.D.), is credited with the authorship of three Buddhist dramas, of which one, *Sariputra Prakarana,* was definitely written by him. Its subject matter refers to the conversion of Maudgalyayana and Sariputra, the hero, by the Buddha. All the rules laid down for the composition of a *Prakarana* or prologue in the *Natyasastra* are followed here. Bhasa, the author of *Svapnavasavadatta* and several other dramas, is considered to be later than Asvaghosha. The dramas are generally based on the epics and most of them are one-act plays. Two derive their theme from the *Ramayana* and some, including the famous *Pratijnayaugandharayana* and *Svapnavasavadatta* and the non-existent *Charudatta,* are based on the then current literature. The first two are complementary. The latter picks up in the thread of the story of king Udayana of Ujjayini. Written in Bhasa's style it is simple and direct though the plot construction is crude since it includes magic giving it an air of unreality. Another interesting drama is the *Mrichchakatika* or 'clay cart' written very probably by Sudraka whose date is uncertain. This play deals with the love of Vasantasena a rich courtesan and Charudatta, a Brahman merchant, and ends with their coming together. The variety of incidents and quick dramatic appeal makes the play fairly interesting.

A number of good Sanskrit dramas, nearly a dozen, were written between A.D. 400 and 800 by great dramatists like Kalidasa, Bhavabhuti and others, some of whom very probably dedicated their contributions to their patrons and benefactors like Sudraka and Harsha. Kalidasa, famous as an epic and lyric poet, was the most eminent dramatist as well. His three dramas are *Sakuntala, Vikramorvasi* and *Malavikagnimitra.* The first two describe the amorous adventures of two famous legendary kings while the third concern a historic personality of the Sunga period (second century B.C.). It is a palace drama of love and intrigue. *Sakuntala* describes the romance of king Dushyanta and the daughter of a celestial nymph (*apsara*). Watering her favourite plants in the grove of the sage Kanua, her guardian, Sakuntala enchants Dushyanta, engaged in a chase. The king falls in love with her and marries her, but returns home alone. The guardian sage sends the bride to her lord's house after sometime, but the latter fails to recognise her due to a curse pronounced by an angry sage. After passing through many vicissitudes, the lovers are finally united when the ring given earlier by Dushyanta to his bride is found. In this drama, Kalidasa describes the communion of the lovers with nature, their fantasy and tender sentiments.

The second play *Vikramorvasi* or 'Urvasi won by valour' deals with the Rig Vedic story of the Puruvas and the nymph Urvasi, the former rescuing her from demons but parting with her due to Indra's summons, and finally reuniting with her by the grace of the gods. The *Malavikagnimitra* centres round the court room scene of King Agnimitra of Vidisa. His love for Malavika, a Vidarbha princess, who became one of the attendants of the queen, is intriguing but none-the-less serious and steady. When her identity is revealed the obstacle is removed and they are united in marriage. Harsha of Kanauj and Thaneshwar (seventh century) is the reputed author of two plays, *Ratnavali* or the 'Pearl Necklace' reflecting the court life of the age, and *Nagananda*—a sensational play in a Buddhist setting. The former is the story of the love of king Udayana of Vatsa and Sagarika, an attendant of his queen Vasavadatta. The heroine finally appears to be Ceylonese princess Ratnavali who was shipwrecked and had found her way to Udayana's court. The real author of this play might have been Bana, who is supposed to have written another extant drama, *Paravatiparinaya* or the 'marriage of Paravati'.

The eminent dramatist Bhavabhuti (eighth century), a Brahman native of Ujjain who enjoyed the patronage of Yasovarman of Kanauj, wrote three plays which are unique in character. They differ from the earlier ones in various ways. In his dramas, the jester (*vidusaka*) is absent, and the comic element is entirely lacking. Moreover he is not interested in the delicate and mild aspects of nature but one suggestive of grandeur and sublimation. The most popular of his plays is *Malati-Madhava* portraying the love of Madhava, a young student, and Malati, daughter of a minister at the Ujjain court. The king wants to marry her to someone of his choice. The girl resents this and finally marries the person of her own choice. The other two dramas are *Mahaviracharita* or 'the adventures of a great hero' based on the *Ramayana* with slight differences, and *Uttara-rama-charita* or 'Later Adventures of Rama' which is more of a dramatic poem than a play. The plot begins with the banishment of Sita and ends with her restoration to the throne of Ayodhya after twelve years of solitude. Hence, it does not have the usual tragic ending.

Visakhadatta is the author of two dramas, the *Mudrarakshasa* or 'the signet ring of Rakshasa' and *Devi-Chandraguptani*. The former is a play of political intrigue, full of action and sustained interest. The plot centres round the personality of the Brahman diplomat, Chanakya, and his attempt to win over Rakshasa, the former minister of the Nandas. The reader's interest in the work never flags, and one is delighted to find maxims of politics flowing from the mouth of both Chanakya and his rival Rakshasa. Two other plays ascribed to Visakhadatta, or Visakhaveda, are *Devichandragupta* and *Abhisarikavanchitaka*. The former deals with the story of Dhruvadevi who was saved from being surrendered to a Saka ruler by her coward husband Ramagupta by Chandragupta, her brother-in-law. The play itself is lost, and is preserved only in citations in the *Natyadarpana* by Ramchandra and Gunachandra. The second play *Abhisarika-vanchitaka* relates the love story of Udayana and Padmavati who in a disguised form regains the lost love of her husband.

A few important plays have survived between AD. 800-1100. These include the *Venisamhara* or 'Binding of the Hair in a Braid' by Bhatta Narayana. The plot is based on an incident from the *Mahabharata*. The dragging of Draupadi, the wife of the Pandava brothers, by Dshuasana, one of the Kauravas, by her hair and her vow never to braid her hair again until the insult is avenged, as it ultimately is, forms the main theme. The drama lacks literary merit and its popularity stems from its partiality for the cult of Krishna who was invoked by Draupadi for help at the time of the insult.

Rajasekhara (ninth century) was probably the last of the great Hindu dramatists. He was preceded by Murari, author of *Anargharaghava,* now available only in quotations. It is based on the epic *Ramayana* and he borrowed from Bhavabhuti's *Uttara-ramacharita*. Rajasekhara, noted for his grace and fluency of diction, wrote several dramas. The *Karapuramanjari* or 'the camphor cluster', probably his first play, entirely in Prakrit, was composed and staged at the instance of his wife Avanti Sundari. The three other Sanskrit plays are the *Viddhasalabhanjika* or the 'Pierced Statue', the *Balaramayana* or 'Little Ramayana', and the *Balabharata* or 'Little Bharata'. These plays are supposed to be based on earlier works and have unmistakable traces of Kalidasa, Bhavabhuti and Harsha. The first one in the list, *Viddhasalabhanjika,* has several points of resemblance with the *Ratnavali* of Harsha. The *Balaramayana,* probably the longest Indian drama, tells the story of Rama from his betrothal to Sita down to their return to Ayodhya. The other one, *Balabharata*, relates the events narrated in the *Mahabharata* from the wedding of Draupadi down to the departure of the Pandavas for the forest. A play entitled *Chanda-Kausika* or the 'Angry Kausika' was composed by the poet Kshemisvara, probably in the tenth century A.D. under king Mahipala of Kanauj.

A few other dramas of the eleventh and twelfth centuries include the *Hanumana-sataka*, or 'Play of Hanumant' by Damodara Misra who lived at the court of Bhoja, king of Malwa, in the early part of the eleventh century. It is a disconnected piece, dealing with the adventures of Rama and his ally Hanumant. The *Prabodha-Chandrodaya* or 'Rise of the Moon of Knowledge' by Krishna Misra is an allegorical play of theologico-philosophical purport. Here only abstract notions and symbolical figures act as persons in the drama. Its object is to glorify the Vedanta philosophy and to inculcate the worship of Vishnu.

Didactic Literature

The artless tales devoid of moral or instructive purpose and meant only as a past-time were eventually grouped in a connected series within a frame-work. The aim for developing this class of literature was to provide useful advice to young princes in their political and practical affairs. The proverbs and instructions woven into the fables and tales present the best picture of Hindu ethics. The most important collection of such tales and fables is no doubt Buddhist, written in Pali and known as Jatakas or 'birth' stories. In all these, Buddha appears as the wise or successful person or animal and points out the moral of the fable. The two most important Sanskrit collections are the *Panchatantra* and the *Hitopadesa*. The first one or 'Five Books' existed at least as early as the first half of the sixth century A.D. as it was translated into Pahlavi by order of king Khusru Anishirvan (531-579). There seems to have been an original text on which this one was based. It is suggested that there was a proto-*Panchatantra* in which the *kavya* style was applied in a simple form. The oldest form of this version is considered to be the *Tantrakhyayika* or 'Collection of Little Tales' probably a Kashmiri version and it might have been written in the Gupta period. The unknown author of this collection and the *Panchatantra* furnish the set of morals for the average man in story form, e.g., a good householder and a good father should be hospitable and loyal to friends. They are also, in a way, instructive for the king who is expected to protect the innocent and rule the country with the help of able ministers. The *Hitopadesa* or 'Useful Teaching' has the same didactic object. Its author Narayana wrote it for the young princes of his patron, a certain Dhavalachandra, who may have been in Bengal.

Fresh matter is introduced in this work in the form of seventeen new stories. Many verses from the *Kamandaki Nitisastra* are introduced by way of illustration. This work may roughly be placed in the twelfth century A.D. Both these works are handbooks of practical ethics (*Nitisastras*).

The *Brihat-katha* or 'the Great Romance' of Gunadhya, *Katha-sarit-sagara* or the 'Ocean of story', and *Suka Saptati* or 'the Seventy Tales of the Parrot' are some other interesting works dealing with narrative and didactic literature with tales and fables as their main theme. The first work, unfortunately lost, is preserved in a few verses in the Prakrit Grammar of Hemachandra. It was written in the *Paisachi* language, a dialect of Prakrit. The *Brihat-katha* in its Kashmiri version was used by Kshemendra and Somedeva, both of the eleventh century A.D. The former wrote his *Brihat-katha Manjari* or the 'Bouquet of the Great Romance', while the latter is noted for his *Katha-sarit-sagara* with its three hundred and fifty episodic stories loosely connected, covering different periods and backgrounds. It is composed in verse and contains 22,000 slokas or couplets. The main narrative, however, begins with the hero Udayana and his wife Vasavadatta. Another collection of pretty and ingenious fairy tales is *Vetala-panchavimsatika* or the 'Twenty-five Tales of the Vampire' by an unknown author of an unspecified period. There is still another collection of fairy tales namely *Simhasanadvatrimsika* or 'Thirty-two stories of the Lionseat' supposed to be told to Vikrama by his throne. The *Suka-Saptati* is also a work of the same type, relating stories from the mouth of a parrot. Their object is to reproach the lady of the house who was anxious for a meeting with a stranger in the absence of her husband. All the stories relate to the faithlessness of women which is shown as reprehensible. The maxims introduced into the *Panchatantra* and the *Hitopadesa* from earlier works are found scattered elsewhere in Sanskrit literature.

Scientific Literature

Sanskrit is equally rich in literature dealing with scientific subjects like medicine, surgery, mathematics, astrology and astronomy and with the humanities like grammar, etymology, lexicography, prosody, rhetoric, music and architecture. The ancient Hindu mind did not distinguish between literary creation and scientific presentation. All the disciplines have a rich literature in Sanskrit, written in different periods. The Vedic glosses of Yaska, or the *Naighantukas* and the *Nirukta* and the *Pratisakhyas* or phonetic treatises; the *Ashtadhyayi* or the 'Grammar of Panini' with commentaries by Katyayana and Patanjali, the *Kasika* of Vamanacharya and many other schools of grammar are important contributions. The '*Amarkosa*' or 'Dictionary of Amara-Simha' enjoys the same high position in lexicography as Panini's work does in grammar. Other works in lexicography include Sasvata's *Anakartha-Samuchchaya* or 'Collection of Homonyms', Halayudha's *Abhidhanaratnamala* or 'Necklace of Names' (c. 950 A.D.) and the *Abhidhana-chintamani* of the famous Jain scholar Hemachandra (eleventh century). Treatises on Drama and Dramatic Art include Bharatas *Natyasastra* (sixth century) while those on poetry include Dandin's *Kavyadarsa* or 'Mirror of Poetry' (c. A.D. 600), and Rajasekhara's *Kavyamimamsa* or 'Discussion on Poetry' (ninth century).

The achievement of ancient Indians in the field of mathematical sciences as inventors of numerical figures and the decimal system was also considerable. The oldest extant mathematical writings are the Vedic *Sulva Sutras* representing a kind of ritual geometry applied to the construction of altars. This includes the construction of right angles, squares and rectangles and also the Pythagorean theorem stating that the square of the hypotenuse equals the square of the other two sides. The later mathematicians made progress in trigonometry with the invention of the sine table. The greatness of the Indian mathematicians including Varahamihira, from the fifth century onwards, lies in their enquiries into algebra and arithmetic. The mathematical chapters of astronomers are composed in verses. The earliest works of Indian astronomy, scientific in nature beginning about A.D. 300 include *Siddhantas* or canonical text-books of which only one, namely the *Suryasiddhanta,* is now available. The founder of Indian astronomy was Aryabhata (fifth century) who was the first to propound the theory of the earth rotating on its axis. His work is entitled '*Aryabhatiya*'. Varahamihira (sixth century), the great astronomer, is noted for his *Pancha-siddhantika,* a practical astronomical treatise, and *Brihat-Samhita* written in the style of the great epics. Brahmagupta (seventh century) wrote his *Brahma-*

Sphutika-Siddhanta while the last one in the series of astronomers was the famous Bhaskaracharya (twelfth century) who wrote the *Siddhanta-Siromani* or 'Diadem of system'.

The treatises on medicine and surgery include the *Charaka-Samhita* and *Susruta-Samhita* named after the authors dealing with these two subjects respectively. Both belonged to the second century A.D. References to the science of medicine or the art of healing are noticed in the Atharva Veda in that many diseases are mentioned along with the important healing plants. The most notable writer on medicine after Charaka and Susruta was Vagabhata (c. 600), author of the *Ashtanga-hridaya*. Many works on medicine were translated into Arabic by orders of the Caliph of Baghdad.

Reference is not made here to Sanskrit works dealing with religion and philosophy or legal matters, as these are mentioned elsewhere. So also contributions in the field of art and architecture are dealt with in a separate study. The area of Sanskrit literature is so vast and of such a diverse nature that a general survey of the religious and secular, literary and grammatical, prose and poetry and literary criticism would be inadequate. The influence of Sanskrit literature, particularly on Pali and Prakrit and on Dravidian and vernacular literature, is notable both in theme and in presentation. Sanskrit words have found an appropriate place in all the languages that were subsequently developed in different parts of the country and produced a literature of their own. A proper assessment of the impact of Sanskrit language and literature on these languages is neither feasible nor desirable in this context.

Pali Literature

The entire mass of Buddhist literature is preserved partly in Pali and partly in Sanskrit. Pali as the sacred language of Buddhism in Ceylon, Burma and Thailand, preserves the Hinayana literature, while the Mahayana literature is mostly preserved in Sanskrit. The Pali canon is called the '*Tri Pitaka*' or 'The Three Baskets', comprising the *vinaya* or canon law, *Sutta* or Discourses and *Dhamma* or Doctrine of Moral Law. The *Vinaya-Pitaka*, 'The Basket of Discipline', contains the regulations for the management of the Buddhist order (*Samgha*) and for the conduct of the daily life of monks and nuns. It also includes rules for incorporation into the order, for the periodical confession of sins, for life during the rainy season, for housing, clothing, medicinal remedies, and legal procedures in case of schism. The second 'Basket' contains *Suttas* or Discourses and is known as *Sutta-Pitaka*. It contains in prose and verse lectures and discourses of the Master which are grouped together in five minor collections, known as *nikayas*. Extensive use of parables and similes make these discourses lively and interesting. They throw light on the daily life of the people. The *Dighanikaya* is a collection of lengthy lectures, consisting of 34 *suttas* each dealing at length with one or more points of Buddhist doctrine. The first one entitled *Brahmajalasutta* or 'Lecture on the Brahman net' enjoins the Buddhist monk to avoid the snare of the Brahmans. The second, namely, the *Samannaphalasutta* or 'Lecture on the reward of asceticism', contains a discourse on the views of number of non-Buddhist teachers and founders of other sects. The *Ambatta-Sutta* relates the history of castes and Buddha's attitude towards the caste system. The discourses relating to Brahmanism and its relations with Buddhism are included in *Kutadanta-Sutta*, 'Lecture on the sharp tooth', and *Teujja-Sutta*, 'Lecture on the followers of the three Vadas'. Doctrines of Buddhism, including instructions for the layman are included in the *Mahanidana-sutta* or 'Great lectures on Causation', *Sigalovadasutta* or 'Admonition of Sigala', *Mahaparnibhanasutta* or 'Great lecture on the complete Nirvana', a continuous lecture on the last days of the Buddha. The *Majjhima-nikaya* or 'Collection of lectures of middle length' consists of 15 sermons and dialogues dealing with the main points of Buddhism. These throw light on the life of the Buddhist monks, on Brahmanical sacrifices, various forms of asceticism, the relation of Buddha to the Jains, and also on superstitions and contemporary socio-religious conditions. The *Samyutta* or 'collection of combined lectures' deals with the four truths and contains the famous *Dhamma-Chakka-ppavattana-sutta*, 'Lecture on setting in motion the wheel of law', which the Lord delivered at Sarnath. The *Anguttara-Nikaya* or 'Collection of lectures arranged according to increasing number' consists of over 2300 *suttas* in 11 sections. It contains a number of *suttas* and stanzas from other texts, by way of quotation. The *Khuddu-nikaya* or 'Collection of small pieces' is a later compilation. It contains all the most important works of Buddhist-Indian poetry. The *Dhamma-pada* or 'words of religion' forms a part of this *nikaya* or collection. It is the most familiar and longest known work of Buddhist literature and is an anthology of maxims concerning the ethical doctrines of Buddhism. The *Suttanipata* is a collection of poetical *suttas* supplying information on the original doctrine of the Buddha. The Jataka is a book containing about 550 stories of former births of Buddha in the character of a Bodhisattva or a 'Buddha in the making'.

The *Abhiddhama-pitaka* or 'Basket of higher religion' is more scholastic than the previous one, namely the *sutta-pitaka*. The subject matter of both is the same. It is written mostly in the form of questions and answers, like a catechism. As its subject matter is mainly derived from the *Sutta-pitaka* in which are found the beginnings of the *Abbhidhamma* and the *Vinaya Pitaka,* it may be said to be merely the extension of lists mentioned in the *vinaya*. It comprises seven books called *Sattapakarana,* namely the *Dhammasangani, Vibhanga, Dhatukatha, Puggalapannali, Kathavatthu, Yamaka and Patthana*. All these books are later in date and lack originality. The authorship of the *Kathavatthu* is ascribed to Moggaliputta Tissa, who was the president of the Third Buddhist Council, although in its present form it is of a much later date.

Besides the above canonical literature in Pali, the non-canonical includes the *Milindapanda* or 'the Discourse of Milinda-Menander' with the Buddhist philosopher Nagasena. The present text is supposed to be a translation of the original written probably in Sanskrit or some north Indian Prakrit dialect about the beginning of the Christian era. While the original text seems to have been written in north-west India, the translation was done in Ceylon. The Buddhist doctrine of the impermanence of the ego is expounded in this work. The Indo-Greek kings, convinced by the arguments of the Buddhist monk, accepted Buddhism.

The contribution of north India to Pali literature is very meagre in the later period, as Mahayana Buddhism and its gospels were preserved in Sanskrit. The *Theravada* school or 'Doctrine of the Elders' with its different offshoots also has some literature in Sanskrit. Among the Buddhist Sanskrit works the most important include the *Lalitavistara* or 'Detailed account of the plays of Buddha' and a biography of the *Sarvastivadins* and *Mahavastu,* both having traces of Mahayanism. The *Saddharma Pundarika* or 'The Lotus of the True Law' is also a Mahayanist work. Those of a philosophic or dogmatic character include the *Lankavatara Sutra* relating to the visit of the Buddha to Ceylon and his answering the questions according to the doctrines of the Yogachara school founded by Asanga. The *Madhyamakarika* of Nagarjuna and the *Prajnaparamitas* or 'Sutras on the perfection of wisdom' are Mahayanist works in mixed Sanskrit. Vasubandhu's *Abhidharma-kosa* is an encyclopaedic work which deals with ethics, psychology and metaphysics. It is known only through a Sanskrit commentary and Chinese and Tibetan translations.

Prakrit and its Literature

The language of the masses, popularly known as Prakrit, and its different dialects was at first used by the Buddha and Mahavira in their discourses. While the Buddhist scriptures were later on written in Pali, those of Jainism are in Prakrit in the *Ardha-Magadhi* dialect. The language adopted in non-canonical writings differs considerably from this, being a form of Maharashtri which was generally used by the Brahman Prakrit poets. There are also two other forms, *Magadhi* and *Sauraseni.* It would thus appear that unlike chaste Sanskrit, which was uniformly spoken throughout the country, Prakrit, the spoken language of the people, had several forms, based on geographical and regional factors. A large number of Prakrit inscriptions, more than fifteen hundred in number covering a period of eight centuries (third century B.C. to fifth century A.D.) with only a dozen or so in Sanskrit, suggest its prevalence among the masses. Even in Sanskrit drama the ladies and ordinary people speak in Prakrit. The dramas of Asvaghosha, Bhasa and Sudraka are replete with speeches in the different dialects of Prakrit. Besides a number of Jain canonical works, to be noted in the context of Jainism, the Prakrit *kavyas* of a secular nature deserve attention, e.g., the *Setubandha* and *Gauda-vaho*. The former is a narrative poem written in the Maharashtri-Prakrit dialect. It describes the story of the *Ramayana* from the expedition to Lanka (Ceylon) up to the death of Ravana and the recovery of Sita. Its author is supposed to be Pravarasena, identified with king Pravarasena II of Kashmir. The second is the composition of Vakpatiraja, a court poet of king Yasovarman of Kanauj. It was written about A.D. 725 and contains information about the deeds of the hero, king Yasovarman. The *Gatha Sattasai* (Skt. *Sapta-sati*) or 'Seven-Countries' of Hala, an anthology of lyric stanzas, is mostly of an erotic type. The *Karpura-manjari,* or 'Camphor-cluster', of Rajasekhara noticed earlier, is written entirely in Prakrit. It describes in four acts how king Chandapala married Karpura-Manjari, the daughter of the king of Kuntala. The jealousy of the queen, and the intrigues employed in bringing the king and the heroine together, furnish the plot of the play.

Dravidian Literature

The Dravidian group of languages comprises Tamil, Kannada, Telugu and Malayalam. Tamil leads the rest chronologically, and has the greatest Indian literature next to Sanskrit. Dravida, Dramada, Damila and Tamil, and the names suggest, seem to have had the earliest contact with the Sanskrit language and culture, though at present it has comparatively fewer Sanskrit words than the other languages. The history of Tamil literature begins with the so-called three 'Sangams' or academies of learned men where the works of different scholars on diverse subjects were presented. The first two are associated with the north Indian sage Agastya whose *Agastyam* (*Akattiyam*) is supposed to have consisted of 1,000 sutras or aphorisms. The Sangam epoch is said to have lasted about a thousand years, roughly from 500 B.C. to A.D. 500. None of the works of the first Sangam are available, and of the second, only one work, viz., *Tolkappiyam,* has survived. It is encyclopaedic in range and has been annotated by many writers. The principal works of the third Sangam are *Patthupattu* (The Ten Idylls), *Ettuthokai* (The Eight Collections) and *Padinenkilkanakku* (The Eight Minor Didactic Poems). The ten idylls, which include two by the famous poet Nakkiar, constitute a literary heritage of a high order noted for their descriptions and faithful depiction of human feelings. They were composed in the first century of the Christian era. The century following seems to be the golden age of Tamil literature. The five major epics were probably written during this period. They include *Silappadikaram, Manimekhalai, Jivakachintamani, Valayapati* and *Kundalakesi.* Of these, only the first three are available. The first two are considered to be the *Iliad* and the *Odyssey* of Tamil literature. The former records the moving story of Kovalan and Kanaki. Kovalan exhausts his fortune, being infatuated with the courtesan Madhavi. and Kanaki sacrifices herself as a mark of chastity and devotion to her lord despite his lapses. The second is a sequel of the first. In it, Manimekhalai, the daughter of Kovalan by Madhavi but spiritually accepted by Kanaki, sees through the limitations of human love and consecrates herself to the service of the Buddhist Trinity. *Jivakachintamani* is the work of a Jain author, a Chola, who renounces his father's throne, after killing the usurper, and becomes a Jain ascetic.

Religious movements no doubt exercised considerable influence on Dravidian literature. While Jainism and Buddhism exercised strong influence at first, they were eventually overcome by the religion of the orthodox Hindus—namely Saivism and Vaishnavism. From the sixth or seventh century onwards many Saiva Nayanmars and Vaishnava Alvars, who were simple *bhaktas* or devotees, composed devotional poetry which could reach the masses. Tirumular, author of the ten Tirumurais (Saiva hymns), Manikkavachakar and three other Saiva *Samayacharyas* flourished in the Tamil country and contributed to the religious literature of this Hindu sect. The Alvars, who in all probability flourished between A.D. 500 and 550, contributed to Vaishnava devotional songs in Tamil. Andal or Kodai, daughter of a celebrated Alvar Periyalvar, poured forth her divine love into some of the finest poetry in the Tamil language. Seeing herself as one of Krishna's gopis, she is said to have achieved union with him, with single-minded devotion and fervour. The Tevaram and Tiruvachakam of the Saiva *Samayacharyas* and the *Nalayira Prabandham* of the Vaishnava Alvars constitute the greatest elements in the Tamil literature of Hindu medieval India. The poets of the Brahmanical period concentrated on the *Ramayana* and the *Mahabharata* and other Pauranic stories which they adapted into Tamil. Kamban, Ottakuttan and Pugalendi are considered as the three Tamil gems of this period who made great contributions to Tamil literature. Of these Kamban is famous for his Ramayana in Tamil, considered more akin to a luxuriant but limited garden when compared to the vast forest of Valmiki's *Ramayana*.

Kannada, next to Tamil, as the most ancient of the Dravidian languages, started its independent existence about the beginning of the Christian era, as there are references to Karu natar or Karunadu in the famous Tamil classic, *Silappadikaram*. The literature in this language is also enriched by the Jains, Virasivas and Vaishnavas.

Other religions too contributed to the progress and development of literature in this language. The earliest work is supposed to be *Vodda-aradhana* by a Jain *Sivakotyacharya* probably before the eighth century A.D. *Kavirajamarga* by the famous Rashtrakuta king Amoghavarsha was written about A.D. 850. Another writer was Gunavarma I who wrote *Sudraka* and *Neminatha Purana,* also called *Harivamsa*. The three gems of the tenth century, Pampa, Poona and Ranna, are noted for their contributions to Kannada literature. Pampa's *Adi Purana* is a history of the first Tirthankara, also described as the first of the brave heroic souls who crossed the muddy and disturbed sea of human misery and frailty, reaching the shores of an unending indefinable place. The other two were also preoccupied with Jain tenets, traditions and interpretations. Pampa's *Vikramanka-vijaya* and Ranna's *Sahasa Bhima-vijaya* (also called *Gada-yuddha*) are both secular poems based on the *Mahabharata*. Two Brahman authors of the eleventh century, Nagavarmacharya and Chandraraja, and a succession of Jain writers, following the traditions of the earlier trio—Pampa, Poona and Ranna—are notable for their contributions to Kannada literature up to the twelfth century A.D. They were followed by the rise of the Lingayat or Virasaiva movement in Kannada serving as a milestone in Karnataka's progress in religion and literature. Basava, supposed to be the founder of this sect, is glorified in several episodes of a *Basava Purana*.

Telugu and Malayalam literature is not very old. The earliest surviving writings of Telugu authors date from the twelfth century and include a *Mahabharata* by Nannapa or Nanniah, meant for the sophisticated court and urban population, closely resembling the great epic of Vyasa. Besides him, Tikkanna and Errapragada (Errana) form the great Trio or the '*Kavi Traya*' of Telugu literature. The eleventh and twelfth centuries saw little original in activity in the field of literature in the Telugu country, now Andhra Pradesh. Pavuturo Mallana and Fluganti Peddanna wrote mathematical treatises in Telugu based on or translated from Sanskrit originals. The influence of Virasaivism and the earlier Vaishnava movement initiated by Ramanuja was also felt in Telugu life and letters. The Malayalam literature is not too old. The oldest Malayalam literature imitated Tamil poetry, but it soon fell under the influence of Sanskrit. The classical epoch in this language commences with Tunjattu Ezhuthachhan in the seventeenth century.

North Indian Vernacular Literature

The north Indian vernacular literature is divided by a sharp line into poetry and prose. The earlier period was the age of poetry which continued for a long time and was confined to religious devotional songs or was simply bardic poetry eulogising the deeds of battle heroes in verse. The general employment of prose in the vernacular was due to the British influence and to the need of elementary textbooks in the nineteenth century. The richest vernacular literature is in Bengali, of which the oldest examples are found in place-names in inscriptions of Bengal from the fifth down to the tenth century A.D. The *Charyapadas* are the earliest instances of Bengali poetry. These poems were composed by a class of religious teachers known as *Siddhas* who were claimed by the later Mahayana Buddhists as well as by the followers of Gorakshanath of the Saiva sect. The style and technique of these poems were continued in other languages as well, including Assamese, Oriya, Hindi and Maithli. The characteristic of these verses are their religious and emotional appeal. The poets in Bengali before A.D. 1300 used not only Bengali but also western Apathramsa in addition to Sanskrit. Western Hindi and other dialects were also evolving in the art of Apabhramsa during this period. In the same period, great Rajput romances like the *Prithvirajarasau* by Chandrabardai, the *Visaladevarasau*, the *Khumanarasau* and the *Alha-Udal* also took shape. Kabir's predecessors came into the field of Apabhramsa and new Indian literature in this period.

A review of education and literature during this long period of more than fifteen hundred years has to be made in the context of their stages of progress and development. In the first stage the literature was primarily religious and the centres of learning were the hermitages of seers. The language was Sanskrit. Writing gradually replaced the transmission of knowledge by the rote method. Besides Vedic literature, other areas included grammar, philosophy and religion. The age of Sanskrit poetry followed with Valmiki's *Ramayana* and the *Mahabharata* of Vyasa. Smritis or legal texts were also composed in this period. Secular literature and Sanskrit drama seem to have originated about the beginning of the Christian era. The Pali language by that time had established itself since the canonical texts of the Buddhists were produced in this language. The teachings of the Buddha were however in the language of the masses, namely Prakrit. The Jain canonical texts were of course in this language. The period of classical Sanskrit literature was a fairly long one with contributions in the different forms of poetry—lyric, didactic, narrative and romantic. Plays were also written though there are not more than a dozen good ones. Sanskrit prose followed later on. The works of some of the masterminds provided landmarks in the development of Sanskrit literature. The early medieval period was characterised by great progress in literature dealing with technical and scientific subjects, though the one dealing with medicine and surgery can be traced to the second century A.D. The contributions of individual authors, playwrights and intellectuals, besides philosophers and religious thinkers, were considerable and added to the vast mass of literature. Centres of learning like Nalanda and Vikramasila served as forums for discussions among scholars. Besides the literature in Sanskrit, Pali and Prakrit, that in the Dravidian languages, especially Tamil, may also be noted in this context. The vernacular in the north was evolved out of Apabhramsa and had devotional songs as its main theme. This was the base which provided the setting for the growth of literature in different languages in the medieval period.

